G. Tartan

ROYAL HISTORICAL SOCIETY

STUDIES IN HISTORY

New Series

THE GREAT WAR, MEMORY AND RITUAL

THE GREAT WAR, MEMORY AND RITUAL

COMMEMORATION IN THE CITY AND EAST LONDON, 1916–1939

Mark Connelly

THE ROYAL HISTORICAL SOCIETY
THE BOYDELL PRESS

First published 2002

A Royal Historical Society publication
Published by The Boydell Press
an imprint of Boydell & Brewer Ltd
PO Box 9, Woodbridge, Suffolk IP12 3DF, UK
and of Boydell & Brewer Inc.
PO Box 41026, Rochester, NY 14604–4126, USA
website: http://www.boydell.co.uk

ISBN 0 86193 253 6

ISSN 0269–2244

A catalogue record for this book is available
from the British Library

Library of Congress Cataloging-in-Publication Data
Connelly, Mark.
    The Great Wat, memory and ritual : commemoration in the City
and East London, 1916–1939 / Mark Connelly.
       p. cm. – (Royal Historical Society studies in history. New series)
    Includes bibliographical references and index.
    ISBN 0–86193–253–6 (alk. paper)
    1. World War, 1914–1918 – Monuments – England – London.
    2. Corporation of London (England) – Social life and customs.
    3. East End (London, England) – Social life and customs.
    4. Armistice Day – England – London.   5. London (England) –
Social life and customs.   I. Title.   II. Series.
D680.G7 C66 2002
940.4'65421 – dc21   2001035275

This book is printed on acid-free paper

Printed in Great Britain by
St Edmundsbury Press, Bury St Edmunds, Suffolk

The pallor of girls' brows shall be their pall;
Their flowers the tenderness of patient minds,
And each slow dusk a drawing-down of blinds.
Wilfred Owen, 'Anthem for Doomed Youth'

For Jacqui

City of London Regiment, Royal Fusiliers' memorial, Holborn Bars

Contents

List of Illustrations

Frontispiece/jacket illustration: City of London Regiment, Royal Fusiliers'
memorial, Holborn Bars

Photographic Acknowledgements

Plate 1, 4, 5, 7, 8 and the frontispiece/jacket illustration are reproduced by kind permission of the Imperial War Museum; plate 2 of the Isle of Dogs Local History Trust; plates 3, 6 and 9 of the Tower Hamlets Local History Library. The map is reproduced from *The citizen series maps of London*, London 1912, by permission of the Guildhall Map Library.

Acknowledgements

This book is based largely on my PhD thesis and so my first thanks go to my supervisor, Professor John Ramsden. He always had the art of saying exactly the right thing at the right time: his praise, criticism and comment were of the highest value. I would also like to thank all the librarians, clergymen and archivists who helped me to dig out some very obscure scraps of evidence. Of particular help were the staff of Tower Hamlets Local History Library, of Newham Local History Library, and of the Guildhall Library, as was Eve Hostettler at the Docklands Settlement, and the clergy and parish church councillors of St Clement's Ilford, St Paul's Chadwell Heath, All Saints' Goodmayes, and St Sepulchre Holborn.

I should also like to thank the Royal Historical Society for taking an interest in this work and providing very patient editors in Peter Mandler and Christine Linehan. I am extremely grateful for their help and dedication.

Finally, I should like to thank my colleagues and my friends for putting up with me throughout, and above all else my family who took all my financial worries, every tantrum and every gloomy patch I could throw at them and provided solutions. I therefore dedicate this work to Karen, Brian and Danny and to those men and women with 'splendid hearts' who answered the call and paid the price in so many ways.

Mark Connelly

Abbreviations

BGWMC   Bethnal Green War Memorial Committee
NUWM   National Unemployed Workers Movement
PCC   Parochial church council
RUDC   Romford Urban District council

Newspapers and journals

Co-Part   *Co-Partners: Journal of the Gas Light and Coke Company*
CP   *City Press*
EEN   *East End News*
EHE   *East Ham Echo*
EHTCSSM   *East Ham Technical College and Secondary School Magazine*
ELA   *East London Advertiser*
ELCM   *East London College Magazine*
ELO   *East London Observer*
EP   *Eastern Post*
ET   *Essex Times*
GERM   *Great Eastern Railway Magazine*
HAC   *Honourable Artillery Company*
HAC Journal   *Honourable Artillery Company Journal*
HKG   *Hackney and Kingsland Gazette*
IR   *Ilford Recorder*
JC   *Jewish Chronicle*
JESM   *Jewish Ex-Serviceman: Journal of the Jewish Ex-Servicemen's Legion*
JG   *Jewish Graphic*
JGuard   *Jewish Guardian*
PB   *Prudential Bulletin*
RR   *Romford Recorder*
RT   *Romford Times*
SE   *Stratford Express*

Archives

CoLRO   City of London Records Office
GBL   Guildhall Printed Books Library
GML   Guildhall Manuscripts Library
GLRO   Greater London Records Office
HHL   Havering Local History Library
NHL   Newham Local History Library

RFM   Royal Fusiliers Museum
RHL   Redbridge Local History Library
THL   Tower Hamlets Local History Library

Note
Primary sources quoted without a named repository indicate material *in situ*.

Introduction

The memory of the Great War, as a subject for academic investigation, is now receiving a great deal of attention. The genre is relatively new, but almost as much work is now being done in this area as on aspects of the military and political conduct of the conflict itself.[1] The most recent works of historians such as Jay Winter, Adrian Gregory and Alex King have attempted to show the massive public response to the war in the years that followed its conclusion. They have demonstrated that the memory of the war was constructed by official attempts to orchestrate remembrance and by genuine popular inspiration.[2] Jay Winter's work, for example, has stressed the roles of both institutional religion and the strictly uncanonical practice of spiritualism as ways in which ordinary people sought to come to terms with bereavement and loss. Though these were seemingly unreconcilable developments the result was the same – an intensified sensation of communion with the dead. Both Winter and Gregory have also shown that the effect of the various forms of commemoration was usually to allow grief to flow but at the same time to buttress a socially conservative message. Memorialisation tended to stress that the men had not died in vain, that it was the duty of the living to continue to make sacrifices in order to be worthy of the dead. In the troubled times of the twenties and thirties this was a powerful way of maintaining the continuity and quiescence of British society. Thus, whatever the intention of the forms of remembrance, the overwhelming result was to stimulate and maintain a desire to remember and revere the dead.

The aim of this book is to place these conclusions within a particular, and indeed peculiar, locality. Both Winter and Gregory use a broad brush covering the entire nation, and in Winter's case the empire and Europe too. It is the intention here to test the established thinking on the memory and commemoration of the Great War in Britain by looking in detail at a geographically homogeneous but socially and economically diverse location – the City, East London and metropolitan Essex. The intensive nature of this study has allowed for an extremely detailed investigation into how memorials were planned and funded, how Armistice Day rituals developed and how those rituals changed during the twenties and thirties. Running through the narrative is an additional thread: to what extent did the specific nature of the

---

[1] For a good example of recent work on this topic see B. Bushaway. 'Name upon name: the Great War and remembrance', in R. Porter (ed.), *Myths of the English*, Cambridge 1992, 136–67.

[2] See, for example, J. M. Winter, *Sites of memory, sites of mourning*, Cambridge 1995, and also A. Gregory, *The silence of memory: Armistice Day, 1919–1946*, Oxford 1994.

communities involved throw up their own particular variants. It is the 'fine toothcomb' approach, the trawl through innumerable informal, local archives that give this work its originality and importance as a test of more general conclusions. By adopting this approach it has been possible to 'get under the skin' of particular communities, to show that the nuances of the local atmosphere often influenced the form of the war memorial and the style of the Armistice Day commemorations.

The memory of the war examined here is far different from the popular image of the war, which is one of an horrific slaughter for no particular reason followed by a botched peace in which ex-servicemen were cast aside and left to atrophy on street corners or in the dole queue. The twenties and thirties, according to popular memory, were a time when the words 'God', 'King' and 'Country' were shown to be empty baubles; it was the bitter, disillusioned period of the long weekend.[3] This image was fixed by the experience of the Second World War – a war less costly in British lives, fought for a new Britain and against the evils of the death camps. Such an experience threw the Great War into a different light and in the 1960s a host of different media combined to create the image of the Great War we have today.[4] In 1961 Alan Clark published his provocative account of the Western Front battles of 1915, *The donkeys*. For Clark, the Great War was already ancient history and not just a few decades ago: it was a great watershed and like L. P. Hartley's view of the pre-1914 world the past was truly a foreign country where things were done differently: 'My generation did not fight in the Second World War. To many of us the First is as remote as the Crimean, its causes and its personnel obscure and disreputable.'[5]

Clark had sounded the charge of the bunking and debunking brigades. This was followed in 1963 by the hugely popular stage play *Oh! What a lovely war*, which satirised the British high command and celebrated the good humour and endurance of the ordinary Tommy. In 1969 Richard Attenborough directed the film version and created a potent image of a futile war conducted by conceited, foolish generals.[6]

At the same time John Terraine 'hoisted a standard emblazoned *Douglas Haig*, and along with Correlli Barnett, sought to justify the battles of attrition

---

3 This phrase was used by Robert Graves and Alan Hodge in their book on Britain during the twenties and thirties: *The long weekend: a social history of Great Britain, 1918–1939*, London 1940.
4 For a wider debate of these issues see A. Danchev, 'Bunking and debunking: the controversies of the 1960s', in B. Bond (ed.), *The First World War and British military history*, Oxford 1991, 263–8.
5 L. P. Hartley's novel *The go-between* (London 1953) centred on an Edwardian family teetering on the verge of a violent crisis which presages the great conflict to come. The author recreates the atmosphere of a well-to-do East Anglian family with painstaking care as he attempts to find his way around the irrecoverable foreign country of pre-1914 England. See also A. Clark, *The donkeys*, London 1961, 11.
6 See Danchev, *Bunking and debunking*, 281–8.

fought on the Western Front and with it the reputation of Haig as one of the great modern generals.[7] Terraine was then made scriptwriter on the biggest television documentary series made in Great Britain to that date, *The Great War* (1964); despite the editorial wranglings, the final script followed Terraine's theories about the conduct of the war. But far from re-educating the public all it did was buttress the 'futility myth'. Danchev quotes the response of an anonymous housewife to the series: '[it] should be seen by *all* to bring home the horrors of war and the dreadful waste of young manhood'.[8] In the late sixties Martin Middlebrook seemed to find confirmation of this 'from the horse's mouth' in his interviews for his book about the first day of the Battle of the Somme:

> Many's the time I've gone to bed, after a day of 'tramp, tramp' looking for work, on a cup of cocoa and a pennyworth of chips between us; I would lay puzzling why, why after all we had gone through in the service of our country, we have to suffer such poverty, willing to work at anything but no work to be had. I only had two Christmases at work between 1919 and 1939.[9]

And this was not the only example Middlebrook found. Intrinsic to this statement is the irony between the idealism and loyalty of the service given and the ingratitude shown by the state afterwards. It is precisely this element that Paul Fussell took as the key result of the Great War; irony made the post-war world fundamentally different from the pre-war world. According to Fussell, Philip Larkin expressed an essential truth about the nature of the experience of the Great War in his poem *MCMXIV*, written to mark the fiftieth anniversary of the outbreak of the War, as there could 'Never [be] such innocence again'.[10] Fussell's book *The Great War and modern memory* (1975) pioneered research into the question of the Great War's legacy and remembrance. The theories this work contains are now coming under increasing pressure.[11] Samuel Hynes has written a more balanced account of the effect of the war on English culture in which he explores the continuities and differences between the pre- and post-war worlds. But, for him too, the war caused the loss of a language; he stated that: 'Graves had called his anti-rhetorical poem *Big Words*, and that, you might say, was the common issue: how to get rid of the big words.'[12] The important point about both Fussell and Hynes is their over-riding dependence on high art and culture and their desire to draw

---

[7] Ibid. 263; J. Terraine, *Douglas Haig: the educated soldier*, London 1963, rev. edn 1990.

[8] See Danchev, *Bunking and debunking*, 279–81.

[9] The recollections of Private C. A. Turner quoted in M. Middlebrook, *The first day on the Somme*, London 1971, 309.

[10] P. Larkin, *The Whitsun weddings*, London 1964, 28.

[11] In particular see R. Prior and T. Wilson, 'Paul Fussell at war', *War in History* 1 (1994), 63–80. Professor Brian Bond has also challenged the view that the war largely produced ironic literature in his unpublished paper, 'The anti-war writers and their critics', given at a conference on '1914–1918: the war experienced', University of Leeds, September 1994.

[12] S. Hynes, *A war imagined: the First World War and English culture*, London 1990, 167.

general conclusions from these sources. It is the contention of this work that no such all-pervasive language of paradox and satire descended like a curtain, obscuring the real meaning of the 'Big Words' of 1914, and that their use continued unimpaired via the remembrance movement throughout the twenties and thirties.[13]

War memorials were completely ignored by Fussell and only briefly mentioned by Hynes. Two reasons can be suggested for this: first, war memorials are singularly lacking in ironic content; secondly, a great many of them cannot be considered as high art. Alan Borg has written that 'It is probably because they are so common that these memorials seldom attract much attention, although they represent the biggest communal arts project ever attempted.'[14] Recently this neglect has been transformed as interest in war memorials has proliferated. Quite a number of popular works are now available, such as Borg's, and this is matched by the work being carried out in British universities.[15] Much of this confines itself to the nature of the war memorial schemes and aspects of the symbolism; studies are taken up to the unveiling and dedication services but no further. This approach, although very necessary and of great interest, largely misses the point of the memorials, that they were built to serve the cause of remembrance in order to ensure that the names of the dead did indeed live for ever more. By extending the scope of this book to include Armistice Day rituals as well it is intended to give a fuller picture of the nature of commemoration in the twenties and thirties.[16]

The rationale for a local study

This study, unlike the works already mentioned, which take the form of general surveys, is firmly fixed in terms of location. The most important studies of East London during this period, Julia Bush's *Behind the lines: East London Labour, 1914–1919* (1984), and Jon Marriott's *The culture of Labourism: the East End between the wars* (1991) are very illuminating on how far the war affected political allegiances and trade unionism. They are not, however, concerned with the direct shadow of human loss; the addition of a

13 A balance to the concentration on the high literature of the war can be found in R. M. Bracco, *Merchants of hope: British middlebrow writers and the First World War, 1919–1939*, Oxford 1993.
14 A. Borg, *War memorials: from antiquity to the present*, London 1991, p. ix.
15 See, for example, D. Boorman, *At the going down of the sun: British First World War memorials*, York 1988; C. McIntyre, *Monuments of war: how to read a war memorial*, London 1990; A. King, *Memorials of the Great War in Britain: the symbolism and politics of remembrance*, Oxford 1998; C. Moriarty, 'Narrative and the absent body: mechanisms of meaning in First World War memorials', unpubl. PhD diss. Sussex 1995.
16 In *Memorials of the Great War*, Alex King does mention some aspects of remembrance services, but his approach is rather different. Gregory, *Silence of memory*, however, provides a a solid general study of Armistice Day.

work on East London which does attempt to deal with that issue will provide balance and help to put their conclusions into a wider context.

The City, East London and metropolitan Essex were deliberately targeted for attention for a number of reasons. It was a compact area, but displayed great variety within its confines: at one and the same time it was typical and unique. It was, and still is, extraordinary in its racial mix, matched by no other district: it also exhibited a wide variety of social and economic conditions, from the merchants of the City to the dock labourers of Poplar, from the white-collar clerks of East Ham to the dairymen of Romford market. Walter Besant, the most celebrated historian of East London, stated exactly this point when he noted that it was an area of *All sorts and conditions of men* (London 1882). These are exactly the elements which also make it typical: in one area it is possible to emulate a general sampling technique – a variety of conditions and types placed against, and tested by, a set of theories. Added to these elements is the general mystique and peculiar atmosphere of the area (reflected in both popular perception and serious scholarship) which seems to demand attention.[17]

But this study is not simply to satisfy some romantic or nostalgic whim, for there is a clear need for a local study in order to test the general theories. Angela Gaffney, Jane Leonard and Fiona Douglas are working on aspects of remembrance in Wales, Ireland and Scotland respectively, thus seeking to balance the anglocentric nature of much of the work in this field. But no one has yet attempted a local study on this level. In some ways the most comparable work is Geoffrey Moorhouse's *Hell's foundations: a town, its myths and Gallipoli* (1992), in which he examines the memory of the Great War in Bury as filtered through a whole range of local traditions, beliefs and *mores*, most particularly the Bury regiment – the Lancashire Fusiliers. Adrian Gregory has noted the need to uncover these peculiar sorts of remembrance: 'More studies are needed at a local level to penetrate this memory, although the problems of uncovering it are methodologically profound. I happily leave those studies to others.'[18]

Gregory has stated that his work is largely a study of the use of language in

---

[17] Perhaps the best exponent of both the 'romance' of the cockney East End and serious work is Bill Fishman. Richard Cobb stated in his foreword to Fishman's *East End, 1888* (London 1988) that 'W. J. Fishman's history is social history as it should be: *walked* (and what a walker he still is), seen and heard. His awareness of locality is unrivalled, and one senses the contribution of the powerful combination of family loyalty, childhood and adolescent memory and tenderness . . . and his ability to recreate an urban topography of one of the most distinctive and unusual quarters of any of the great cities of the late nineteenth century.' And, as Alan Palmer has noted, 'Everyone knows the East End, at least as a generalised concept. A popular television series, together with media coverage of the boom in Docklands keeps it firmly in the public eye; and over the last hundred years no part of London has remained so consistently newsworthy. But the whole area between the City and metropolitan Essex is rich in a history which is of national significance rather than merely of local curiosity': *The East End: four centuries of London life*, London 1989, preface.
[18] Gregory, *Silence of memory*, 6.

commemoration and remembrance rituals.[19] Alex King has also tried to define the meaning of memory and its place in the community.[20] But neither of them really attempts to understand remembrance at its most intimate level, on the streets and in the parishes. It is the aim of this study to uncover exactly what community meant in the face of such human disaster and how those communities expressed themselves; the various sub-communities will also be explored and this will show how each exerted a different kind of pull and therefore subtly shaped the memory of both the dead and the conflict itself. This will highlight what is known as the 'urban mosaic' of city life, as identifed by the American sociologist R. E. Park:

> In the course of time every sector and quarter of the City takes on something of the character and qualities of its inhabitants. Each separate part of the City is inevitably stained with the peculiar sentiments of its population. The effect of this is to convert what was at first a mere geographical expression into a neighbourhood, that is to say, a locality with sentiments, traditions and a history of its own.[21]

In turn these neighbourhoods further subdivide: the sociologists Michael Young and Peter Willmott put this pattern into the specific context of this study:

> Sometimes a person's relatives are in the same turning, more often in another nearby turning, and this helps to account for the attachment which people feel to the precinct, as distinct from the street, in which they live. A previous observer [P. J. O. Self in *Voluntary organisations in Bethnal Green*] remarked: 'There is further localism within the borough. People are apt to look for their friends and their club within a close range. The social settlements draw nearly all their members from within a third of a mile, while tradition dictates which way borderline streets face for their social life. The main streets are very real social barriers, and to some residents the Cambridge Heath Road resembles the Grand Canyon.' In Bethnal Green the one-time villages which have as elsewhere been physically submerged and their barriers usually obliterated – Mumford talks of London as a 'federation of historic communities' – live on in people's minds.[22]

In many cases memorials were therefore chosen in order to reflect a pre-existing self-perception. At the same time, for the new communities of the rapidly expanding suburbs, the war and the planned memorials were the first test of an embryonic sense of community and the first badge of honour – the war gave them a history and heritage to pass on. Set against this is the

[19] Ibid.
[20] King, *Memorials of the Great War*, 1–17.
[21] Quoted in D. W. G. Timms, *The urban mosaic: towards a theory of residential differentiation*, Cambridge 1971, 1.
[22] M. Young and P. Willmott, *Family and kinship in East London*, London 1957, 87.

glittering heart of the British empire – the City of London – with its own very definite sense of history and its place within it. This will test the theory of J. M. Mayo, who has stated that 'memorials help to form the community's identity . . . [and] commemoration of war reshapes how a society views its political history'.[23] Finally, this work will seek to show that in many ways it was the acts of remembrance that shaped the war – an inversion of history and time. It is this aspect that it is so pervasive and so haunting, perfectly expressed by Geoff Dyer in his impressionist book *The missing of the Somme*:

> The young men [in the 1914 photographs of the enlistment offices] are queuing up to be slaughtered: they are already dead . . . the Great War urges us to write the opposite of history: the story of effects generating their cause.
>
> The war, it begins to seem, had been fought in order that it might be remembered, that it might live up to its memory.[24]

Ted Hughes seemed to be making exactly the same point in his poem, 'Six Young Men', which describes a photograph of six men taken on the eve of the Great War. The last line of the first stanza bluntly states: 'Six months after this picture they were all dead.' Hughes then reverts to describing the peaceful countryside of the photograph, but it no longer matters as the reader knows that 'they are already dead'.[25]

Methodology

In trying to uncover the East London of the twenties or thirties, and its attitudes towards the war dead, I was confronted with a fascinating task: defining the feeling of the period, the landscape of its memory, was crucial. An important indicator of temperament and outlook can be found in local newspapers, which often regarded themselves as the guardians of, and conduits for, the feelings of a community. The sorrow, the pity and the pride engendered by the war was thus palpable in the pages of the local press.

Then, as people attempted to come to terms with their loss they often turned to religion. Church records contained much information on how memorial committees came to be formed, the debates over the form of the memorial and the plans for fund-raising. In an area as racially diverse as East London, however, far more than Anglican Church records were needed to build up an accurate picture. Nonconformist, Roman Catholic and Jewish communities all had deep roots in East London. In order to understand the responses of these communities records of their activities had to be found and examined. Pursuing such material often meant much detective work,

---

[23] J. M. Mayo, *War memorials as political landscape*, New York 1988, introduction, 249.
[24] G. Dyer, *The missing of the Somme*, London 1994, 6, 15.
[25] Quoted in J. Stallworthy (ed.), *The Oxford book of war poetry*, Oxford 1984, 224–5.

enduring the bitter cold of church vestries in winter and breathing lungfuls of dusty air from cupboards unopened for years.

The collection of personal memoirs in the form of diaries and letters was difficult. State education was rudimentary in Britain prior to 1914, and did not improve much after the Great War, a problem exacerbated by large areas of East London stricken by poverty. However, the advent of oral history studies from the late 1960s has managed to fill out some of the missing sections of the mosaic of the past. Various local history projects and initiatives have collected oral data and encouraged the writing of autobiographies. But the survivors of the Great War are now very few and far between, and even people too young to have served in the conflict, but old enough to remember the 1920s and 1930s clearly, are difficult to find. In addition, it is very hard to recover the 'pure' spirit of the time from people who have experienced bombing and rationing. The Second World War fundamentally altered people's memories of the Great War. It was only after the Second World War that the British people gained a comparator with the Great War; only then were they given a 'yardstick of futility'. Until the British people had faced mass bombing, mass rationing, faced a much greater risk of invasion; until they had seen images of Belsen and Auschwitz the Great War retained its hallowed integrity. The experience of the Second World War suddenly made Prussianism seem not so bad after all; compared with Nazism it seemed to be only a mildly objectionable political system. Fighting to defend the poor Belgians from their Prussian invaders was, ironically, relegated to being a futile waste of lives.

The testimonies of East Enders illustrate the way in which layers of memory can effect, affect and infect each other. Writing in the 1980s, Harry Pepper of Poplar recorded his memories of his childhood. He claimed a clear memory of the unveiling of the Upper North Street School memorial, erected to commemorate children killed in a zeppelin raid. Without doubting the clarity of his memory, I found it difficult to believe that his child's mind – he was six or seven at the time – actually placed this interpretation on the event:

> I couldn't help but think of all these young men, who now shared the same sad epitaph and whose deaths were not front page news, had themselves not long been out of classrooms like those at Upper North Street School.[26]

Whiffs of 'Oh! What a lovely war' seem to permeate this statement. It has the element of irony and the dichotomy between innocence and experience that only becomes apparent long after the original event.

Similarly, Fred Wright, writing in 1992 about events in his mother's family, mixed a little knowledge with a thick slice of received opinion to make a statement about the Great War:

[26] H. Pepper, *Seven-days soup: growing-up in London's Chinatown*, London [1981], 27.

The eldest son, swept along by the hysteria that followed the declaration of war in 1914, joined up and within six months was mown down like the 1,054,000 other young men of the British, French and German armies in that holocaust that history has labelled the Battle of the Somme. To remember his contribution to 'the war to end wars' one must visit Limehouse churchyard where his name appears on the War Memorial.[27]

Again, it is hard not to be impressed by the sheer passion, but it is one heavily influenced by the 'lions led by donkeys' school, and it is a long way from the *leitmotif* of the time. For this reason post-1945 recollections did not help in the struggle to recover the East London of the 1920s and 1930s, the world in which the community of the bereaved desperately wanted to know that the dead did not grow old, as they that were left grew old, that their lost loved ones had died in the noblest of causes.

Investigation of the spirit of that world is best achieved by looking at the war memorials erected by the various communities of East London. Interpreting the clues and signs they offer helps us to understand how these communities reacted to the war and how they viewed themselves. As each war memorial was built to serve a continuing commemorative function, the nature of Armistice Day celebrations shows how communities refined their memories, how certain rituals and a special language came to be associated with the dead, and how this in turn created a highly stylised interpretation of the nature of sacrifice. As the 1920s and 1930s were years of contradiction and flux, Armistice Day can be seen as an anchor, a constant reminder of seemingly timeless values. The extent to which those values were commonly accepted across social classes, religions and even languages, by the communities of East London helps us to understand a country looking for comfort in the wake of a traumatising conflict.

The structure of the book

This book is divided into two parts. The first part looks at the war memorials erected at the various different levels of community. It seeks to show the variations in the iconography of the war dead, how they were used to serve different purposes and what elements and considerations shaped the eventual form of the memorial. The second part looks at Armistice Day from 1919 to 1939. It shows how, in the twenties, the day established itself in the City and East London and went on to become a key event in the communal calendar. Discussion centres on the language and rituals of the day, and the degree to which these were conditioned by the size and nature of the community involved. It then goes on to demonstrate how in the thirties wider problems, both local and international, came to have a much higher profile during

27 F. Wright, 'The Ingles of Limehouse', *East London Record* xv (1992), 15–18.

remembrance services. The study ends with an examination of Armistice Day 1939, in order to identify the memory of the Great War against the background of another conflict with Germany: this will enable us to see just how far the memory of the war and its dead had changed over the intervening twenty years – if at all. The final chapter, on one specific community, that of Jewish ex-servicemen, is designed to show how the dead continued to play a distinct role in the lives of survivors. It shows how important they were to the debates surrounding Britain's entry into the Second World War, as well as their importance in defining a community within the East End of London.

PART I

THE ICONOGRAPHY OF WAR MEMORIALS

1

The City, East London and Metropolitan Essex

In order to understand the nature of memorials erected to commemorate the Great War in the City, East London and into metropolitan Essex, the processes that led to their construction and the way in which Armistice Day developed and was celebrated it is first necessary to survey the district. It is important to have some grasp of the nature and psyche of the area as these traits shaped the form the memorials took, where they were sited and how much money could be raised and spent on the various projects.

Romford Urban District

Romford Urban District (since 1965 part of the London Borough of Havering) was formed in 1895 and provides the easternmost boundary of the London conurbation.[1] Its growth was slightly different to the other suburban districts studied insofar as its expansion was steady rather than spectacular during the forty years between 1871 and the outbreak of the Great War: its real explosion came in the twenties and thirties. In 1871 the population stood at 8,239, by 1901 it was 13,915, in 1921 it had reached 19,442 and by 1931 it had climbed to 35,918.[2] In 1914 it was therefore still a small town clinging to the eastern edge of London.

The economic character of the town was split between its ancient trades and newer industries and occupations. Romford was (and indeed still is) famed for its thriving market, which, lying in the shadow of the parish church of St Edward, dominated the town, supplying London with meat, grain and vegetables.[3] Of similar fame was the Ind Coope brewery in the High Street; by 1908 it employed 480 workers and had laid down railway lines connecting it to Romford Great Eastern Railway station.[4] It was the Great Eastern Railway that pulled Romford toward London: it not only linked the town to Liverpool Street, but was also a major local employer for the main stores department and the railway tarpaulins and sacks factory were based in the town.[5]

The residential areas of Romford reflected the various characteristics of a

1 VCH, *Essex*, vii, Oxford 1978, 78.
2 Ibid. vii. 57.
3 *Kelly's directory of Essex [1911]*, London 1911, 106.
4 *Official guide to Romford, 1908*, Romford 1908, 3.
5 GERM, Aug. 1920, 125.

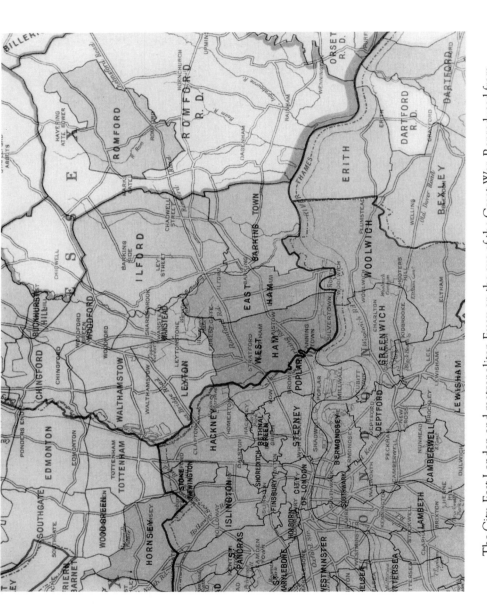

The City, East London and metropolitan Essex on the eve of the Great War. Reproduced from *The citizen series maps of London*, London 1912

suburban, small industrial and rural market town. By the 1880s a series of middle-class housing estates had been built. The most important of these was Mawney's estate, which took up a large square of land and rapidly acquired its own character, due to its relatively isolated nature at the northern point of the town. But by the outbreak of the war it still lacked a church and most Anglican communicants had to attend St Edward's in the market place.[6] In 1910 work started on the Gidea Park garden suburb. This was conceived as a grand estate of mock Tudor houses for the London-based professional classes. Part of its attraction was its proximity to Romford Golf Club; again the GER was influential, for it offered special concessions to members travelling to central London and a subsidised cab fare from the station to the club house. The area around the railway yard and station itself contained the houses of Romford's workers and by 1862 the church of St Andrew had been built to serve this community.[7] The nature of Romford was encapsulated by the description in the *Official guide to the Great Eastern Railway*:

> The chief support of its inhabitants is derived from the surrounding agricul-
> tural and grazing district, but, like many small country towns within easy reach
> of London, it has likewise become a favourite centre for suburban residence. A
> large section of its industrial population finds employment at the celebrated
> Romford Brewery of Messrs. Ind, Coope and Company, Limited, whose ales
> have acquired a high reputation throughout the United Kingdom, India and
> the Colonies.[8]

The religious complexion of Romford was largely Anglican: in 1914, like Ilford, many of its new estates had either half-built churches or iron huts serving as temporary churches; but unlike Ilford and East and West Ham, nonconformity was of only minor significance.[9]

By 1914, therefore, Romford was a town with a split personality, part of rural Essex in some ways, following its ancient trades and customs, but also becoming ever more part of London, shadowing the growth of neighbouring Ilford.

Ilford Urban District

Although Ilford Urban District (since 1965 part of the London Borough of Redbridge) consisted of seven wards in 1922, there was a huge imbalance in its population; the vast bulk of it was concentrated in the five southern and central wards whilst the two northern wards, Hainault North and Hainault

---

6   VCH, *Essex*, vii. 57, 86.
7   Ibid. vii. 59, 85; B. Weinreb and C. Hibbert (eds), *The London encyclopaedia*, London 1992 edn, 323.
8   *Official guide to the Great Eastern Railway, 1892*, London 1892, 87.
9   VCH, *Essex*, vii. 82–91.

South were largely rural and very quiet. The remaining five wards – Clementswood, Cranbrook, Loxford, the Park and Seven Kings – had exploded in terms of house-building and population, transforming Ilford into a commuter town packed with white-collar workers.

The census of 1891 revealed a population of 10,913; by 1911 it was 78,188. Population increase slowed down over the next ten years, affected by the disruption of the war, but had nevertheless reached 85,194 by 1921. The *Victoria county history of Essex* noted that 'between 1901 and 1911 Ilford's rate of growth was exceeded only by that of Southend among English towns of more than 50,000 inhabitants'.[10] The main occupation of Ilfordians was that of clerk; the *Official guide to Ilford* for 1920–1 stated that the town 'has become colonised, so to speak, by the professional class of city workers'. The guide also estimated that on average 10,000 commuters a day passed through the town's GER stations to the City.[11] It has been noted that from 1862, the year the GER arrived in Ilford,

> the growth of the district has been phenomenal. Being in a unique position, only about seven miles from Liverpool Street, and in close proximity to the countryside, it grew rapidly in favour as a residential town.[12]

The wealthiest wards in Ilford were Park and Cranbrook, both centred upon Valentines Park. This area was developed by the Griggs family who were extremely influential in the town: Sir Peter Griggs became the first MP for Ilford in 1918. Two smaller communities were built at Seven Kings and Goodmayes by A. Cameron Corbett, later Lord Rowallan. He persuaded the Great Eastern Railway Company to build stations to serve his estates which were duly completed in 1899 and 1901 respectively.[13] These communities tended to view themselves as individual units apart from Ilford. In fact, Seven Kings was known as 'Klondyke' such was the sense of isolation, and Goodmayes was thought to be even more quiet and remote.[14] The *Official guide to Ilford* stated that 'Although part of Ilford proper, Seven Kings constitutes an almost distinct township.'[15] This is well worth bearing in mind, for the mental parameters of community fundamentally influenced the siting and nature of the war memorials.

The two Hainault wards grew only towards the end of the twenties. Goodmayes was originally part of Hainault South but became a a ward of its own around the same time as the housing developments in Hainault North. Goodmayes also included a small part of the large LCC estate of Becontree.

---

10 Ibid. v, Oxford 1966, 6.
11 *Official guide to Ilford, including Seven Kings and Goodmayes*, Ilford 1921, 17. The title of this guide reveals the separate natures of Seven Kings and Goodmayes.
12 *Ilford charter day, October 21st 1926, souvenir book*, Ilford 1926, 13.
13 VCH, *Essex*, v. 251.
14 *Ilford charter day, souvenir book*, 15.
15 *Official guide to Ilford*, 23.

The poorest part of Ilford, relatively speaking, was the ward of Loxford, which included many workers for the factories of Barking, East Ham and Ilford.[16]

The churches of Ilford provided a familiar point of reference for the town's large migrant community: the Scottish community was particularly centred around the Presbyterian church. *Kelly's directory* for 1921 lists fourteen Anglican churches, one Roman Catholic, three Baptist, three Congregational and one church each for the Presbyterians, Primitive, United and Wesleyan Methodists, Unitarian and one Society of Friends Meeting House.[17] The *Victoria county history* stated that 'only two English towns of over 50,000 inhabitants had among their population a smaller number of their own natives than Ilford'. But this was part of a general pattern: 'the percentage of natives in each of the chief Essex suburbs was: West Ham 42.6, East Ham 20.2, Ilford 18.6'. If the birthplaces are grouped by counties then the chief sources of population in the Essex suburbs, expressed in percentages, were:

West Ham: Essex 49.5, London 31.6, Kent 1.8.
East Ham: Essex 39.4, London 38.3, Kent 2.3, Middlesex 1.8.
Ilford: Essex 37.5, London 33.9, Middlesex 2.7, Kent 2.1, Scotland 1.6, Suffolk 1.6 [a quarter, therefore, came from outside London].[18]

This also seemed to encourage a keen interest in community and the reports of the Ratepayers Association meetings show them to have been extremely active. The *Official guide to Ilford* boasted that it was the 'largest such Association in the United Kingdom'.[19]

The county boroughs of East and West Ham

The London Borough of Newham was formed in 1965 by the amalgamation of the old county boroughs of West and East Ham. West and East Ham provide the middle ground, geographically, socially and ideologically between the proletarian boroughs of Poplar and Stepney immediately to the west and the bourgeois Ilford on their north-eastern fringe.[20]

In 1914 both boroughs had just completed a period of rapid growth, starting around 1860 in the case of West Ham, and 1880 for East Ham. By this time they had also developed an atmosphere of solid respectability.[21] The bourgeois districts which made up the 'respectable' elements of the boroughs formed part of a northern ribbon running from east to west, straddling the

---

16 VCH, *Essex,* v. 251.
17 *Kelly's directory of Ilford [1921],* London 1921, 107.
18 VCH, *Essex,* v. 6–7.
19 *Official guide to Ilford,* 24.
20 Weinreb and Hibbert, *London encyclopaedia,* 563.
21 Ibid.

boundary line of East and West Ham. Sedate estates with genteel names such as Upton Park, Woodgrange, Forest Gate, Manor Park and Plashet Grove dominated this area. The *Victoria county history* referred to the 'long terraces of small but well-built dwellings . . . for clerks and skilled workers'. (Many of the West Ham estates were built by Thomas Corbett. His son, A. Cameron Corbett developed much of East Ham and Ilford. The influence of this Scottish builder may well go some way towards explaining the Scottish population of Ilford.)[22] In 1907 it was noted of Upton that 'practically the whole of the ward belongs to the middle class, and a large proportion has some unearned income'.[23] Stanley Holloway, the actor and comedian, came from East Ham and later served on the Western Front, first as an officer in the London Rifle Brigade and then in the Connaught Rangers. In his autobiography he described his early life in Manor Park and East London:

> But, when I was born [1890], Manor Park was full of big, well-built houses and solid citizens. Not glamorous, maybe, but reasonably prosperous. My father was a lawyer's clerk. I have no idea what his income was, but we certainly lacked for nothing. Manor Park, a few stations away from Liverpool Street station, is not now, perhaps, the most elegant place to live but in the late years of the nineteenth century and when the century turned it was a very comfortable place. Areas like Bow and Burdett Road in the East End housed many comfortably off business-men. They used to commute the few miles to and from Cornhill, Throgmorton and Threadneedle streets or else ran small but prosperous businesses locally.[24]

It would be the respectable areas of the boroughs that provided the initial impetus in war memorial activity.

The southern districts of East and, in particular, West Ham were very different. West Ham was an industrial giant with a huge population: in 1924, standing at 300,860, it was exceeded in England only by London, Birmingham, Liverpool, Manchester, Sheffield, Leeds and Bristol.[25] Industrial development followed a peculiar pattern in West Ham, being concentrated in a band running from the Great Eastern Railway locomotive works at Stratford in the north-west, then hugging the River Lea and railway spur southwards down to the Thames, making a rough 'L' shape. Marriott states that ' Heavy industry had a considerable presence, particularly in the south where the massive factories of Henley's cable works, the sugar refineries of Tate & Lyle, the Beckton gas works, Silver's India Rubber, Gutta Percha and Telegraph Co. among others lined the Thames.'[26] Industry was supplied with labour from the poor-quality housing estates of Canning Town, Silvertown,

22 VCH, *Essex*, vi, Oxford 1973, 5, 49.
23 E. Howarth and M. Wilson, *West Ham: a study in social and industrial problems*, London 1907, 4.
24 S. Holloway, *Wiv a little bit o' luck*, London 1967, 43, 58.
25 J. Marriott, *The culture of labourism: the East End between the wars*, Edinburgh 1991, 17.
26 Ibid. 16–17.

Plaistow and Custom House.[27] Such economic power gave West Ham the ability to envisage a memorial scheme on a grand scale.

East Ham had some poor districts on its extreme eastern fringe in the parish of Little Ilford (the district which provided the borough's most revered son, Boy Seaman Jack Cornwell VC), but compared with its neighbour had a much smaller industrial base. The main industries of the borough lay in the southernmost district of Beckton, which was the home of the King George V dock (opened only in 1921), and the massive gasworks of the Gas Light and Coke Company. It also shared the Royal and Victoria Docks complex with West Ham.[28] But, as a result of the strange meandering of the London, Tilbury, Southend Railway, these had little to do with East Ham as most of the labour came from West Ham. Beckton was further separated by the fact that it had been originally developed by Simon Beck, chairman of the Gas Light and Coke Company, for his workers. Beck gave his name to the district and built the parish church: this meant that the community was defined by its major employer and this had a significant effect on memorial activities in the area.[29] East Ham was effectively a dormitory suburb of London, rather than an industrial town in its own right like West Ham.[30]

West Ham therefore perceived itself to be the more important of the two boroughs, as an extract from the Mansfield House University Settlement magazine fully reveals:

West Ham is the largest County Borough in the whole country [sic]. . . . It may be noted that West Ham is the largest town within a hundred miles of London. All such Boroughs as Croydon and East Ham have considerably smaller populations than that of West Ham.[31]

None the less each borough took a keen interest in the affairs of the other, as will be seen in the rival memorial schemes, and they did share some interests. Great mutual pride was invested in the football team, West Ham United: although originally based in West Ham it had moved to East Ham in order to attract the bourgeois shopkeepers of the area. During the war the West Ham (Service) battalion of the Essex Regiment had recruited under a slogan based on the club's nickname; 'Join the "Hammers" and Hammer the Huns'.[32] Both boroughs revelled in the Cup Final appearance of 1923; indeed West Ham used the team to promote their war memorial plans.[33]

Politically West Ham was quite an explosive place: West Ham South

[27] Ibid. 76.
[28] VCH, *Essex*, vi. 6, 16.
[29] Ibid. vi. 6, 29.
[30] Weinreb and Hibbert, *London encyclopaedia*, 255–6.
[31] NHL, *Way Down East; The Magazine of Mansfield House University Settlement*, Dec. 1926, 4.
[32] NHL, Councillor Dyer's cutting book, 1914–15.
[33] C. Korr, *West Ham United*, London 1986, 31, 82; *SE*, 18 Apr. 1923.

elected Keir Hardie as the first Labour MP in 1892 and it had the first Labour council in England in 1898. During the war years Will Thorne of the Gasworkers and General Workers' Union (along with Jack Jones in Silvertown) came to dominate the borough.[34] The north of the borough was more traditional and alternated between Tory and Liberal MPs.[35] East Ham mirrored this pattern; when in 1918 it was split into two divisions, the north followed the old and influential Liberal MP, Sir (later Lord) John Bethell, whilst the south became a Labour stronghold. But in 1923 East Ham North caused a shock by returning the first female Labour MP in Susan Lawrence.[36] Both Thorne and Bethell played a considerable part in the development of their boroughs' war memorials.

The metropolitan boroughs of Poplar, Stepney and Bethnal Green

The London Borough of Tower Hamlets was created in 1965 by amalgamating the former metropolitan boroughs of Poplar, Stepney and Bethnal Green.

Bethnal Green was the most northerly of the three boroughs and was bordered by Hackney and Shoreditch on the north and west and Poplar and Stepney in the south and east. In 1921 the population stood at 117,238, a relatively steep decline since 1901 when it stood at 129,680, but it was still densely populated.[37] It was also poor; in 1932 the New Survey of London Life and Labour published its findings and stated that 'poor and overcrowded conditions are found in many parts of the borough'.[38] The main forms of employment in Bethnal Green were the woodworking and furniture and clothing trades and boot and shoe manufacturing.[39]

Despite the economic and housing situation, Bethnal Green perceived itself to be slightly superior to its neighbours Poplar and Stepney. The impressive Victoria Park and the actual Bethnal Green gave the small borough a sense of space and gentility, elements largely missing from the crammed industrial boroughs of Poplar and Stepney.[40] This was reflected in the continued Liberal presence in the two parliamentary divisions of the borough.[41]

---

34 Marriott, *Culture of labourism*, 26, 30–8.

35 VCH, *Essex*, vi. 112.

36 Ibid. vi. 25.

37 *London statistics, 1921–23*, xxviii, London 1924, 36.

38 *New survey of London life and labour*, III: *Survey of social conditions: the eastern area*, London 1932, 345. This survey used the same methods as Charles Booth's great investigation of 1889 and plotted the social complexion of London via colour-coded maps.

39 W. Besant, *East London*, London 1903, 22–3.

40 The sociologists Michael Young and Peter Willmott later remarked upon the peculiar village atmosphere of Bethnal Green: *Family and kinship in East London*, London 1972 edn, 87–9.

41 See P. Thompson, *Socialists, Liberals and Labour: the struggle for London, 1885–1914*,

Stepney lay to the south of Bethnal Green and east of the City; it was bordered by Poplar to its east with the Thames providing its southern edge. In 1921 it too had a declining population: 249,657 in 1921 compared with 298,600 in 1901.[42] The population was poor and contained a great racial mix: Jews concentrated in Whitechapel, Irish in the parish of St George's-in-the-East, Chinese in Limehouse and Germans and Scandinavians in the dock areas.[43] The chief sources of employment were dock labour, the clothing industry (in which many Jews were employed), furniture manufacture and commercial occupations in warehouses and shops.[44] Many of London's breweries were also based in Stepney: Charrington, Mann, Crossman and Paulin, Truman, Hanbury and Buxton and Taylor Walker.[45]

Poplar extended from Hackney to the north down to the Thames and was flanked by the River Lea and West Ham on the east and Bethnal Green and Stepney to the west. In 1921 its population stood at 162,578 down from 168,822 in 1901.[46] However it suffered the most acute post-war housing shortage: the borough guide referred to 'appalling over-crowding' problems.[47] The population was poor, despite some middle-class pockets around Bow Road, and the New Survey found it to be the poorest borough in London. Racially the borough was not as mixed as Stepney, although an Irish community had settled in Wapping and Jews and Chinese were also found in the area.[48] The principal occupations of the borough were the docks, railways and canals – all requiring unskilled and casual labour. Unemployment rose rapidly in the wake of the post-war depression and led to the famous rates dispute in 1921, led by the radical socialist George Lansbury.[49]

All three metropolitan boroughs, therefore, had a surface similarity in their poverty and overcrowding. Poplar and Stepney, however, were far more comparable as was reflected in the fact that the two boroughs served as a recruiting base for the 17th battalion, London Regiment, the Poplar and Stepney Rifles.[50] Religiously the three boroughs were a great mix, reflecting the racial composition of the districts. Julia Bush has analysed Richard Mudie-Smith's figures for church attendance in London and has noted the general lack of religious feeling among the working classes. Nonconformity

London 1967, 183–4; J. Bush, *Behind the lines: East London labour, 1914–1919*, London 1984, 243.

[42] *London statistics, 1921–23*, xxviii. 36.

[43] *New survey of London*, iii. 353–4; Besant, *East London*, 190–2.

[44] *New survey of London*, iii. 353.

[45] Weinreb and Hibbert, *London encyclopaedia*, 86–8.

[46] *London statistics, 1921–1923*, xxviii. 36. See also G. C. Rose, 'Locality, politics and culture: Poplar in the 1920s', unpubl. PhD diss. London 1989.

[47] *Official guide to the metropolitan borough of Poplar*, London 1927, 35.

[48] *New survey of London*, iii. 365–6.

[49] N. Branson, *Poplarism 1919–1925: George Lansbury and the councillors' revolt*, London 1979, 31.

[50] R. Westlake, *The Territorial battalions: a pictorial history, 1859–1985*, London 1986, 221–2.

was spreading, but not among the working classes. Only Jews and Irish Catholics seemed to have a genuine religious identity, largely because it also defined their community.[51] Despite the criticisms of the hold of Anglicanism in the heart of the East End made by Mudie-Smith's contributors, the Established Church was still important through its network of clubs and missions. This work was supplemented by the university and public school missions such as Oxford House in Bethnal Green. Ben Thomas, a Limehouse resident, noted in his autobiography that: 'The Church was of more importance than it is today, so that more attended either morning or evening at the places of worship. Our Lady's Catholic Church and St Anne's Limehouse Parish Church both had big congregations.'[52] But the war was to bring both the Anglican and the other Churches into the lives of East Enders as never before. Ironically Mudie-Smith did stumble upon one of the reasons for this in his 1902–3 survey; he stated that novelty and special events did have the effect of pulling the people into church, even if he did doubt the strength of High Church ritualism.[53]

The City of London

The square mile that makes up the City of London has a unique history which permeates every part of its existence: that ancient and unique history had a fundamental effect on the way in which it commemorated its war dead. Custom, tradition and honour were the forces that shaped the City's reaction to the war. It simply drew upon its inheritance and its overwhelming sense of its own history, dignity and importance:

> London, and by this I mean a very small portion of the great area that bears that name, is something more than the premier municipality of the greatest Empire that the world has ever known. It is a little kingdom in itself.[54]

So wrote a historian of the City in 1932. Presiding over this square mile – stretching from the bars at Holborn and the Temple in the west to the Tower of London in the east, and from Smithfield and Moorfields in the north to the River Thames in the south – was (and still is) the Corporation of the City of London. Centred on the Guildhall, the Corporation annually elected a Lord Mayor from the ranks of the aldermen; decision-making was in the hands of

51 Bush, *Behind the lines*, 16.
52 B. Thomas, *Ben's Limehouse: recollections by Ben Thomas*, London 1987, 48.
53 R. Mudie-Smith (ed.), *The religious life of London*, London 1904, 19–42, 294–301. Mudie-Smith initially conducted his survey from November 1902 to November 1903 through the columns of the *Daily News*. A team of investigators examined church attendance in London via a census of attendance on fixed dates. The results were collated by Mudie-Smith and published in book form in 1904.
54 R. J. Blackman, *London for ever the sovereign city*, London 1932, 1.

the court of common council and the court of aldermen elected from the twenty-six City wards.[55] The Corporation was the fount of all pageantry and custom:

> The Corporation of the City of London cherishes its ceremonials with the greatest tenacity. No feature of a procession must be altered or omitted, as it was in the beginning so must it remain for ever. Woe be unto the man who seeks to make any change.[56]

In turn, the Corporation was fed and replenished from the ranks of the livery companies. Originally the twelve great guild trades of the City, slowly other trades were admitted and by 1921 there were seventy-three. Economic and commercial power were therefore at the heart of influence in the City; Britain's industrial revolution and empire meant that the City was 'the economic centre of the world'.[57]

As the City had become more and more dedicated to trade, finance and commerce its residential population declined. The 1921 census found that it had a day-time population of 436,721 and a night-time one of only 13,701.[58] This meant that the nature of the community was markedly different from that of the other districts studied. Community was defined by the bonds of trade and commerce rather than residence. None the less the Anglican Church was still extremely important: in 1921 the City could still boast forty-seven parish churches (prior to the Great Fire ninety-seven were crammed into the City walls). The churches were connected by new and ancient bonds to certain trades and were still of great significance as the focus of the communities.[59] Indeed in 1924 one commentator noted: 'In these ancient and noble shrines, the City owns a treasure which all its gold could not buy.'[60] By studying the City, it will be possible to see how these alternative bonds of community affected remembrance.

History, custom and honour placed a huge burden on the City to uphold the war effort and mark it properly. It supported the war vigorously. 'London took the lead in the nation's life. *London roused the cities and towns of England to greater activity.*'[61] This was most clearly revealed in the pride taken in the exploits of the various units directly connected with the City,[62] an impressive list which included the City of London Regiment, the Royal Fusiliers, the

---

[55] Weinreb and Hibbert, *London encyclopaedia*, 177–80, 496–8. All the above-mentioned bodies and processes are still in existence.

[56] A. J. Glasspool, *The Corporation of the City of London; its ceremonies and importance*, London 1924, 1.

[57] Weinreb and Hibbert, *London encyclopaedia*, 166–77; P. H. Ditchfield, *The City of London*, London 1921, 121.

[58] Quoted in the *City of London guide*, London 1939, 4.

[59] J. Betjeman, *The City of London churches*, London 1974, 2–4.

[60] M. E. Tabor, *The City churches*, London 1924, 15.

[61] Blackman, *Sovereign city*, 185.

[62] Many of the City battalions, along with the City Imperial Volunteers, had fought in the

London Rifle Brigade, the City of London Rifles, the 7th battalion City of London Regiment, the Post Office Rifles, the Inns of Court Officer Training Corps, the City of London Yeomanry and the Honourable Artillery Company.[63]

The City workers largely came from the eastern suburbs. The Great Eastern Railway terminus at Liverpool Street was 'the largest terminus, not only in London, but in the kingdom'.[64] In 1905 the Royal Commission on London traffic found that it handled the greatest number of season ticket journeys of any station at 20 million a year and the greatest in terms of total journeys at 65.3 million. By 1921 Liverpool Street was handling 229,073 passengers a day and the two other City stations serving the east, Broad Street and Fenchurch Street, were handling 50,000 and 80,000 a day respectively. In contrast, London Bridge station, the City's great southern exit handled 11.7 million season ticket journeys in 1905 and 29.8 million total journeys.[65] The City thus forms both a link and a comparator to the areas more usually known as 'East London'.

South African War. The City gave them a rapturous reception on their return: C. Messenger, History of the British army, London 1986, 101.

[63] For the details of these units see their various war histories: The Royal Fusiliers in an outline of history: 1685–1938, Aldershot 1938 (the City was most intimately connected with the four Territorial battalions attached to this regiment and the two service battalions raised during the war, the 10th [Stockbrokers] and the 26th [Bankers], as they had their headquarters in and around the City, whereas the regular battalions were stationed at Hounslow); The History of the London Rifle Brigade, 1859–1919, London 1921; E. G. Godfrey, The Cast-Iron Sixth: a history of the 6th battalion, London Regiment (The City of London Rifles), London 1938; C. Digby Planck, History of the 7th (City of London) battalion, the London Regiment, London 1947; C. Messenger, Terriers in the trenches: the history of the Post Office Rifles, Chippenham 1981; F. H. L. Errington, The Inns of Court Officer Training Corps in the Great War, London 1922; A. S. Hamilton, The City of London Yeomanry (Roughriders), London 1936; G. Goold Walker (ed.), The Honourable Artillery Company in the Great War, 1914–1919, London 1930.

[64] A. H. Beavan, Imperial London, London 1901, 289.

[65] Figures from A. A. Jackson, London's termini, London 1985 edn, 99, 119, 139, 374.

2

War Shrines: The Origins of the War Memorials Movement

Gallipoli and the Battle of Loos in 1915 had brought the first real rumbles of war to the people of East London and metropolitan Essex. Local men took part in both. Though both campaigns, particularly Loos, were to become a part of the post-war commemoration there seems to have been little direct memorial activity at the time. Rather it was the battle of Jutland, closely followed by that of the Somme fought throughout the summer of 1916, that forced home the reality of war to most East Londoners and most Britons as well. The first memorial activity of note came out of these great struggles in the form of street war shrines. The first shrine was erected in South Hackney under the auspices of the rector in August 1916.[1] But it took until the autumn of 1916 for the movement to really spring into life; the catalyst was an article in the London *Evening News* on 4 October 1916 which commended the shrines and prompted a letter from the Lord Mayor of London urging their erection across the capital. A fund was started and a standard design was published consisting of a triptych with space for the names of the dead and serving on the wings, a shelf for flowers and a centre panel containing a small calvary and Union Jack, along with a promise of financial aid to the most deserving applicants. Selfridge's, the department store, took up the cause and donated £150 to the fund and by the end of October more than 250 shrines had been erected or put in hand.[2]

But what was the true significance of these shrines; what emotions and concepts did they embody? Crucially, the shrines reflected a desire to turn the sublime and abstract emotions of grief, pride and hope into tangible symbols; and the precedents and patterns set at this time provided the blueprint for the permanent memorials erected at the end of the war. The shrines were set up because people wanted them and needed to feel that they were doing something to remember their dead, and to provide some sort of superstitious protection for those still serving at the front. That the vicar of St Michael and All Saints', Bromley-by-Bow, perceived the shrine to be of equal importance to the bereaved and to those with serving relatives can be seen in the parish magazine, which stated that the parish shrines would have 'a shelf for

[1] See A. Wilkinson, *The Church of England and the First World War*, London 1978, 171.
[2] *Evening News*, 4, 6, 10, 13, 27 Oct. 1916.

flowers, which will no doubt be gladly provided by the relatives of those who are serving'.[3]

The shrine was also a symbol of community and belonging at its most intimate level – the parish and the streets. People turned to certain leaders, secular and religious, in order to articulate their feelings. In middle-class areas the leaders were more likely to be ordinary members of the community and the collections were organised amongst themselves. Thus a female parishioner of St Andrew's, Bethnal Green, paid for a large wayside cross to be erected in her back garden, dedicated to the dead and serving men of the parish; the bishop of Stepney himself dedicated it.[4] The first shrine in East Ham was erected by a female Catholic resident of Coleridge Avenue; according to the *East Ham Echo* 'it was her own idea thus to provide some record of the sacrifices made by her neighbours'.[5] One woman therefore provided her street with a focus for its emotions. Much the same pattern was followed in Sixth Avenue, East Ham, where a resident designed the shrine and a second man organised the street collection.[6] In Browning Road, East Ham, the Gothic triptych shrine was designed by the son of the organiser, while his daughters collected the donations.[7]

Small neighbourhoods consisting of a few streets or one of the relatively new housing estates were the units of community that gave life to the war shrines movement. The apogee of this can be seen in the middle-class Mawney's estate in Romford, a large estate of villas but clearly cut off from the rest of Romford by four wide roads. Its physical state therefore encouraged a sense of being a separate community. Residents organised their own roll of honour and shrine, which was unveiled in December 1916. It contained the names of 356 men, twenty-three of whom, recorded separately, had been killed. Mr Ashby, the scoutmaster, made a brief speech in which he emphasised the bonds of community: 'Many of those present had been for some time scanning the casualty lists day by day, but the names upon the Roll of Honour had a personal interest for them.' The shrine was of their community, for their community.[8] But that was not the end of the story as the scroll was updated and in May 1917 a new one was unveiled containing 480 names including thirty-seven dead. The *Essex Times* emphasised the special nature of the estate when it stated that it was 'a patriotic structure worthy of the Mawney's district'.[9]

At the other end of the social scale were the tenement blocks of the Prestons Road estate in Poplar. R. G. Burnett's biography of the Revd F. W. Chudleigh, warden of the East End Mission, noted that 'Every tenement

---

3   THL, St Michael and All Angels', Bromley-by-Bow, parish magazine, Jan. 1917.
4   THL, St Andrew's, Bethnal Green, parish magazine, Nov. 1916.
5   *EHE*, 20 Oct. 1916.
6   Ibid. 3 Nov. 1916.
7   Ibid. 17 Nov. 1916.
8   *ET*, 9 Dec. 1916.
9   Ibid. 19 May 1917.

building in the East End slums was represented in France by many Tommies.'[10] This stimulated a desire to remember equal to that of the middle-class districts. But the great difference in the shrine erected on this estate lay in the organisation: instead of the residents taking matters into their own hands, the *East London Observer* credited the Revd Cyril Winn of St Nicholas's as the driving force behind the scheme.[11] Working- class communities seem to have been shepherded towards a response by the clergy to a greater extent than residents in middle-class districts. That is not to imply that there was not a desire to mark sacrifice and service. The parish magazine of St James the Great, Bethnal Green, stated that:

> Those who have been collecting the names of the soldiers and sailors in the Parish have been struck by the remarkable keeness of their relatives to have their names put on the shrines; only once or twice in each street has anyone declined to have a name put up. The people in each street are paying for the material from which the shrines are being made, and we are sure that fresh flowers will be placed on them.[12]

At St Matthew's, Bethnal Green, the vicar and vestry noted the great demand for war shrines and agreed to organise a scheme.[13] The parish of St Michael and All Angels' eventually erected eighteen shrines containing 1,506 names: of the forty-eight individual subscribers fourteen were directly associated with the church and six of the shrines were built by members of the congregation.[14] As can be seen, the administrative and organisational burden fell onto the local Anglican church.

Shrines were also the result of initiatives taken by individual benefactors. In the City of London traditional concepts of largesse and of making bequests to churches shaped the response: in the parish of St Andrew-by-the-Wardrobe the alderman of the ward offered to pay for a churchyard shrine to contain the names of the servicemen who lived and worked in the parish. In so doing he was demonstrating his own beneficence as well as his pride in his fellow-parishioners.[15] In Romford H. E. Mitchell, owner of the Eastbury estate, paid for and unveiled a shrine on his estate. The *Romford Times* noted that the estate was made up of three roads and 133 houses, and seventeen of the residents had been killed: 'the proportion of residents who have made the great sacrifice in the war is therefore a large one'.[16]

---

[10] R. G. Burnett, *Chudleigh: a triumph in sacrifice*, London 1932, 110.
[11] *ELO*, 23 Dec. 1916.
[12] GLRO, P72/JSG/118/1, St James the Great, Bethnal Green, parish scrapbook, cutting from the parish magazine, Nov.–Dec. 1916.
[13] GLRO, P72/MTW/244/1–11–265/1–12, St Matthew's, Bethnal Green, parish magazine, Dec. 1916.
[14] THL, St Michael and All Angels', Bromley-by-Bow, parish magazine, Apr., May 1917.
[15] GML, L92 MS 8014, St Andrew-by-the-Wardrobe, vestry minutes, 21 Dec. 1916.
[16] *RT*, 7 Aug. 1918.

As the shrines sprang from the community of the streets it was natural that they should become objects of local pride and honour. The parish magazine of St Michael and All Angels' stated that the erection of eighteen shrines was a fine achievement and that 'it will be cause of pride for all of us to know how splendidly this place has responded to the call of duty'.[17] Carrie Lumsden, writing her memoirs of Poplar in 1991, aged seventy-nine, vividly remembered the shrine at the corner near her local Catholic church: 'On the corner of Canton Street I remember a more than life-sized Christ fixed to a huge cross.'[18]

The services of dedication revealed much about the collective psyche of the time. Words spoken at these services became the standard matrix for all later memorial ceremonies; the rhetoric was merely tinkered with in order to justify the sacrifice and console the bereaved. The Revd Hugh Guy of St Paul's, East Ham, linked the desire to remember to the meaning of the war: 'the shrine was erected as evidence of their desire that those who had gone forth from the parish to fight for King and Country in this Holy War should be remembered'.[19] He was repeating almost word for word the message of the Revd H. V. Eardley-Wilmott of St Mary's, Ilford, who unveiled and dedicated the church war shrine 'in remembrance of the gallant men who had gone forth from them to serve their King and Country in this holy war'.[20] Death in a holy war was therefore a glorious sacrifice made in imitation of Christ: it was a comforting and consoling thought. A. F. Winnington-Ingram, the bellicose bishop of London and formerly bishop of Stepney, was absolutely convinced of the justice of the British cause and the value of every sacrificed life. He dedicated the Prestons Road estate shrine with the words: 'This nation had never done a more Christ-like thing than when it went to war in August 1914 . . . the world had been redeemed again by the precious blood shed on the side of righteousness.'[21] Eardley-Wilmott made a similar statement; he said that the figure of Christ on their shrine would remind them 'of the great sacrifice of Christ and [make them] ready to follow His example and that of our soldiers and sailors in making sacrifices for Him and for our King and Country'.[22]

In turn, by laying flowers and offering a prayer at the shrines relatives could assure themselves that they were maintaining their covenants with their loved ones. Indeed, living in the constant shadow of death must have increased the desire to do something to try to help the loved one in danger.

17 THL, St Michael and All Angels', Bromley-by-Bow, parish magazine, May 1917.
18 Carrie Lumsden, My Poplar Eastenders, Stepney 1991, 62.
19 EHE, 17 Nov. 1916.
20 IR, 3 Nov. 1916.
21 ELO, 23 Dec. 1916. A. F. Winnington-Ingram was fond of such imagery and it can be found in his book of collected sermons, The potter and the clay, London 1917, 229. His influence on East London will become apparent. For his quite extraordinary career see his autobiography, Fifty years work in London (1889–1939), London 1940.
22 IR, 3 Nov. 1916.

Kit Bradley, of West India Dock, Millwall, told of the psychic trauma of that time:

> Morning after morning you'd dread to see the postman going to the doors, because the postman used to come round with the notices, 'killed' or 'missing' you know. And of course, we were at work when my mum got the letter to say he was killed [Kit's brother] and Dolly Williams told me about it afterwards. 'I always remember your mother, the day she got the letter to say Tom had been killed, I saw her run by the shop, she had the letter in her hand, she was going to the priest, and I went into mum and said, "I think Tommy Bradley's been killed because Mrs Bradley's just run down the road with a letter in her hand." But she was one of many, really.'[23]

The Revd J. Clementi-Smith caught this feeling when he wrote about the proposed shrine for St Andrew-by-the-Wardrobe: 'Let us pray that the sight of this shrine, with the names of those who are in Paradise will help many a passer-by to offer some short prayer for them, and for themselves, to Him who said "I, if I be lifted up, will draw all men unto Me." '[24]

But the services of dedication and the symbolism of the shrines went beyond the assurance and comforting of those at home. Messages of duty and obligation were also imparted at these services, once again a formula that was maintained in the post-war period at war memorial unveilings. In the autumn of 1916 this took the form of stressing the need for further sacrifice, a fact all too real at the end of the bitter struggle on the Somme. At a street shrine unveiling, Alderman E. Edwards of East Ham stated that 'we were engaged in such a great struggle that in the end it might well be that the nation that could stand the longest would win'.[25] When the bishop of Stepney unveiled the shrine at St Stephen's, Bow, he told the crowd that 'if we never knew it before we know it now with all our hearts that the price of victory would be an effort such as England has never yet made'.[26] Duty, endurance and a spirit of willing sacrifice were the qualities needed in the winter of 1916–17. At Denmark Road School, West Ham, the boys were lined up in front of the roll of honour and, the *Stratford Express* explained, 'as the Union Jack which covered the roll was withdrawn the scholars came smartly to the salute and sang Lord Nelson's immortal words "England expects that every man will this day do his duty" '.[27] At Pelly Road, West Ham, the dignitaries took the chance to rectify some popular misconceptions about the role of the Royal Navy in the war. The navy had played a dour, though essential, role in the conflict; even the great battle of Jutland (May 1916) had not provided a slice

---

[23] Quoted in E. Hostettler (ed.), *Memories of childhood on the Isle of Dogs, 1870–1970*, London 1990, 30.
[24] *English Churchman*, 11 Jan. 1917.
[25] *EHE*, 22 Dec. 1916.
[26] *ELA*, 16 Dec. 1916.
[27] *SE*, 18 Oct. 1916.

of real glory.[28] Therefore, when the wife of Admiral Jellicoe performed the unveiling ceremony, Colonel Conway-Bishop put the record straight. He noted that the country's debt to the navy would only be known at the end of the war when a true history of the conflict was written.[29]

Some saw the war as the test of the nation: the Revd S. F. L. Bernays spoke at the St Stephen's unveiling of his belief that the war was a purifying force and spoke of the years immediately before the war when:

> the rich young man went about looking as if he was too tired to talk; the work-ing man who seemed to think about nothing but cricket and football [but the war had brought out their latent patriotism and ought to lead to a moral refor-mation of the nation] the Union Jack for which we fight, must stand before the nation, not for drunkeness, not for fornication, not for gambling, but for righteousness and for God.[30]

Bernays also seems to have been motivated by the National Mission of Repentance and Hope inaugurated that October. The mission was partly the brainchild of Winnington-Ingram as 'an attempt by the Church of England to respond to the spiritual needs of the nation in wartime; an attempt to discharge its sense of vocation to act as the Christian conscience of the nation'.[31] Thus the war shrines became symbols not just of who was fighting, but how and why the nation was fighting as well.

An ambiguous message was certainly contained in the first war memorial to be erected in the City. In the form of a wayside cross in the churchyard of St Botolph, Bishopsgate, it was unveiled in August 1916. The cross had four inscriptions at its base in memory of Lord Kitchener, Jack Cornwell, the men of Bishopsgate and the men of the Honourable Artillery Company. Of this list only the last two had any direct connection with the church, the HAC being based nearby. But the purpose of the memorial was obvious: local heroes were juxtaposed with national ones. The City was living up to its self-appointed role as leader of the nation, this time in the commemoration of its glorious dead. Pride, and more especially the honour of the City of

---

28 On the Armistice in 1918 the Admiralty admitted as much in a dull statement of victory. 'The surrender of the German Fleet, accomplished without the shock of battle, will for all time remain the example of the wonderful silence and sureness with which sea power attains its ends': *Encyclopedia of sea warfare*, London 1975, 75.

29 *SE*, 27 Jan. 1917. It was a theme picked up by others notably Kipling whose 1916 poem 'The verdicts' (Jutland 1916) stated: 'They are too near to be great/ But our children shall understand/ When and how our fate/ Was changed, and by whose hand': Brian Gardner (ed.), *Up the line to death: the war poets 1914–1918*, London, 1986 edn, 76.

30 *ELA*, 16 Dec. 1916. The war as a cleansing force has been discussed by Samuel Hynes. He noted that for many 'what the war did was to make the condition of England a social disease for which war was the cure. War, with its male asceticism, its discomforts and deprivations, was the physical opposite of Edwardian luxury. But in its demand for dedication and sacrifice it was also the spiritual opposite': *A war imagined*, 13.

31 Wilkinson, *The Church and the war*, 70.

London, over-rode every other emotion as was writ large in the Lord Mayor's unveiling speech:

> We are assembled here today to unveil one of the earliest of the many thou-sands of memorials which will be set up all over the kingdom in connection with the war. *It is, I think, right that the City of London should take the lead in gratefully perpetuating in this public manner* the services and sacrifices of its well-remembered citizens [emphasis added].[32]

Grief and mourning clearly had no role to play:

> Though this monument thus recognises the statesman-warrior, the citizen sol-dier, and the humble sailor-lad, they are each and all types and examples of the same self-sacrificing devotion to the very death, which, looking back upon our history, I think we have a right with pride to claim as an outstanding attribute of our national character.[33]

Most of the above examples reveal a genuinely popular response to the losses, as streets and residents took matters into their own hands. However, the shrine never remained totally free of 'genuine' authority, for the words of invited clergymen and councillors meant that a conformist message was always part of the package. Remarkably, there was little variation in organisa-tion and execution throughout East London other than the fact that the middle class areas were better at making their own arrangements. Despite class differences and the massive variation in religion, from the Catholic areas of Wapping to the nonconformist strongholds of East Ham, there was great conformity of approach. Precedents were set in the autumn of 1916 and into the winter of 1916–17; machinery was in place to organise permanent schemes at the end of the war and a whole stock of images, concepts and words were ready to be buttressed and confirmed once victory crowned the efforts of the righteous. The shrines were obviously regarded as a special phenomenon. Elma Paget, in her biography of her husband Henry Paget, bishop of Stepney, wrote that:

> At this time War Shrines were beginning to appear in the back streets. They had sprung up spontaneously, and no one seems to have planned them; they were entirely of the people – imagined, carried out and paid for by them. The usual form was a simple triptych, with a shelf beneath for flowers, recording the names of all who had gone out from the street to serve the Colours. Inter-cessions were constantly made at the shrines and they quickly proved of real spiritual value. The Bishop was always ready to dedicate these little stations; he loved nothing better, for they drew him yet more closely to the people and associated him with their innermost anxieties and aspirations. Once when a shrine was dedicated in Bethnal Green, the street was crowded from end to

---

[32] *CP*, 5 Aug. 1916.
[33] Ibid.

end with women, bare-headed Englishmen, and head-covered Jews. The Bishop, after giving the Blessing in English, turned to the Jews and thanked them for joining in, and then gave the blessing in Hebrew. He had quick observation and quick sympathy and always the same instinctive love of brotherhood.[34]

But this does not quite tell the whole story, for there was one major outburst of dissent directed against war shrines. This happened in Ilford and was aimed at Eardley-Wilmott's shrine on St Mary's church railings in the High Road. It caused some disquiet in the town as members of both the Anglican congregation and nonconformists saw it as a Catholic innovation contradicting Protestant theology. Tempers exploded in late November 1916 when a group of protestors gathered outside the church and a few days later the shrine was desecrated by an unknown perpetrator.[35] One man wrote to the *Recorder* asking whether the vandal had 'boasted of his glorious deed to a returned soldier and been commended for it', but another wrote in favour of the action against 'those who are in love with papal superstitions'.[36] At this point J. H. Kensit entered the fray. He gave his address as St Paul's Churchyard EC4, but did not reveal his role as leader of the Protestant Truth Society. His letter urged the ending of illegal, uncanonical practices in the grounds of English churches.[37]

The climax came with a public meeting in the town hall on 16 January, chaired by a local Baptist minister, the Revd H. F. Smith. It was a rowdy evening and very well-attended, though Eardley-Wilmott refused to be present. Smith expressed his sympathy with the bereaved and stated that he understood their desire to commemorate the dead, but he could not condone 'misleading superstition – (cheers and counter cheers) – viz, that we could benefit the dead by our prayers which was at least outside the revelation of the New Testament'.[38] Smith raised the objection that many of the names on the roll were not even communicants at St Mary's and thus betrayed a certain sense of inter-church rivalry. Kensit then made his speech in which he connected the justification of the war with the protection of English Protestant values – the basis of Englishness and patriotism:

> Mr Kensit declared his subject to be of appealing interest both from the standpoint of religion and of patriotism, the very greatness of our nation was bound up with our patriotism, and this war would be waged in vain if during the course the foundation of our patriotism were sapped and undermined. (cheers.)[39]

34 E K. Paget, *Henry Luke Paget*, London 1939, 197–8.
35 *IR*, 8 Dec. 1916.
36 Ibid. 22 Dec. 1916.
37 Ibid.
38 Ibid. 19 Jan. 1917.
39 Ibid.

The evening concluded with the motion that the meeting call upon the bishop of Chelmsford to interview Eardley-Wilmott with a view to removing the shrine, which was duly carried.

But this was not the end of the controversy which continued to rage in the letters column of the *Recorder* until the editor declared the matter closed on 16 February. That it still a genuine matter of contention is demonstrated by an extract from a letter from J. W. Pointer:

> I cordially endorse the remarks of Mr Kensit contained in the open-letter in your last issue to the Bishop of Chelmsford, I am a churchman and a parishioner of St Mary's, but unfortunately, like many others am debarred from attending the parish church on account of the illegal practices indulged by the vicar.[40]

The bishop of Chelmsford replied to Kensit, via his chaplain, tartly stating that:

> he feels that the holding of a meeting mostly consisting of Nonconformists and presided over by a Nonconformist minister for the purpose of passing a resolution on Church matters is not helpful to the position which you state, and brings at once other issues into question such as the relation of the Church and Nonconformity. . . .[41]

At this point Kensit was riding high as he also forced the rector and vestry of St Andrew-by-the-Wardrobe to abandon their plans to erect a shrine.[42] It was a pyrrhic victory. By the spring of 1917 war shrines covered East London and that winter Kensit met his Waterloo. He attempted to disrupt the unveiling of a calvary at St Bartholomew-the-Great in the City, continually barracking the bishop of Willesden as he dedicated the memorial, asking him to repeat the Second Commandment (*see* plate 1). This provoked a furious reaction from the crowd. Led by an officer on leave, he was taunted as a 'pacifist', a near riot ensued and police were called.[43] Such a reaction is highly significant as it displays the depth of respect for the dead and, by extension, belief in the war; no one would countenance any form of slight, real or imagined, or entirely accidental.

Many of the shrines were retained at the end of the war; the emotional significance invested in them was obviously very high. At St Michael's, Romford Road, East Ham, they were gathered in and placed on display in the church; the same thing happened at St Michael and All Angels' where they were placed in the church hall.[44] In some parishes they remained *in situ*: the

[40] Ibid. 26 Jan., 2, 9, 16 Feb. 1917.
[41] *English Churchman*, 8 Feb. 1917.
[42] GML, L92 MS 8014, St Andrew-by-the-Wardrobe, vestry minutes, 1 Mar. 1917.
[43] *Daily Mirror*, 19 Nov. 1917.
[44] *EHE*, 10 June 1921; THL, St Michael and All Angels', Bromley-by-Bow, parish magazine, June 1919.

Plate 1. War shrine, St Bartholomew-the-Great, Smithfield

parish magazine of All Hallows', Bromley-by-Bow, for November 1933 reminded the people that the usual Armistice parade from shrine to shrine would take place.[45] They became firmly entrenched in the community. Such was the pride in the shrines at the corner of Tagg and Mace streets, Bethnal Green, for example, that in 1936 the residents collected enough money to replace the decaying wooden ones with York Stone tablets.[46] The meaning and significance of the shrines was passed on to each new generation: in 1957 the sociologists Willmott and Young noted that fresh flowers were continually being placed on the shrine in Cyprus Street, Bethnal Green.[47]

The war shrines of East London laid the foundations for later remembrance and started the process of encapsulating the dead in fixed concepts with a whole set of iconographical images. It is now necessary to turn to the permanent war memorial schemes in order to see how far the experience of erecting war shrines influenced that movement.

[45] GLRO, P88/ALL2/13/4/26/27, All Hallows', Bromley-by-Bow, parish magazine, Nov. 1933.
[46] Bethnal Green News, 18 Jan. 1936.
[47] Young and Willmott, Family and kinship in East London (1972 edn), 86.

3

War Memorials in Places of Worship:
Seeking Solace in Religion

At the end of the war the various sub-communities of East and West Ham, Ilford, Tower Hamlets and the City instigated their own war memorial schemes. The most important of these groups were the various religious communities. By studying the memorials of the different Churches it will be possible to identify the marked consistency in the way the dead were remembered and commemorated, and to highlight the progression from war shrine to permanent memorial, and from memorial to Armistice Day ritual. Jews, Catholics and nonconformists all turned to their places of worship to erect their own memorials. The Anglican Church played its role as the Established Church by not only memorialising its own communicants, but often including all those who resided in the parish as well.

War memorials as symbols of community

After a war that had cost so much in terms of human lives it was natural that people should turn to the Churches. Only Christianity, disseminated through the various denominations, could both make sense of the whole issue and provide comfort. Christianity was equipped with a language of consolation and hope. Alan Wilkinson has noted that the Church drew many people into a new relationship with it via remembrance rituals.[1] It was not just the spiritual element that made the Churches important, however, for they were also symbols of community and friendship: they made up an extended family that included patriarchal and trusted figures. Religion and the Churches provided a sense of belonging and inter-dependence. This fact, perhaps more than any other, explains why so many memorials were erected in religious buildings. The smaller units of identity, the streets, provided the focus for the shrines, while permanent memorials sprang from the family of the Church. Indeed, memory seems intrinsically to link the war memorial, Church and community. Carrie Lumsden's recall hooked them together:

> I remember Father Bartlett as a rather tall man, striding out vigorously past our street door, on his way between the little Chapel in Giraud Street and the

---

[1] Wilkinson, *The Church and the war*, 292–311.

Vicarage in Arcadia Street, on the corner of which we lived. The Roll of Honour to the War Dead was fixed to the outside wall of the Chapel.[2]

When the Forest Gate Congregational church council first discussed the question of a memorial, it was in terms suffused with a sense of belonging and loss:

> Our Roll of Honour contains the names of almost 150 of our young men, Members of our Church and Congregation, of our Sunday School, of the Boy Scouts or in some way connected with the Church. The three who were prisoners of war have been released. Several men have been wounded, more or less seriously, and 23 have made the supreme sacrifice. All honour to the noble dead. These young men went from our midst at the Country's Call, most of them voluntarily, not knowing what danger they might have to encounter. They did their duty and did it right well.[3]

In 1920 the pastor wrote in the church manual: 'our thoughts have been turned for some time in the direction of a worthy memorial to *our lads* who have fallen in the war, laying down their lives for our sakes' [emphasis added].[4]

The dead therefore still belonged to their churches, and their relatives ensured this by erecting memorials. Consequently, on the unveiling and dedication of the memorials it was images of possession, of belonging that dominated. When the Plaistow Congregational church held their unveiling ceremony, the Revd G. C. Britton stressed the role the dead had played in their community:

> These men were no unknown warriors, most of them were well known and honoured among them. Some of them had begun to serve them, they had dedicated their lives to the service of Christ, and found their part and place in the work of the Church and the Sunday School. It was no exaggeration to say that most of those who remained at home only lived because such heroes died.[5]

Exactly the same sentiments were expressed at Bruce Road Methodist church, Bow. The mayor unveiled the tablet and stated that 'They were not mere strangers, but known to them, and had lived among them, and they had brought honour to Bow-and-Bromley by their valour. They had died in a noble cause, and this tablet would perpetuate their memory.'[6] Likewise at St Alban's, Ilford, where the memorial was inscribed 'To the Glory of God these

---

[2] Lumsden, *My Poplar Eastenders*, 11.

[3] NHL, Forest Gate Congregational church, church council minutes, 2 Apr. 1919.

[4] NHL, Forest Gate Congregational church, annual manual 1920, 11.

[5] *SE*, 13 Nov. 1920. The memory and spirit of the dead remained the property of the local church just as the physical bodies of the dead remained the property of the state, lying in imperial war cemeteries: P. Longworth, *The unending vigil: a history of the Commonwealth War Graves Commission, 1917–1984*, London 1985, 41–2.

[6] *ELA*, 13 Sept. 1919.

Windows are dedicated in/Memory *of these our brothers*, members of the Congregation/of this Church, who laid down their lives in the Great War/1914–1918' [emphasis added].[7] The Revd M. Wills then gave a sermon which revealed the links between locality and sacrifice. The implication was clearly that the men had died for their own part of Ilford and now belonged with them even in death:

> He had known personally nearly all the young men who were commemorated by the new windows. Epitaphs and funeral orations were sometimes insincere, but in this case he felt he could refer to their departed friends as truly Christian soldiers. He knew from the letters he received from them during the War what a reality their religion was to them, and how great a role St Alban's played in their lives.[8]

Anglican churches had a slightly wider definition of community and memorials in these churches often included all the men of the parish as opposed to just the communicants: the church of All Saints', Goodmayes, decided to erect just such a memorial.[9] Alternatively, the local church became the only fitting location for ostensibly civic memorials. In many ways this was a tribute to the subliminal power of the Established Church. A good example of this can be seen in Old Canning Town: instead of placing the memorial on a piece of civic ground, it seemed to find a natural home within the large shadow of St Gabriel's church. Indeed, the vicar noted on its dedication that: 'all the church had done was to provide a site where it could be erected'.[10] In this instance the parish church was not the sole instigator of the memorial, nor was it the crux of a large community in the manner of the nonconformist churches; rather it was the agreed symbol of locality and belonging. The memorial erected at St Mark's, Silvertown, followed much the same pattern. It commemorated over 200 men of Silvertown but it is difficult to believe that they were all regular communicants at the church.[11] But this clearly did not effect the emotion invested in the memorials or the belief that the church was an accepted definition of the community. James Inskip, bishop of Barking, wrote in his autobiography that:

> In my earlier days as Bishop I dedicated many War Memorials. These services gave me a valuable opportunity of coming into touch with the people in various parishes. . . . At St Matthias', Canning Town, the Memorial was a carved

---

7 St Clement's, Great Ilford, parish magazine, July 1921.
8 Ibid.
9 All Saints', Goodmayes, parish magazine, Mar. 1919.
10 *SE*, 9 June 1920.
11 Ibid. 1 June 1920. Evidence for poor church attendance can be found in an essay entitled 'The problems of greater London' which appeared in Mudie-Smith's survey of religion in London. The author was extremely depressed at the lack of genuine religious interest displayed by the workers of Canning Town, Silvertown and Stratford: *Religious life of London*, 340.

oak chancel screen with the names of the parishioners concerned inscribed on it. The church was crowded with working folk, who were moved beyond words by the pathos of the occasion.[12]

At St Michael and All Angels', Bromley-by-Bow, the vicar felt that the memorial was for the entire parish 'and not only of the congregation'.[13] It was 'to commemorate all those men, irrespective of creed, who have given their lives for their country in the Great War'.[14] A similar pattern was followed at St Anne's, Limehouse. In March 1919 the parish magazine announced that 'The Memorial is to be the outward expression of gratitude of the inhabitants of Limehouse to these brave men. . . . The names will of course be restricted to men who have lived in the parish.'[15] Interestingly, this reveals that an outward expression must be made, and that the memorial was to be primarily one of 'gratitude' and not an expression of grief. In August 1919 the all-embracing nature of the memorial was once again stressed, emphasising its role as a memorial for the whole community: 'we should like to emphasise that the Memorial is for the civil parish, which is much wider than the bounds of the ecclesiastical parish and embraces Limehouse as a whole'.[16]

The desire to appeal to all faiths and to promote the parish church as the true heart of the community was most marked in the cosmopolitan boroughs of Poplar and Stepney. In the parish of Christ Church, Spitalfields, for example, the rector asked the Jewish residents for their help and it was suggested that 'Mr Goldstein and several other Jewish leaders on the council be approached as to their views'.[17]

Some Anglican churches opted for a second memorial to commemorate communicants only. In Ilford and Romford two daughter churches decided to erect their own memorials despite the fact that the mother churches were erecting umbrella memorials for the parish. The desire of the parishioners of St Alban's to erect their own memorial was not shared by the Revd A. W. Ottaway of St Clement's, vicar of Ilford. He stated that the PCC had already decided that St Clement's was the only fitting place for a war memorial.[18] But the St Alban's PCC members persisted and eventually got their own way. In April 1920, Ottaway stated in the parish magazine that

> They have been anxious to erect a War Memorial in St Alban's Church in memory of those who were associated with the worship of the Church and have collected nearly £200 by private subscription for this purpose. The

---

[12] J. T. Inskip, *A man's job: the autobiography of James Inskip, second bishop of Barking*, London 1948, 128.

[13] THL, St Michael and All Angels', Bromley-by-Bow, parish magazine, Sept. 1917.

[14] Ibid. Nov. 1919.

[15] THL, St Anne's, Limehouse, parish magazine, Mar. 1919.

[16] Ibid. Aug. 1919.

[17] GLRO, P93/CTC1/20, Christ Church, Spitalfields, PCC minutes, 27 July 1920.

[18] St Clement's, Great Ilford, PCC minutes, 26 Nov. 1917.

Parochial Church Council at its last meeting rescinded its resolution on the subject, as far as it concerned St Alban's, and sanctioned the necessary steps for erecting Memorial Windows in the north aisle.[19]

In Romford the parishioners of St Andrew's appear to have had no such difficulties with the Revd G. M. Bell of the mother church of St Edward and set about erecting their own memorial.[20] This shows communities breaking down into their smallest, most intimate blocks. At All Hallows', East India Dock, an oak shrine for the communicants was erected as well as a parish memorial.[21] When memorial schemes were discussed by the PCC of St Matthew's, Bethnal Green, Mr Pratt stated that he 'preferred another form of memorial which should be for the church members only'.[22] But it was the regular congregation of St Anne's, Limehouse, who showed the psychological importance of a memorial to those who really belonged to the church. The pride and grief of the community was obvious:

> For the members of our congregation there is perhaps something even more intimate and personal in the simple but most beautiful memorial which was unveiled in the church porch at Evensong on Armistice Day.
>
> It is, as it were, the work of our own hands, to which we have contributed according to our ability, in honour of those of our own members who gave their all for us. . . . There was an exceptionally full congregation, including a large number of ex-servicemen. The Rector in his address, taking as his text the inscription on the memorial, 'This is the victory that overcometh the world, even our faith' dwelt upon the fact that the thirty-five men singled out for record were men who in their lives before the war had closely identified themselves with the church's work in our parish: one as priest, one as organist, several in the choir, some servers, and nearly all communicants. This was no ordinary war memorial, but was erected that these men might still deliver to the world their message. Being dead they still speak and tell us of a greater warfare – the spiritual warfare; and a great victory – the spiritual victory, the victory won only by Christ and His Sacrifice. *'This is the victory that overcometh the world even our faith'.*[23]

The Anglican Church was also at the heart of memorialising in the City, but there parishioners were, in the main, made up of non-residents: parish communities were therefore only partly defined by the few residents they did contain, and instead the firms, businesses or livery gilds lying within the parish boundary had the greatest effect on the parochial character. Soon after the Armistice, the *City Press* gave clear advice as to its preferred form of commemoration, stating that:

[19] St Clement's, Great Ilford, parish magazine, Apr. 1920.
[20] St Andrew's, Romford, vestry minutes, 25 Oct. 1920.
[21] THL, All Hallows', East India Dock, parish magazine, Dec. 1920.
[22] GLRO, P72/MTW/190, St Matthew's, Bethnal Green, PCC minutes, 13 Apr. 1920.
[23] THL, St Anne's, Limehouse, parish magazine, Dec. 1921.

A memorial in stone or in glass will serve no useful purpose, and, therefore we venture to think, may be dismissed from our minds as far as the Corporation itself is concerned. What is needed is something practical – something that will benefit the living while it immortalises those whom it is designed to honour, and those whose deeds it is desired to hold for all time in loving remembrance as an inspiration to generations yet unborn.[24]

Such advice was completely ignored. Aesthetic memorials were adopted by virtually every institution, ecclesiastical and secular. Tradition demanded that great events be marked by aesthetic memorials. Six months later, the editor of the *City Press* bemoaned the fact that 'there is still far too much of a tendency to decide on useless war memorials, instead of acting on the principle that the best way of perpetuating the memory of the honoured dead is to establish something that will benefit the living'.[25]

The parish church was not simply the most recognisable symbol of community in the City, but also the actual symbol of community for the bonds between certain trades and their adopted churches stretched back to the Middle Ages. City churches were already the repository of a great number of monuments and memorials, and hence the natural place to house any form of war memorial. The millinery firm of Woolley Sanders placed their memorial in St Vedast-alias-Foster as their head office was in the next street. St Vedast was also the livery church of the Saddlers' Company; when the parish memorial was unveiled, the Company displayed its largesse by providing hospitality for the congregation and the bishop of London.[26] St Bride's erected a memorial for the men of the newspaper and press advertising trade; indeed, as a church in an alley adjacent to Fleet Street it could hardly do otherwise.[27] But the resident parishioners of the City also wanted their own memorials, and they too saw the parish church as the agreed symbol of community. The vestry of St Botolph-without-Bishopsgate revealed the problems of defining that community, for when they discussed their memorial they debated whether it should be confined to communicants alone. Eventually, they decided that it was a memorial for the entire parish, resident or worker, and a plan to make it a ward memorial was dropped when it was revealed that St Helen's, Bishopsgate, was also erecting a memorial.[28] St Olave's, near the Tower of London, saw both a City institution and residents use the church as their communal home and only fitting place to remember their dead. Every level of remembrance can be seen in this church: four memorials were erected, one for Trinity House (the organisation entrusted

---

[24] CP, 28 Dec. 1918.
[25] Ibid. 12 July 1919.
[26] GML, L92 MS 18,319/43, St Vedast-alias-Foster, faculty papers, 22 Apr. 1920; L92 MS 779,801, St Vedast-alias-Foster, vestry minutes, 22 July 1921.
[27] GML, L92 MS 6554, St Bride's, vestry minutes, 8 Dec. 1919.
[28] GML, L92 MS 4526, St Botolph-without-Bishopsgate, vestry minutes, 24 Apr., 19 June 1919.

with the care and staffing of all Britain's lighthouses), one for the parishioners and two family memorials.[29] When the St Michael's, Cornhill, memorial was unveiled the Revd J. H. Ellison stated that

> It was with a family feeling in their hearts that they met, for the houses of business of the parish had co-operated with him in making the roll, and had subscribed generously to the memorial now unveiled. [This was a two-way process as it was the] . . . desire of the church to promote sociability, comradeship, goodwill and a good feeling among the many thousands who worked beneath the shadow of St Michael's.[30]

And the war memorial was the greatest symbol of these bonds.

Organising war memorial schemes

Churches therefore acted as badges of community and belonging, providing fitting homes for memorials. But who organised these schemes and how were the funds collected? At the risk of appearing impudent, it might be argued that the memorials were erected because the leaders of the church communities demanded them. All the schemes were certainly arranged and organised by small groups: although the opinion of the congregation was canvassed it was usually after many of the key decisions had already been taken. When Ottaway wrote about the St Alban's war memorial scheme, he said that it was 'the long cherished wish of several of the *leading members* of St Alban's Congregation' [emphasis added].[31] The deacons and committee of Forest Gate Congregational church discussed their war memorial for eight months before the pastor put the matter to the congregation; a further month passed before he visited the bereaved to ask for their opinions.[32] A similar situation developed at St Andrew's, Romford, where the vestry members discussed the memorial on four separate occasions before the parishioners were invited to examine the designs.[33] The members of St Clement's, Great Ilford, PCC, first discussed their memorial on 31 July 1916; fund-raising started that winter and the congregation do not appear to have been consulted.[34]

Those most intimately connected with the church community were the driving forces behind most of these schemes. At Stratford Presbyterian church, it was noted that 'To Mr Webster and Mr John Weir we owe the

---

[29] GML, L92 MS 18,319/47, St Olave's, Hart Street, faculty papers, 10 June 1920.
[30] CP, 6 Nov. 1920.
[31] St Clement's, Great Ilford, parish magazine, Apr. 1920.
[32] NHL, Forest Gate Congregational church, council minutes, 26 Feb., 29 Oct., 3 Dec. 1919.
[33] St Andrew's, Romford, vestry minutes, 25 Oct. 1920, 15 Mar. 1921, 27 Apr. 1922, 25 May 1922.
[34] St Clement's, Great Ilford, PCC minutes, 31 July, 9 Oct. 1916.

inception of the scheme, Mr Webster, as chairman of the Memorial Committee, had the delicate task of securing a suitable plan that should satisfy all, and was responsible for the collection of the funds.'[35] Two leaders of the church community therefore took it upon themselves to formulate a permanent communal expression of pride and grief. On certain occasions the leadership was determined by very obvious vested interest of the best possible sort: it came as no surprise to the parishioners of All Saints', Forest Gate, when Mr F. Drewry was confirmed as treasurer of the memorial fund – his son had won the Victoria Cross at Cape Helles.[36] Occasionally, however, parishioners did not wait for their leaders to initiate plans on their behalf, but took the initiative themselves. The vestry members of St Sepulchre, Holborn, noted that

> Many parishioners having expressed a desire that a memorial tablet be erected to the honour of those gallant men of this parish who have so nobly answered the call of King and Country in the great war – a Committee was formed and appeal for funds made – and we are pleased to know the subscriptions are most readily made for this to be done. The vicar and churchwardens acquiescing in the wish of Committee and subscribers to erect such a memorial in the Church porch propose making an application to the Consistory Court for the necessary faculty.[37]

At St Michael and All Angels', the vicar and the vestry members started to discuss a permanent war memorial in August 1917, but a public meeting on the subject did not occur until June 1919.[38] The church was determined to make the scheme look like a genuine community effort. The public meeting was chaired by the mayor of Poplar and supported by the local Liberal MP Sir Alfred Yeo.[39] But when the committee was formed in August the true power behind the scheme was revealed. It consisted of Messrs Blackmore, Badcock, Matthews, Maule, Mills, Saunders and the Revd C. G. Langdon. Of the laymen, three were churchwardens or sidesmen and the other two were ordinary members of the congregation.[40] Despite the alleged ecumenical nature of the scheme, it was clear from the very first meeting that the memorial would be sited outside the church.[41] Down at St Anne's the story was the same. When in March 1919 the committee met for the first time, it consisted of a variety of parish officers but also included the local Unionist MP, Sir William Pierce, Councillor Newell and the Jewish Councillor Marks. Later the committee was augmented by the Revd T. Rose of the local Wesleyan

[35] THL, Stratford Trinity Presbyterian church magazine, Apr. 1921.
[36] *EHE*, 11 Apr. 1919.
[37] St Sepulchre, Holborn, vestry minutes, 12 Apr. 1917.
[38] THL, St Michael and All Angels', Bromley-by-Bow, parish magazine, Aug. 1917, June 1919.
[39] Ibid. July 1919.
[40] Ibid. Aug. 1919.
[41] Ibid. July 1919.

Mission and a representative of the Roman Catholic Church.[42] The siting of the memorial in the churchyard raised little objection, indeed Pierce received backing from a relatively odd quarter:

> Sir William Pierce then addressed the meeting, and, in conclusion, proposed that a War Memorial should be erected in the Churchyard. This was seconded by Mr Councillor Marks.
>   This resolution was carried after discussion and after the defeat of an amendment that the memorial should be erected at the corner of one of the main thoroughfares.[43]

The people making these decisions were hardly remote and faceless bureaucrats; they were members of the community, sensitive to its feelings, and there is no evidence of any large-scale dissent. In any case the simplest form of expressing disagreement would surely have been the withholding of contributions.

The real need for war memorials lay in the fact that the bereaved had no graves to grieve over and through which to exorcise emotion. The mass casualties of the war led to the establishment of the Imperial War Graves Commission, which acted on behalf of the empire. The commission decided to uphold the decision that it was impossible and unethical to repatriate the bodies of the dead. So many had no known grave that it could be unfair to many of the bereaved. It was therefore agreed to erect permanent cemeteries on or near the battlefields.[44] This created a desire to make alternative arrangements; the bereaved had to feel that they were doing something to mark and remember their dead. Much the same reasoning had driven the war shrines schemes; it was a way of proving that the memory of a loved one still lived. By contributing to a memorial scheme the bereaved paid for a surrogate headstone or grave. In that sense a war memorial was not a communal thing at all, but a convenient frame for any number of substitute, individual graves. A mourner saw only the name of their particular loved one when looking at a memorial, although he or she could also take comfort at the proof of a shared fate. The comparison with a grave can be seen in the practice of placing flowers on shrines and memorials. At St Michael's, Romford Road, East Ham, the Revd J. Davidson told the congregation that 'Flowers could still be brought to the church by relatives of the fallen and placed upon the shrines in the porch; those intended for the permanent shrine would be arranged by members of St Mary's Guild.'[45]

During the war, requiem masses had been held regularly at St Anne's, Limehouse. The rector put the success of these services down to the fact that 'mourners for the fallen sadly miss the funeral service which we give to our

---

[42] THL, St Anne's, Limehouse, parish magazine, Apr. 1919; *ELA*, 9 Aug. 1919.
[43] THL, St Anne's, Limehouse, parish magazine, Apr. 1919.
[44] Longworth, *Unending vigil*, 47.
[45] *EHE*, 10 June 1921.

dead'.[46] A war memorial service gave the mourner the chance to attend a substitute interment. All the traditional mourning rites were included and flowers were vital. When the St Alban's, Ilford, memorial was unveiled the parish magazine noted the fact that 'representatives of the Church and Congregation had grouped themselves round the table which had been placed beneath the windows to receive the many flowers, brought by relatives of the fallen'.[47] Writing about the installation of the last part of the St Clement's war memorial, Ottaway stated that 'when they are in position, we propose to remove the vases that have been supplied with flowers week by week by the relatives of those whose names are recorded on our Roll of Honour'. Once the work was completed the vases were replaced.[48] One of the negative features of the St Matthew's, Bethnal Green, memorial was that it was 'not well situated for offerings of flowers. However a certain number can be placed on one or two suitable stools just in front'.[49] The vicar of St Andrew's, Romford, requested some sort of receptacle for flowers to be placed on the plinth of the memorial.[50] The orphaned son of a soldier, wearing his father's medals, laid a poesy at the St Anne's, Limehouse, memorial.[51] The parish magazine perfectly caught the role of the memorial as a substitute grave and the unveiling as an alternative funeral: 'Floral tributes were laid on the base and steps by many relatives and friends, as they passed out, feeling – we are sure – so thankful they were at last able to honour by outward tokens those whose memorials will be for ever green.'[52]

As well as laying flowers, contributions to the scheme were perceived as important gestures: it was a positive signal and commitment to perpetuate the memory of a lost loved one. The distinction between memorials for communicants and those for all parish residents occasionally caused some confusion. All Saints', Goodmayes, decided to erect a memorial for everyone in the parish but the vicar confined collecting to the congregation: 'As it is a church memorial contributions will be solicited from members of the congregation only.'[53] At All Hallows', East India Dock, the memorial was also for all residents, but in this poorer parish the chance for all to contribute was promoted: 'The appeal will be sent to every house in the parish, as we wish everyone, whether connected with the Church or not, to have an opportunity of contributing, just as we wish to inscribe the names of all the parish who have laid down their lives.'[54]

46 THL, St Anne's, Limehouse, parish magazine, May 1918.
47 St Clement's, Great Ilford, parish magazine, July 1921.
48 Ibid. Feb. 1920.
49 GLRO, P72/MTW/44/1–11–265/1–12, St Matthew's, Bethnal Green, parish magazine, Aug. 1922.
50 St Andrew's, Romford, vestry minutes, 15 June 1922.
51 ELA, 4 June 1921.
52 THL, St Anne's, Limehouse, parish magazine, June 1921.
53 All Saints', Goodmayes, parish magazine, Mar. 1919.
54 THL, All Hallows', East India Dock, parish magazine, July 1917. The importance of the

There was a further option for those who could afford it – the personal memorial, erected by the family of the deceased. Of the two such in St Olave's, the first unveiled was to Captain F. C. Man. It was in the form of a stained-glass window, picturing the Virgin and Child, St George in armour and St Olave as an Anglo-Saxon warrior: thus a highly traditional form of ecclesiastical beautification was employed, blending concepts of sacrifice and struggle. The rector assured the grieving family and friends that 'he and his brave comrades had left a light by which the path of peace and deliverance could be seen. Those brave boys had not died in vain. Their sacrifice would be immortal'.[55] A second window was unveiled in memory of Lieutenant Arthur Kerr, son of one of the churchwardens. The Revd T. Wellard offered an explanation of the sacrifice designed to answer all questions and remove any doubt:

> When they were confronted with the mystery of sorrow and suffering and sep-aration of life, and were tempted to ask why, they knew that behind the veil there was the Master Mind, who could and would in His own good time let them see and know that behind the discords of life there was a harmonious purpose or plan for the benefit of mankind.[56]

In Ilford, the parents and sisters of Charles Wiffin, who was killed in Mesopo-tamia, donated an ewer to St Alban's. Mr and Mrs Edward Page donated a paten and chalice to St Andrew's inscribed with the message: 'A. D. M. G. In loving memory of Eddie Page, Server at the Altar of this Church, who died of wounds in Palestine on December 20th 1917 during the Great War. The gift of Edward and Nancy Page.'[57] Similar gifts were deposited as memorials in churches throughout East London. Mr and Mrs Jones, for example, presented a Lamp of Remembrance to the Poplar and Stepney Rifles chapel in St Stephen's, Bow, in memory of their two sons.[58] At East Ham Presbyterian church, the mother of a dead soldier donated silver communion cups in his

---

individual desire to contribute was also noted by the Imperial War Graves Commission. Although the headstones in the cemeteries were erected by the imperial governments 'it was felt nevertheless that relatives should be allowed to contribute something personal to what would otherwise have seemed unrelievedly institutional memorials. They were there-fore allowed to choose and pay for an inscription or text for the headstone'. The Canadians insisted that payments be purely voluntary however, and this solution was adopted: Longworth, *Unending vigil*, 44. The City of London-based London Rifle Brigade established a scheme to purchase memorial silver for the battalion chapel; the committee stated that 'it is felt that many next-of-kin of our fallen will be glad to have the opportunity of actually contributing some of the silver required and, by so doing, be able to feel that they have the most intimate connection possible with this memorial': *LRB Record,* Feb. 1921, 5.

[55] *CP,* 26 Feb. 1921.

[56] Ibid. 30 July 1921.

[57] St Clement's, Great Ilford, parish magazine, July 1919.

[58] *ELA,* 17 Nov. 1934.

memory.[59] A bereaved mother established a memorial prize of specially inscribed bibles to be presented annually to the best pupil in the Sunday School at Woodgrange Baptist church, West Ham. The bibles contained ornate inscriptions on the fly leaves giving details of her son and his death on the Western Front. This touching story reveals the complex nature of remembrance and memorialising: one woman channelled her grief and pride into a practical memorial in order to glorify God and perpetuate the example of her son among the younger members of her particular community.[60]

The parishioners of St Luke's, Ilford, witnessed the execution of a particularly lavish set of personal memorials. The scheme took the form of badges carved into the corbels in memory of eight boys connected with the choir, bible class or the Lads' Institute. On the north side of the sanctuary memorials were erected to Arthur Imrie-Jupp, William Pain, Percival Gibbons and H. E. Jones. The carvings consisted of St George, St Michael, the London Rifle Brigade badge and that of the Royal Regiment of Fusiliers. On the south side A. L. Gibbons (brother of Percival), Walter Fox, B. A. Hall and E. W. Gulliver were commemorated in the form of a crusader with sword and pennant, and the badges of the Essex Regiment, the Machine Gun Corps and the City of London Rifles. The carving was carried out by Mr A. Pope of Stratford and paid for by the relatives of the deceased. It seems, however, to have been largely arranged by John Baldwin, whose nephew and adopted son was Gulliver. Baldwin owned a stationery business in Ilford and regularly attended the town's war memorial committee meetings. These memorials made a very definite statement about the wealth and rank of the families involved for, although no record of cost survives, any form of special carving cannot have been cheap.[61] Such memorials follow the ancient Christian tradition of making bequests to beautify churches whilst also serving a memorial function for both families and members of guilds or other corporate bodies.[62]

The process was sometimes reversed when the church offered families personal memorials to be kept in the house. The pastor of Stratford Presbyterian church spent months on a labour of love as he produced a memorial volume containing biographical details of the church's dead:

> In the meantime I am greatly encouraged by the warm welcome given to our other Memorial – 'The Book of Remembrance'. I had almost despaired at one time of being able to publish it, the cost of production was so great; but I am glad that I persevered, and I am sure that you will also be glad. It is a book of

59 NHL, East Ham Trinity Presbyterian church of England, *Jubilee handbook, 1900–1951*, London 1951, 10.

60 NHL, 'A brief synopsis of the history of the Woodgrange Baptist Church', manuscript [1940].

61 *IR*, 18 Apr. 1919.

62 See J. A. F. Thomson, *The transformation of medieval England, 1370–1529*, Harlow 1989 edn, 340–4.

which any congregation might be proud; and I hope that a copy will find its way into every home. It is published at a price which brings it within the reach of all; but we must dispose of at least 300 copies to make it pay.[63]

War memorials in places of worship were primarily for the bereaved and not for ex-servicemen. Occasionally, a different reason for erecting a memorial was cited. The Revd R. Warburton of Bow Road Wesleyan Methodist church, said that their memorial was erected in order 'that any of the lads returning from the front either on leave or after the war, would see they had not been forgotten by those they had left at home and how they had a warm interest in our prayers'.[64] But comfort and catharsis for the bereaved was the major reason. Comfort was exactly the word used by the mayor of East Ham when he spoke at the unveiling of the Tennyson Road Free Church tablet: 'none of them could appreciate the anguish of mind which those who had lost their nearest and dearest had suffered, but possibly it gave them some little comfort to realise that their loved ones were not forgotten by their friends'.[65]

Funding war memorial schemes

Funding these memorials was a large task, requiring much dedication and organisation. The memorial schemes for St Clement's and St Alban's churches in Ilford provide good case studies. PCC members of St Clement's first discussed their war memorial project in July 1916 when it was agreed that a sub-committee be appointed 'to consider the best means of perpetuating the memory of, and expressing thanks for, those who have served in the war'.[66] Fund-raising for the project appears to have started in the autumn of 1916 as the PCC minutes of 18 December reveal that £94 0s. 14d. had already been collected.[67]

---

[63] NHL, Stratford Trinity Presbyterian church magazine, Jan. 1921. The state provided the family of the deceased with a bronze plaque embossed with Britannia and the name of the dead as a memorial to be kept in the home. It was accompanied by a scroll which bore the facsimile of King George V's signature and expressed his gratitude for the service of the dead. This memorial was known as the 'dead man's penny': P. Dutton, ' "The dead man's penny": a history of the next of kin memorial plaque', *Imperial War Museum Review* iii (1988), 60–8. The bereaved were also entitled to receive the medals of the deceased although the right to wear them in memory remained a disputed point: Gregory, *Silence of memory*, 40–1. The IWGC also offered the bereaved the chance to reclaim the original wooden crosses from the cemeteries and as the cemeteries were completed the registers became available for purchase: Longworth, *Unending vigil*, 126–7; C. Moriarty, 'Christian iconography and First World War memorials', *Imperial War Museum Review* vi (1991), 66.
[64] GLRO, Acc 1850/147/1, Bow Road Wesleyan Methodist church, minutes of Leaders meeting, 21 Sept. 1918.
[65] *EHE*, 3 June 1921.
[66] St Clement's, Great Ilford, PCC minutes, 31 July 1916.
[67] Ibid. 18 Dec. 1916.

The July meeting proposed various memorials including an East Window, a new boys and lads institute and a brass plaque. It was estimated that around £700 needed to be raised. The suggestion of a new club for boys shows the links between church and community and how Anglican values had created a situation whereby patriotic fervour could easily be tapped in 1914. Muscular Christianity was a strong force and the public school ethos fostered by St Clement's is easily recognisible. The sub-committee was formed under Edwin Hodnett and A. W. Green, churchwardens of St Clement's, with three other members, one for each of the daughter churches. In the autumn the PCC invited C. A. Nicholls, manager of the London County and Westminster Bank, to become treasurer of the fund. He was joining a committee of fellow professionals. It was also agreed that the war memorial should take the form of a new East Window depicting the saints of the four churches.[68] Messrs Tinson, Leyland and Green proposed and seconded the window and stated that it would beautify the church. This points to an interesting duality of motives, the desire to remember in a fitting way and the desire to have a church to be proud of. The memorial was therefore not one *per se* but part of an architectural whole. This implies that the memorial was primarily for the Anglican parishioners and the qualification for inclusion on any roll of honour became a little more ambiguous.[69] It was also very clearly a memorial reflecting mainstream Anglicanism, lacking the High Church atmosphere of those of the working-class areas of East London. The middle-class areas of East and West Ham, Romford and Ilford seemed to avoid what they probably perceived as some of the excesses of the High Church in their choice of memorial. Though this cannot be taken too far: Ilford was at the heart of the shrines controversy and St Andrew's, Romford, was to adopt a calvary for its memorial.

From January 1917 the war memorial dominated St Clement's parish magazine. Every edition included a progress report on the fund-raising, with carefully printed tables of contributors. The implication that contribution was not only the mark of a Christian but that of a patriotic citizen of Ilford and the empire was obvious. It is possible to speculate on motives for contribution and certain patterns can be perceived by careful study of the lists. It may be cynical to suggest that the leaders of Ilford society contributed in order to maintain a prestigious facade, but whether they genuinely felt the need to make a donation or not the great tradesmen of the town and residents

[68] Ibid. 9 Oct. 1916.
[69] Ibid. 31 July 1916. When the All Saints', Forest Gate, war memorial was unveiled its aesthetic qualities were also stressed. The Revd W. E. R. Morrow stated that the memorial not only commemorated the dead but served 'to beautify an already beautiful church' as well: *EHE*, 18 June 1920. Similarly, when the war memorial committee of Stratford Presbyterian church discussed their scheme, they noted that 'if carried out in its entirety [it] will be a permanent enrichment of the Church, and will also make for its greater comfort': NHL, Stratford Trinity Presbyterian church magazine, Mar. 1919.

of the parish must certainly have been aware of what the vicar and the PCC expected of them. St Clement's also had a great advantage, for it served the district around Valentines Park, the wealthiest residential streets in the town. The donation lists read a little like *Kelly's directory of Ilford* or the town's official guide. The pressure to make multiple contributions was also apparent, particularly as costs spiralled once tenders were put out.

Sir Peter Griggs MP and his extended family, including Lady Griggs, Captain J. W. Griggs and Mr and Mrs A. P. Griggs, made many contributions. Mr and Mrs A. W. Green were also regular contributors. As well as being a grocer by trade, Green was also chairman of the local Church Naval Brigade and Cadets, was a member of the Ilford War Pensions Committee, representative of the Soldiers' and Sailors' Help Society and a member of the district council education committee. In short he was the epitome of the new suburban Sunday School zealot, combining Christianity with civic obligation. The Bodger family, owners of a large draper's store in Ilford, were also contributors, as were Mr E. J. Beal JP, another store owner, Councillor and Mrs J. Lowe and their relatives, Miss L. Willis, headmistress of a local ladies college and Mr John Farrow, the registrar of births and deaths, and his wife. Such were the notables who contributed to the St Clement's memorial.[70]

The second striking fact to emerge from the lists is the atmosphere of a tightly-knit young male society, obviously shaped and influenced in some way by the church and its activities: St Clement's Sunday School Cricket Club; St Clement's Young Men's Guild Swimming Club; Valentines Bowling Club ('in memory of W. J. Roffey'); Barkingside Company Naval Cadets ('in memory of Midshipman J. H. Lowe' – son of the councillor); members of Mr A. J. Hazleton's bible class ('in affectionate memory of Eddie Higgins, Fredrick Miller, Harry Spencer, Frank Roper M. C., William Ward and John Anthony'). All these groups contributed, all bound by masculine Christianity.[71]

As expected the great majority of the contributors did so in memory of close relatives or friends. Whole families often contributed together: Mr, Mrs and Miss Bennett (in memory of F. Bennett); Mrs E. Spencer (in memory of H. V. Spencer); Mr and Mrs R. W. Bolland (in memory of F. W. H. Bolland); Mr and Mrs Miller (in memory of Fred Miller). W. J. May MC attracted two contributions from his sisters, the Misses May, whilst Mr and Mrs Simmons donated in memory of their only son Second Lieutenant F. W. Simmons. The examples go on and on. It leaves a very deep impression of the scale of loss. Psychologically, the war memorial fund must have provided the impotent sense of grief with a channel through which to pour emotion, a convenient and fitting way to show piety, patriotism, love, pride and grief. Some people responded by making frequent contibutions: Mr C. M. Hodgson made quar-

[70] St Clement's, Great Ilford, parish magazine, Jan. 1917–Nov. 1920; *Kelly's directory of Ilford, 1916–1920*, London 1916–20, passim.
[71] St Clement's, Great Ilford, parish magazine, Jan. 1917–Nov. 1920.

terly contributions and Mrs Jeffrey made the same arrangement. The subscription lists also reveal many 'Misses'. The temptation is to regard these women as fiancées of the dead, although they are just as likely to be sisters and spinsters. The parish magazine of December 1919 carries a large list of 116 contributors which includes donations from Miss Elsie Pearson, Miss W. England, Miss G. M. Tabor, Miss Phyllis Thirkettle, Miss Ethel Hoslam, Miss K. W. Bell, Miss M. Cattermole, Miss B. Gray, Miss E. A. Coombes, Miss Rapkin, Miss M. E. Broadbank, Miss J. Bayne, Miss Lee and Miss E. Jeacock.[72] It can be seen that the men contributed as a group and out of comradeship whereas the women did so from a sense of personal loss.

In spite of the enthusiastic response of the congregation there was obviously some concern about the ability of the parish to meet the costs. The PCC meeting of 26 June 1917 made two decisions The first was to distribute collecting cards worth £1 and 10s., and the second that qualification for inclusion on the war memorial be restricted to former Sunday School members, active churchmen and Men's Guild members. Those outside these categories could be included only if a relative made a specific contribution.[73] This made the memorial a lot more restrictive than the many other Anglican memorials. Perhaps the PCC remembered the controversy over the St Mary's war shrine when many nonconformists had expressed their objections to non-Anglican names appearing on the memorial. The plans for St Clement's took on a very definite meaning. It was going to be a memorial for the 'active' parish and no one else. The decision to issue collecting cards implied a duty or obligation in the same manner that payment of government taxes was an obligation in return for citizenship. It also implied a fair distribution of the load with no shame on those who could not afford more ostentatious offerings. The parish magazines of August and November 1917 stressed this, stating that Collecting Cards were being issued so 'that all can share from the least to the greatest' and that 'the Collecting Cards are already being returned and include many small sums from some of the poorest homes in the parish'.[74] The September 1917 issue stated proudly that 'to Master Winston Whitten belongs the distinction of having filled and returned the first within twenty-four hours of receiving it'. Master Whitten's card was no. 34 worth 10s.: the pathos of a child reacting first was played upon.[75] The distribution of these numbered cards points to an efficient parish organisation clearly capable of tapping every available source. In order to boost this, in March

---

[72] Ibid. The general importance of women to these schemes was also seen at St Matthew's, Bethnal Green, where it was noted that 'Mrs Colegate, one of the communicants, whose son's name appears on the board, has been asked to take charge of the flowers and arrange any that are sent in, and will remove them when they fade': GRLO, St Matthew's, Bethnal Green, parish magazine, Aug. 1922.
[73] St Clement's, Great Ilford, PCC minutes, 26 June 1917.
[74] St Clement's, Great Ilford, parish magazine, Aug., Nov. 1917.
[75] Ibid. Sept. 1917.

1918 Edwin Hodnett, one of the churchwardens, wrote in tones implying that everyone should 'do their bit':

> As the 10s and £1 cards offer to everyone a means of making a weekly thankoffering, we trust that many more members of our congregations will apply for one. No time limit is fixed for their return. May we still plead for that sustained help which can alone enable us to do honour to those who have given their lives for us, as we pray that Christ may accept the offering of their self-sacrifice and grant to them a place of refreshment and peace in His Kingdom? Greater Love hath no man than this, that a man lay down his life for his friends.[76]

Concerns over financing continued however. On 18 March 1918, at a time when the total amount collected stood at £410 19s. 9d., a PCC meeting proposed a series of weekly collections.[77] The Armistice appears to have given the fund a boost as at the meeting of 9 December Hodnett boasted of good progress, a current total of £603 13s. 1d. It was further resolved to add an oak screen or stalls to the chancel out of the fund. But in spite of the fact that a roll of honour was envisaged, the windows were still the only part of the scheme definitely agreed upon.[78]

The next significant stage came in May 1919 when the parish architect, Edwin Dunn, invited tenders for the work including an oak reredos.[79] The reredos was to include the roll of honour, but at the PCC meeting on 24 June Green announced that due to the tremendous increase in the cost of materials the memorial would now cost £1,700. He was confident that this sum would be raised by November.[80] In order to ram the message home Ottaway wrote a thought-provoking piece in the parish magazine for October 1919 stating that:

> those whose homes have been spared seem to be forgetting that it belongs even more to them to see that 'The Glorious Dead' are worthily commemorated. . . . There must be something like 2000 people that enter the Parish Church alone in the course of a month. If each of them was to give or collect 5s a month for the next two months, we should have enough to spare by November 1st, and our War Memorial would be dedicated as it ought to be, free from debt. We are counting on you. Will you try?[81]

---

[76] Ibid. Mar. 1918.
[77] St Clement's, Great Ilford, PCC minutes, 18 Mar. 1918.
[78] Ibid. 9 Dec. 1918.
[79] St Clement's, Great Ilford, parish magazine, May 1919.
[80] St Clement's, Great Ilford, PCC minutes, 24 June 1919.
[81] St Clement's, Great Ilford, parish magazine, Oct. 1919. Ottaway's fellow Ilfordians appear to have shared this idea. The Revd Hector Reindorp of All Saints', Goodmayes, wrote in his parish magazine that 'I feel that there are many who are thankful to God for sparing their dear ones and bringing them safely back home. Would it not be a nice idea to give a thank offering to the Reredos Fund as a token of gratitude? I shall be most happy to receive any such donations. Surely we ought not to let the onus of raising the amount fall on

In November 1919 the total stood at £1,495 11*d*., but a phenomenal effort meant that by December it had shot up to £1,980 17*s*. 7*d*. By February the £2,000 limit that Hodnett had set had been surpassed and all debts were cleared. Ottaway wrote to thank Hodnett 'for bringing us all to share in such a worthy Memorial'.[82] It was not until a PCC meeting on February 1921 that the war memorial sub-committee was formally wound up, with a letter of thanks proposed for Hodnett and Nicholls 'expressing the indebtedness of the Council to them for their labour in the cause, which had been completed successfully in the face of many difficulties'.[83]

The daughter church of St Alban's was also determined to have a memorial, so it too formed a committee and started to raise funds. The committee consisted of Mr Hustwayte (who was a member of the council education committee), Mr Fidler as the treasurer and Mr Barnes as the secretary. The committee followed the example of St Clement's in issuing collecting cards, but they had to contend with the fact that they were now asking people to contribute to a completely new scheme. The St Alban's scheme also meant the duplication of names as the men they were going to commemorate were already due to be included on the St Clement's roll of honour. But this does not appear to have impeded the fund-raising and once again the contributors reveal the nature of community and the individual reasons for responding. J. A. May donated 'in memory of his son W. J. May, a server at St Alban's'. W. J. May's sisters had already made at least two contributions to the St Clement's fund. Mr and Mrs W. Furness gave 'in memory of Lieut. M. S. Furness'. Hodnett contributed – he could hardly do otherwise – and an anonymous donor who went under the title 'ditto' made quarterly donations of 6*s*. 6*d*. The plans for the window were submitted to the vestry in September 1920 and an application was duly made to the chancellor of the diocese.[84]

A rather more eclectic approach to fund-raising was adopted by St Michael and All Angels', Bromley-by-Bow. In January 1920 the first subscriptions and donations started to come in. The parish magazine noted that many of the poorest streets had donated more than the wealthier ones. Pubs were noted to have collected large amounts, hardly surprising given the importance of drink in working-class culture in general and the East End in particular.[85] The Revd G. C. Langdon, determined to promote the project as an ecumenical one, even managed to enlist the Revd A. Tildsley of the Poplar and Bromley Tabernacle as a fund-raiser.[86] Fund-raising activity gained pace

the shoulders of those who have been bereaved': All Saints', Goodmayes, parish magazine, Sept. 1919. Later the chairman of the Ilford War Memorial Fund made a very similar point (see ch. 5).

82 St Clement's, Great Ilford, parish magazine, Nov., Dec. 1919, Feb. 1920.

83 St Clement's, Great Ilford, PCC minutes, 1 Feb. 1921.

84 St Clement's, Great Ilford, parish magazine, May–Nov. 1920; vestry minutes, 20 Sept. 1920.

85 See L. L. Shiman, *The crusade against drink in Victorian England*, London 1988, 131.

86 THL, St Michael and All Angels', Bromley-by-Bow, parish magazine, Jan. 1920.

in the spring with a wide range of events and what appears to have been a deliberately ambiguous statement on the nature of the memorial. The committee advertised their events with circulars headed with the seal and coat-of-arms of the borough and entitled 'Public War Memorial, Central Ward of Poplar'. The memorial was therefore given a civic, official status despite the fact that it had such heavy connections with the Anglican Church. Even more audacious was the decision to collect cash from every ward in the borough.[87] This certainly shows a more imaginative approach than the orthodox collecting schemes of St Clement's and St Alban's in Ilford. By November £880 had been raised and £80 more was needed. The memorial was unveiled in December and by January 1921 the debts had been cleared. The final subscription totals revealed that £353 17s. 3d. had been raised by direct subscriptions and donations, while house-to-house collections had raised more than £171. The grand total, including proceeds from all the fund-raising events, stood at £1,000 17s. 11d.; the surplus was handed over to Poplar Hospital.[88]

The St Anne's, Limehouse, scheme eventually raised £1,200 for its memorial project. The subscription list revealed the nature of the Limehouse community and the fact that the church leadership was trusted even by those of other faiths. Taylor Walker, the brewers, made the largest single donation of £100, once again displaying the importance of brewing and drink to the East End.[89] Immigrant and Yiddish names also appear on the lists: Councillor Rosenthal, Mrs Schultz, George Cohen and Sons and Messrs Hermann Ltd.[90] By November there was £1,053 in the fund but suddenly the flow of donations dried up.[91] Almost a year later the fund had not increased by much and the rector was forced to admit that many people were wondering whether the scheme would ever be completed.[92] There must have been a renewed effort after this as the memorial was ready to be unveiled by April 1921.[93]

The iconography of the memorials

The symbolism contained in the memorials was fitting to their role as substitute graves; religious concepts of comfort and catharsis were naturally at a premium. Names were also of great importance and the duplication of memo-

87 THL, public war memorial, central ward of Poplar, fund-raising circular, 17 Apr. 1920; St Michael and All Angels', Bromley-by-Bow, parish magazine, Feb. 1920.
88 THL, St Michael and All Angels', Bromley-by-Bow, parish magazine, Nov., Dec. 1920, Jan. 1921.
89 The Mile End New Town memorial was largely paid for by Truman, Hanbury and Buxton; ELO, 21 June 1919.
90 ELA, 9 Aug. 1919.
91 THL, St Anne's, Limehouse, parish magazine, Nov. 1919.
92 Ibid. Oct. 1920.
93 Ibid. Apr. 1921.

rials meant the duplication of names. Those inscribed on the St Alban's memorial were also on the St Clement's memorial; the same occured in Romford where the parishioners of St Andrew's were also on the memorial of the mother church of St Edward.[94] Sometimes a man could be commemorated on the memorials of all the communities he belonged to: William Scotcher, for example, appears on the memorial where he worshipped, St Clement's; at his place of education, Ilford County High School; where he studied as a young man, East London College; and on the Ilford civic memorial.[95]

As the memorials erected at this level of society were so personal and the cash supply limited, the form of the memorials was necessarily aesthetic and utility was rejected. The St Michael and All Angels' committee discussed various ideas for a memorial including a plan to endow hospital beds, childrens' cots, a trough for horses and a drinking fountain. The committee said such things as hospital beds were fine concepts, but 'would not serve as the reminder which is so necessary to the generations which are yet to come of the sacrifice which has been made on their behalf. We need a memorial "Lest We Forget" '.[96] The memorial was clearly perceived as something to comfort the present generation and serve as a didactic instrument for those yet to come; the only way to do this was felt to be via traditional memorial architecture and sculpture. Exactly these sentiments were aired at St Anne's: 'What the committee has set out to do is erect a Memorial which shall be a *permanent* record of the men of Limehouse . . . a record to be seen and read by our children in days to come.'[97]

Christian imagery quite naturally dominated and the cross was a key feature of most memorials.[98] Not only was it the symbol of triumph over death, the promise of everlasting life, but it was also associated with the physical nature of the war on the Western Front; calvaries dotted France and Belgium and were regularly remarked upon by soldiers and observers.[99] The High Church parishes of the East End were particularly attracted to the idea of calvaries as war memorials. The St Michael and All Angels' PCC debated the question of a calvary and noted that:

---

[94] *IR*, 7 Nov. 1919, 21 May 1921; *ET*, 19 Feb. 1921, 5 Aug. 1922.
[95] *IR*, 7 Nov. 1919; *ICHS Chronicles*, spring 1921, 35; *ELCM*, Mar. 1921, 24; RHL, *Ilford War Memorial Gazette*, no. 8 (June 1927), 62.
[96] THL, St Michael and All Angels', Bromley-by-Bow, parish magazine, July 1919, Jan. 1920. 'Lest we forget' is a quote from Kipling's poem 'Recessional' (1897). The poem exhorts the people to remember and trust in the Lord at all times; it was therefore regularly quoted on Armistice Day and at memorial unveilings: *Rudyard Kipling's verse: definitive edition*, London 1966 edn, 328.
[97] THL, St Anne's, Limehouse, parish magazine, Aug. 1919.
[98] For a general discussion of Christian symbolism and war memorials see Moriarty, 'Christian iconography', 63–76.
[99] Wilkinson has noted that 'All over France British soldiers came across crucifixes, often for the first time in their lives. An area of the Somme was called "Crucifix Valley" because of the calvary which stood there': *The Church and the war*, 190.

The suggestion to have a Calvary is one that will appeal to almost everyone, as the Sign of our Redemption, and all the more so for the fact that wherever our soldiers go, in France or Belgium, the Village Cross is the most familiar sight, and also, as we hear, is often the only thing that is untouched by bullets and shells.[100]

All Hallows' adopted a calvary as its war memorial as it would remind passers-by 'of the Great Sacrifice, and will especially remind our soldiers of the Wayside Crucifixes they have so often seen abroad'.[101] At the unveiling of the Mile End New Town memorial the bishop of Stepney stated that 'these Calvaries are new in the East End. It is all the better, therefore, that our people should feel that this representation of the Saviour of the World should be properly saluted, as has always been the case in France and Belgium'.[102] It was not just the parishes of the East End that adopted calvaries for the City church of St Bartholomew-the-Great erected one (see plate 1). St Andrew's, Romford, erected what was described curiously as 'an old English Calvary'. This description was rather ironic given the argument that nothing was more unEnglish than a calvary. But the symbolism was certainly comforting. At the base were carved the names of 117 men of the parish and from that the eye was led up to the Crucified Christ; there was no doubting the validity of the sacrifice or its reward.[103]

The St Anne's war memorial committee discussed a calvary as a suitable memorial, but eventually decided to erect a figure of Christ the Consoler. The choice was, symbolically, one stage on from a calvary; although the significance of the calvary contains the victory over death via the cross, a figure of Christ the Consoler is the Risen Christ, the true proof of life over death. It was decided to adopt a figure of the Risen Christ 'as a symbol of our faith in the immortality of the Dead'. No objections were raised to this suggestion and, incongruously, the Jewish Councillor Marks seconded the proposal and obviously had no qualms over the symbolism.[104] The influence of the Anglo-Catholic, High Church tastes of the working-class areas of East

100 THL, St Michael and All Angels', Bromley-by-Bow, parish magazine, Aug. 1917. The miraculous survival of crucifixes has also been remarked upon by Wilkinson: 'In almost every village a crucifix stood somewhere, sometimes the only object left standing, and this was said to impress even the most callous, though some scorned the survival of crucifixes as evidence of the providential love of God. In 1916 a small book of meditations was published by A. H. Baverstock, a parish priest (with a preface by G. K. Chesterton) entitled *The unscathed crucifix*, which was interleaved with several photographs illustrating the title': Wilkinson, *The Church and the war*, 149–50.
101 THL, All Hallows', East India Dock, parish magazine, Nov. 1916.
102 *ELO*, 21 June 1919.
103 *ET*, 5 Aug. 1922. The general impact of the French and Flemish calvaries on British life was clearly illustrated by R. H. Mottram in *The crime at Vanderlynden's* (London 1927) the last of his novels that make up *The Spanish farm trilogy*. The book rests upon the desecration (p. 571) of a shrine by British soldiers.
104 THL, St Anne's, Limehouse, parish magazine, Apr. 1919.

London is also very clear here. The emphasis this branch of the Church placed on rituals, ceremonial and ornament gave it a powerful affinity with the Roman Catholic Irish communities of the area. At this time of deep spiritual shock and search for consolation the strengths of these liturgical practises came to the fore. High Anglicanism and Roman Catholicism offered consolation through both the overt symbolism of their memorials and the rituals of prayers and intercession for the dead. This will become more apparent when the observation of Armistice Day is examined.

Comfort came through an element that only the churches could confidently provide: namely that each dead man had achieved Paradise. Anglican clergy tended to go one step further and openly associate the sacrifice with the sufferings of Christ, a trait very rarely seen in nonconformist churches. But all were agreed on the important point; death in a just war meant the reward of Paradise. 'Their keen eager eyes are upon us . . . from their place among "the great cloud of witnesses", to see if we are proving ourselves worthy of the sacrifices made for us' wrote the pastor of Stratford Presbyterian church.[105] By adding the obligation of living worthy lives he also gave the congregation a positive task. Each individual could glorify their lost loved one by maintaining this covenant with them. At the unveiling of the All Saints', Forest Gate, memorial the Revd W. E. R. Morrow reassured those mourning by arguing that the dead would never be forgotten 'because they had died for ideals for which Christ had died. . . . If there was ever a war which had principles so near akin to the principles of Jesus Christ it was this war. It was a war of the nailed hand against the mailed fist'.[106]

Such words, which came from a sermon given by the bishop of London in 1915, reveal the entrenchment of wartime concepts in peacetime.[107] At St Gabriel's, Old Canning Town, the vicar put his message across with equal vigour: 'They died as Christ had died, that other men might live, and therefore were sharers in the great sacrifice of Jesus Christ. They could feel with absolute certainty that if these men shared that sacrifice with Christ they would share his kingdom.'[108] This approach confirmed that the Great War really had been a victory for the civilised world; it also immortalised the dead as the crusaders of the age, residing in eternal peace with Christ and the saints.

The Revd C. A. Duthie certainly subscribed to this concept when he commended the souls of the 458 men of Limehouse to the keeping of God

---

[105] NHL, Stratford Trinity Presbyterian church magazine, Jan. 1921.
[106] EHE, 21 July 1919.
[107] The bishop said that the war was being fought 'because we are called to save the freedom of the world and the national honour, and to see the Nailed Hand prevailing over the Mailed Fist': Winnington-Ingram, *The potter and the clay*, 202. This image permeated the language of remembrance; the Revd Herbert Dunnico, addressing an Armistice service in Ilford in 1929, stated that international co-operation would eliminate the 'mailed fist' and ensure that 'might was not right': IR, 15 Nov. 1929.
[108] SE, 9 June 1920.

with the words: 'Accept, O Lord, the offering of their self-sacrifice, and grant to them, with all Thy faithful servants, a place of refreshment and peace, where the light of Thy Countenance shines for ever.' [109] The *East London Advertiser* caught the solemnity of the occasion and noted that 'seldom have the grounds of the old Parish Church of St Anne, Limehouse, been filled to greater capacity, and never have they been used for such an appropriate occasion. . . . Relatives of the fallen have expressed to various members of the Committee their great satisfaction at the impressive service.'[110]

Each dead soldier had followed Christ to his own calvary and glorious resurrection. The new war memorial altar screen at All Saints', Goodmayes, was inscribed 'Mighty by Sacrifice' which 'refers to our Lord who was perfected through suffering on the cross, and in another sense to those who laid down their lives for their country'.[111] When the Revd R. T. Brode dedicated the calvary at St Andrew's, Romford, he said that the men were 'numbered with the saints' and made a further connection between the dead and the sacrifice of Christ when he stated that 'their example was always available, and they could follow in the footsteps of Him who gave the world the example'.[112] The comfort in the thought of a life translated elsewhere and not ended was the key to the bishop of Chelmsford's address at the unveiling of the St Edward's, Romford, memorial:

> Those men were not dead. They were alive. . . . Those were not dead men's names; they were the names of men still living. Those who were parted now would come together by and by. Mother, wife, father, brother, sister, that name on the Roll of Honour was the name of someone who was living in a land that was as great a reality as Australia. He wanted them to take that comfort with them as they went back to their homes.[113]

This was mirrored at the Romford Congregational church where the war memorial windows contained the figures of Courage and Victory holding a scroll inscribed with 'Be thou faithful unto death and I will give thee a crown of life.'[114] The vicar of St John's, Seven Kings, said that the dead, whose names were carved on the memorial, were now 'in Paradise, free from the struggle against temptation, free to make progress'.[115] At the Roman Catholic church of St Margaret and All Saints', Canning Town, a new altar was dedicated to Our Lady of Sorrows. Oak panels contained the names of the 150 fallen of the parish. The bishop of Brentwood unveiled the memorial which for him was a perfect expression of Catholic doctrine:

---

109 THL, order of service for the unveiling and dedication of the St Anne's, Limehouse, war memorial, 30 May 1921.
110 *ELA*, 4 June 1921.
111 All Saints', Goodmayes, parish magazine, June 1920.
112 *ET*, 5 Aug. 1922.
113 Ibid. 19 Feb. 1921.
114 Ibid. 20 Mar. 1920.
115 *IR*, 12 Nov. 1920.

Plate 2. War memorial, St Edmund's Roman Catholic Church, Millwall

the Bishop referred to the permanent character of the memorial, and its connection with the doctrine of the Communion of Saints. The Church militant,
the church suffering, and the Church triumphant were symbolized in that
memorial, and it would serve as a lasting monument to those who had given
up their lives in sacrifice during the great war.[116]

116 *Tablet*, 30 Apr. 1921.

The memorial was also used to promote Catholic beliefs of the after-life as 'the relatives of the fallen men have joined the newly formed sodality of the Seven Dolours of the Blessed Virgin, and will meet on Tuesday to pray for the repose of their souls'.[117]

Mrs Mumford, the mother of one of the dead, unveiled the Ilford Wesleyan war memorial. The Revd E. O. Pearson used the occasion to speculate on the nature of sacrifice:

> He emphasised the sacrifice of Christ for the redemption of the world, of great pioneer missionaries in foreign lands, of Father Damien among the lepers, of the Salvation Army lasses in the slums, and of the millions of the best of our young men in this land in the great war – in all cases for the salvation of others.[118]

St Andrew-by-the-Wardrobe, in the City, furnished a war memorial chapel, the centre-piece of which was a great stained-glass window containing the scene at Golgotha with a soldier looking on in the company of the Virgin, Mary Magdalene and the Beloved Disciple. The archdeacon of London, dedicating the chapel, stated that

> This chapel of remembrance would, therefore be a most appropriate memorial, for we could well, and indeed, might reasonably believe that it would be part of the Heaven of our departed heroes to know that they would be remembered here, and that those for whom they died would forget them not.[119]

The dead therefore looked down upon the living, honoured by grateful remembrance. Six months later the archdeacon was repeating his message at St Bride's: 'it must be their pleasure in Paradise to known that they were not forgotten'. He used the same image for a third time at the unveiling of the St Botolph-without-Bishopsgate memorial.[120] Similar imagery was used by the Revd D. Smyth of St Mark's, Silvertown, in the West Ham docklands. He told the congregation that the men on the memorial were:

> a noble example of self-sacrifice, love and comradeship in difficulties and dangers, and of willingness to suffer for righteousness sake, even to the laying down of their lives. Those present were sorrowful that day, yet they rejoiced in the knowledge that those who had laid down their lives were not extinct – they had simply gone before. They were above encircling that gathering with their spirits, and perhaps looking down on them. They would recognise the conduct of those left behind. They asked for grace and strength to enable them to follow that noble example.[121]

---

117 Ibid.
118 *IR*, 11 June 1920.
119 *CP*, 11 Dec. 1920.
120 Ibid. 25 June, 26 Nov. 1921.
121 *SE*, 1 June 1921.

At the unveiling of the St Mary, Aldermary, memorial chapel Dean Inge of St Paul's Cathedral was absolutely unequivocal in his assurance that the sacrifice was glorious: 'No evil spirit could be exorcised without the suffering of the innocent. Vicarious suffering was the law of the world in which we lived.'[122] The idea that Paradise was full of fit young men anxiously watching those on earth to see if they met the standards they had lived and died for was entwined with the concepts of chivalrous, muscular Christianity. The final choice of memorial at St Michael and All Angels' certainly embodied this spirit: it took the form of a figure of Christ standing with His right hand in blessing, in His left hand was a laurel crown and kneeling before Him was the figure of a crusader (*see* plate 3). The memorial, placed outside the church, was hardly civic in character; it had been a church project from the start and was perceived in entirely Christian terms: 'It was Christian, and therefore fitting to commemorate all those who had followed the example of Christ in their self-sacrifice. It was inspiring, suggesting the thought of victory and not defeat, and of joy not sorrow.'[123]

The medieval atmosphere of the memorial was matched at St Alban's, Ilford, where the memorial took the form of stained-glass windows showing Sir Galahad and Sir Percivale in the Hermit's Chapel on one side of the brass tablet and Christ with a crown of thorns looking over a group of young soldiers on the other. Again it was an exercise in muscular Christianity as it was a memorial by no means in 'the ordinary ecclesiastical groove, away from anaemic saints and emaciated virgins' and sought 'to tell us plainly that Christ may be a living reality to the modern man as He was to many of our soldiers'.[124] The parish magazine fully explored the symbolism of the stained glass:

> The artist has taken his ideas from some lines which occur near the middle of 'The Holy Grail' in Tennyson's 'Idylls of the King'. . . . It is that which makes the Galahad windows a fitting part of the Memorial to the sons of St Alban's, many of whom, as communicants and servers, knew something of the vision of the Altar, but left their church and their homes to go forth on a sacred quest, like Arthur's knights, to take their share in the righting of human wrongs, and 'clash with Pagan hordes and bear them down'. And Sir Percivale? He was a lesser man, but he was inspired by his contact with Galahad, and he too saw the Holy Grail in the distance before Sir Galahad passed on to the spiritual city. We cannot all be Galahads. We cannot all see visions. The picture of Sir

---

[122] *CP*, 16 Oct. 1920. For Dean Inge's wartime career see Wilkinson, *The Church and the war*, 259–60.
[123] THL, St Michael and All Angels', Bromley-by-Bow, parish magazine, July 1919, Feb. 1920.
[124] St Clement's, Great Ilford, parish magazine, July 1921. These sentiments found an amazing parallel at the Honourable Artillery Company Armistice service 1938 (see ch. 9).

Plate 3. Central ward of Poplar war memorial, St Michael and All Angels'

Percivale will remind us lesser men how much help we gain from the friendship and example of the greater knights.[125]

When the archdeacon of London dedicated the war memorial chapel at St
Andrew-by-the-Wardrobe, he told an allegorical story of remembrance based
upon a medieval knight who gave a flower to his damsel as a keepsake.[126]

Christ and the actions of the soldiers were therefore merged. The Ilford
Congregational church memorial consisted of stained-glass windows
depicting the Angel of the Resurrection over the empty tomb and St Paul
shaking the viper into the fire. The religious allegories of life over death were
matched with patriotic ones as the rose, shamrock and thistle were also
depicted.[127] The memorial therefore provided comfort through both religious
and patriotic symbols. Patriotism and the reiteration of the meaning of the
war played a large part in the nature of these war memorials and helped to
frame the memory of the war inherited by Armistice Day.

In a world seemingly transformed the use of familiar images connected the
new situation to the assured, antediluvian world of 1914. The memorial at
All Saints', Forest Gate, was inscribed 'Dulce et Decorum est Pro Patria
Mori'.[128] By employing Horace's most enduring ode the memorial connected
the dead to the glories of classical civilisation, an apt image in tune with the
atmosphere of 1919; the British Victory Medal had the legend 'The Great
War for Civilisation' inscribed on its reverse side.[129] The rural parish of St
Peter's, Aldborough Hatch, on the fringes of Ilford Urban District, erected a
triptych for its dead. The roll of honour was carved onto the wings, the centre
panel bore a female figure of Grief placing a wreath against a tomb. The

---

[125] Ibid. July 1921. Wilkinson has noted that 'Tennyson in *Idylls of the King* (1859), Char-
lotte Yonge in *The Heir of Redclyffe* (1853), and the Pre-Raphaelites had popularised the
ethos of medieval chivalry . . . Scott Holland, in *Commonwealth* for October 1914, called the
Sermon on the Mount "the book of Christian knighthood". Edward Woods, when chaplain
at Sandhurst during the war, wrote a book for the cadets which he called *Knights in Armour*.
Some of the stories of the miraculous deliverance of sacred objects in France reminded R. J.
Campbell of Sir Galahad's vision at Mass as described in *Idylls of the King*. A bereaved mother
writing to Winnington-Ingram described fallen soldiers as "that great band of brave, shining
knights who have given all" ': Wilkinson, *The Church and the war*, 189, 232–3. London and
Essex saw the erection of many chivalrous memorials: St George as a medieval knight for the
Pearl Assurance Company in the City; St George as a knight on horseback slaying the
dragon for St Marylebone; St George on horseback, sword held aloft in triumph for the
Cavalry of the empire in Hyde Park and St George in armour at Colchester. See Borg, *War
memorials*, 99–101.
[126] *CP*, 11 Dec. 1920.
[127] *IR*, 1 Aug. 1919.
[128] *EHE*, 21 July 1919.
[129] For the modern reader, the Horatian lines cannot be read without the thought of
Wilfred Owen's bitter and ironic poem of the same title. However the inscription was
entirely without irony and so rather disproves Fussell's theory that such language could
never be used again after the horrors of the Western Front: Fussell, *The Great War and
modern memory*, 155–190; J. Stallworthy (ed.), *The poems of Wilfred Owen*, London 1985,
117.

inscription displays the pride of a community where everyone had done their bit: 'To the Memory of the brave sons of the empire/who fell on the battlefields of Europe/They fought the good fight in the cause of humanity/that honour might live.'[130] A similar message was propagated at Forest Gate Congregational church, where the pastor wrote that the dead had sacrificed themselves 'in the cause of Freedom and Right' and added 'may the sight of the tablet ever urge us to live in Peace and Brotherhood of mankind'.[131] The unveiling service at St Thomas's, West Ham, saw the buttressing of wartime ethics reach a dramatic apogee. The Revd I. L. Seymour had lost both his sons in the war but had no qualms about their deaths. His message was one of pride and must have boosted the morale of any who doubted whether the sacrifice was justifiable:

> As dear as their boys were, it was a privilege to be able to give so rich a gift to their country in its time of need. It was a grand thing for England that she possessed sons so brave, generous and unselfish as to give their lives for her, so long as the country could breed men of such stuff she would retain her proud position in the world, and prove a boon and a blessing to the human race.[132]

The bishop of Chelmsford left the congregation of St Clement's in no doubt as to the meaning of the war. He said that the men on their memorial had sacrificed themselves for England and its freedom and asked them to consider a German victory with 'the German Eagle flying over Buckingham Palace and the Mansion House'. He then urged them all to do their duty by the dead and lead worthy lives.[133]

The nature of England and its peculiar values was the theme of the Revd J. H. Ellison when he unveiled the memorial at the City church of St Michael's, Cornhill:

> In the hour of England's greatest peril, they gave their lives for the freedom of the world. Those men sought to 'build Jerusalem in England's green and pleasant land' and in so doing set a standard for our race, and showed us the true England, England must see that she never fell below that standard.[134]

---

130 *IR*, 16 Sept. 1921.

131 NHL, Forest Gate Congregational church, annual manual 1921, 9.

132 *SE*, 13 Nov. 1921.

133 *IR*, 7 Nov. 1919.

134 *CP*, 6 Nov. 1920. The use of such rural imagery in the tightly-packed streets of the City shows how far such concepts had permeated the national imagination. During the war the underground railways of London commissioned George Clausen and other graphic designers to produce posters to be displayed on London station platforms and in army huts and canteens in France and Flanders. The aim was to 'awaken thoughts of pleasant homely things' which was reflected in the designs depicting rural idylls. Londoners who travelled on a modern urban underground transport system and Londoners in khaki at the front therefore shared a concept of home as a 'green and pleasant land': J. Darracott and B. Loftus, *First World War in posters*, London 1981 edn, 22; O. Green, *Underground art*, London 1990, 32–3; S. Sillars, *Art and survival in First World War Britain*, London 1987, 133–9.

An extraordinary service took place at the Ilford Presbyterian church when its memorial was unveiled. Ilford had a noticeable Scottish expatriate community connected with the church but interest in the memorial seems to have gone beyond that as the seating was taxed 'to an extent that has seldom been experienced'.[135] Pipers of the London Scottish battalion flanked the memorial and the local branch of the London Scottish Association turned out. A distinctive community, living in a London suburb, was therefore promoting itself and remembering its dead. The Revd D. C. Lusk, formerly of the London Scottish, then linked all of them to the wider concept of the nation:

> He pointed out that the past is strewn with memorials of great sacrifice, and that all that is great in our national life was the result of sacrifice. It was no new thing, for we have always known it to be true that life has been bought with a great price, and we realise afresh in the sacred hour that our lives must in some degree be worthy of this great price.[136]

The dead had set a patriotic standard of duty. Major-General Sir Nevil Smyth VC, commander of the 47th (London) Division, made this point a theme of his speech at the unveiling of the St Michael and All Angels' memorial. He said that most of the 242 dead of the parish had been volunteers who had responded to the call out of a noble sense of duty:

> To the men of the regular forces, war had been prepared for, year in and year out, but these men left behind them at the shortest notice everything that they held dear in life, because they had learnt the meaning of the noblest word of our language – 'Duty'.[137]

The duke of York then unveiled the memorial. He addressed the crowd and put the yoke of duty onto those left behind: 'If we can do our duty with the same unselfish comradeship with which these splendid dead did their task, there can be nothing dark in the difficulties which the future may hold for our country.'[138] Conformity was at the heart of the message. The dead had fulfilled their obligations to duty without fuss or complaint; it was the responsibility of the living to do the same. When General Lord Byng unveiled the memorial at St Anne's, he told the crowd to 'lift their thoughts above the material things, and to try and idealise the future'.[139] When Lord Methuen, the governor of the Tower of London, unveiled the parishioners' memorial at

---

[135] *IR*, 4 Mar. 1921.

[136] Ibid.

[137] *EEN*, 10 Dec. 1920.

[138] Ibid.

[139] THL, St Anne's, Limehouse, parish magazine, June 1921. Lord Byng commanded the Third Army during the war and won great laurels for masterminding the capture of Vimy Ridge as a preliminary to the Battle of Arras in 1917: A. McKee, *Vimy Ridge*, Toronto 1966, 24.

St Olave's, he used patriotic images and the backdrop of the memorial to interpret the present situation. 'He was confident that England could be brought safely through her present industrial and other troubles if all classes would only display the same spirit, and good old British common sense.'[140] The presence of so many military men at the unveiling of these memorials shows that the concept of soldiering was hardly a distasteful subject in the post-war years, despite the alleged reaction against all things military.[141]

The wider message of the memorials

Concepts of duty and obligation infused these memorials with a wider significance. They served as didactic symbols especially to the children and young of the communities. The message of the memorials was used in religious–patriotic catechisms to instruct children in the glories of serving King, Country and God. Framed rolls of honour were erected in the two Sunday Schools of Forest Gate Congregational church. Such memorials served to remind the children of an example set and of their duty to emulate their predecessors if the need arose. In this sense the world supposedly without war was being built upon a foundation of flawed idealism.[142] In April 1918, the St Clement's Young Men's Guild placed in their club room a triptych, its wings inscribed with the 149 Guild members on active service. The young members of the bible class met in the same room and each Armistice Day they gathered to lay a wreath on the triptych.[143] The dead boys were exactly the sort of young men the bishop of Chelmsford referred to in his dedication of the St Clement's memorial:

> Before the war there was a great leavening of the community with Christian sentiment. That had its restraining influence upon the nation; but in the war many of the best spiritual and moral forces were killed off and the nation today was deprived of their influence, and the nation now suffered the loss of the bravest of the brave – the Christian men of the nation.[144]

There were men such as W. G. Scotcher whose communal spirit had resulted in the honour of commemoration on many different war memorials. The war memorial committee at St Anne's recognised the importance of the memorial to the youth of the parish. They set out their aims thus: 'What the committee

---

140 *CP*, 21 May 1921.
141 Lord Methuen, commander of the 1st Division in the South African War, had unveiled the Clifton College South African War memorial: O. F. Christie, *A history of Clifton College, 1860–1934*, Bristol 1934, 148–9.
142 NHL, Forest Gate Congregational church, Sunday School minute books, 10 Apr., 4 Sept. 1919.
143 St Clement's, Great Ilford, parish magazine, Apr. 1918, Nov. 1929.
144 *IR*, 7 Nov. 1919.

has set out to do is to erect a Memorial which shall be a *permanent* record of the men of Limehouse . . . a record to be seen and read by our children.'[145] The dead were portrayed as role-models for the young. The memorial at St Mark's, Silvertown, for example, was a symbol of all the noble virtues of British manhood. The Revd D. Smyth told the crowd that 'To those who were left, these men were an example of fortitude, courage and bravery. They hoped that the memorial would be an inspiration not only to the present generation but also to generations to come.' [146]

For the Catholic youth of Canning Town, the dead played a role in perpetuating their own particular community. A new church and club dedicated to Our Lady of Sorrows was erected as a chapel-of-ease for St Margaret and All Saints'. Councillor Bennett of West Ham spoke at the unveiling and stated that: 'To have a house of their own where the young people of the parish could foregather was an epoch in the Catholic tradition of that locality.'[147]

Memorials also had the role of demonstrating the worth of the communities to each other and to the nation, especially in the case of minorities. Nonconformists made the final step into fully respectable society via the memorials: it was an achievement made possible by sacrifice in a just war for freedom. Anglican clergy were often invited to share their services of dedication and in doing so gave the memorial the official seal of approval. Canon T. G. Rogers spoke at the Stratford Presbyterian church unveiling, assuring the congregation of their 'common churchmanship', and said that 'they did not talk of the Church of England dead and the Presbyterian dead, but only of the Christian dead'.[148] An Anglican clergyman also attended the unveiling of the East Ham Presbyterian memorial.[149]

But perhaps the community with the greatest desire to be recognised as loyal, and yet which had the greatest difficulty in proving it, was East End Jewry. Established Anglo-Jewry had been long engaged in the struggle to knock the segregated ghetto mentality out of the Yiddish-speaking Russian and Eastern European Jews of the East End through such bodies as the Jewish Lads Brigade.[150] In 1914 the Brigade, and similar bodies, urged young Jews to join the Colours. For many Russian Jews, however, conditioned by the brutal treatment they had received as conscripts in the Tsarist armies, service was something to be avoided at all costs. The sight of young Jewish men on the streets fired the claim that Jews were not doing their bit. Serious antisemitic disturbances followed in the East End as Jews became the target of abuse. The government attempted to alleviate the situation by creating Jewish battalions

---

[145] THL, St Anne's, Limehouse, parish magazine, Aug. 1919.
[146] *SE*, 1 June 1921.
[147] *Tablet*, 19 Jan. 1924.
[148] *SE*, 2 Apr. 1921.
[149] *EHE*, 5 Nov. 1920. For a discussion of the nonconformist communities and integration in the Great War see Wilkinson, *The Church and the war*, 202.
[150] See J. Springhall, *Youth, society and empire: British youth movements, 1883–1940*, London 1977, 41–3.

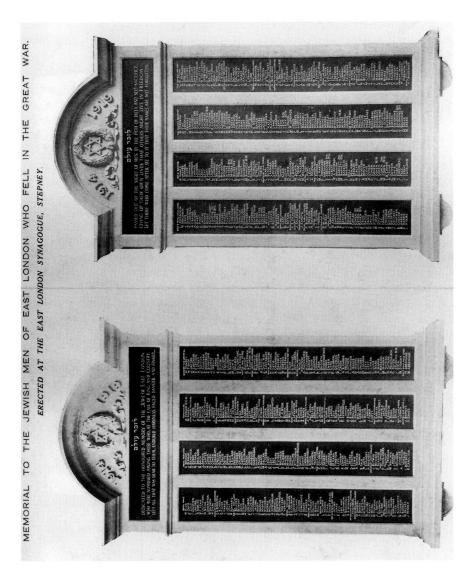

Plate 4. War memorial, East London Synagogue, Stepney

under the umbrella of the Royal Regiment of Fusiliers, to serve in Palestine. Three battalions were eventually formed, the 38th, 39th and 40th, which served solidly, if unspectacularly, but they were still not at all popular with Russian Jews.[151] This left the East End Jewish community in a paradoxical position at the end of the war. Many felt bitter at the treatment handed out to them, whilst others had fulfilled their obligations to King and Country and had the same desire as other communities to remember their dead. It is not surprising that the leaders of the Jewish community decided to use their dead in order to promote a positive image of the community as a whole. Dayan Mendelssohn stated at the unveiling of the West Ham Associate Synagogue that

> the Jews were not cowards. . . . They had not given up their lives as a useless sacrifice. They had upheld the good name of the Jew, and shown their courage, loyalty and devotion. The Jew must learn that the only way to master prejudice was by living a life that would be an example to others. . . . Her sons were buried in all the war zones of England.[152]

The Chief Rabbi, Joseph Hertz, buttressed those comments when he dedicated the memorial at the East London Synagogue, Aldgate:

> Jewish sacrifice is soon forgotten by the world outside, and few remember that 9000 Jews in the British Army alone fell in action or were wounded in this great conflict. In our community, at least, this tablet will for evermore gratefully recount that these Jewish children of East London, added new glories to the name of the Jew vindicating his honour and keeping reproach from the escutcheon of Anglo-Jewry.[153]

But the Jews did have another problem. As their memorials were inside synagogues and therefore out of sight of Gentiles they could not physically impress the outside world with the evidence of their loyalty. This problem was debated throughout the twenties and led the East London based Jewish Ex-Servicemen's Legion to advocate a public Jewish memorial. Lieutenant-Colonel Levy, president of the Legion, wrote:

> why is there no Anglo-Jewish Memorial? Every city, town, village and hamlet throughout the length and breadth of the country has its own local Memorial, but there is nothing in the centre of the East End of London, or the Jewish centres of Manchester or Leeds, which can compare in any way even with that of a local Memorial in a small village. . . . The Jewish Ex-Servicemen are of the opinion that the most practical and effective way of answering the attacks on the loyalty of Anglo-Jewry is to erect in the centre of London a suitable

---

[151] See Bush, *Behind the lines*, 165–92.
[152] *SE*, 14 Apr. 1920.
[153] *JG*, 9 July 1926.

Memorial Hall to be used at the headquarters of the proposed Jewish Ex-Servicemen's Association.[154]

Closely connected with this lack of actual visibility was the general lack of press coverage. The East London newspapers paid scant attention to unveiling ceremonies in synagogues and so the Gentile public were hardly likely to be well-informed as to the nature of Jewish sacrifice. Some of the East London newspapers had pursued generally antisemitic policies during the war and so may have found it convenient to ignore such events in the post-war period, although the *East London Observer*, one of the antisemitic papers, obviously recanted its earlier position. By the end of the twenties it carried a column of Jewish news and events entitled 'Ghetto Gossip'.[155]

Ex-servicemen and memorialisation

The war threw up a distinctive community of its own making; that of the ex-servicemen. These men had their own peculiar view and memory of the war and duly erected memorials in both places of worship and places where they gathered together. The City churches had close links with battalions of the London Regiment and so were natural homes for memorials. As these memorials were for ex-servicemen rather than a wider community, qualities of pride, achievement and belonging tended to be put at a far higher premium than concepts of grief and consolation, though these elements were not entirely dismissed. Like school memorials, their function seemed to be prescribed to a greater degree than in 'ordinary' memorials.

Commercial links played a part in making some of the City military memorials even more specific. Some of the wartime service battalions of the Royal Regiment of Fusiliers were recruited from the trades and professions of the City and so gave London its equivalent of the Pals battalions of the industrial north.[156] The traditional bonds of certain trades with certain churches provided these battalions with natural environments for their memorials. Major Etchells of the 26th, Bankers' battalion of the Royal Fusiliers, asked the church of St Edmund, King and Martyr, Lombard Street, to provide a home for their memorial. The vestry recorded that:

> when the question of a suitable memorial was discussed his [Etchells'] committee at once thought that it would be very fitting if it could be placed in the

---

154 *JESM*, 8–9 (June–July 1935), 32.

155 See Bush, *Behind the lines*, 167. For a good example of the 'Ghetto Gossip' column see *ELO*, 6 July 1935.

156 See C. Hughes, 'The new armies', in I. F. K. Beckett and K. Simpson (eds), *A nation in arms: a social study of the British army in the First World War*, Manchester 1985, 99–127; R. W. Butcher 'A regiment at war', *Stand To! Journal of the Western Front Association* xxi/1 (Spring 1989), 21–4.

church which was situated in the very centre of the daily activities of those who had fallen. He hoped that the association of the battalion with the church would continue.[157]

The men who had worked, fought and then died together were commemorated close to where their surviving comrades continued their lives. It was clearly seen as a great honour by the vestry. Churchwarden Hanbury stated that 'the parishioners of St Edmund the King and Martyr [*sic*] were proud that their church had been asked to house the very handsome memorial'.[158] A similar sense of intimacy inspired the 10th battalion, Stock Exchange, to erect their memorial in St Michael, Cornhill. The battalion headquarters had been within the parish and the Royal Exchange was across the street from the church.[159]

The history and style of each church influenced the choice of design in each case: neither battalion felt the need to stray outside the realms of traditional ecclesiastical ornamentation. At St Michael's the stockbrokers decided that 'nothing should be erected which was not in complete harmony with the church itself'.[160] The bankers' battalion chose a stained-glass window which 'would be a noble embellishment to their church and a great comfort to those relatives of the officers and men of the battalion who had sacrificed their lives'.[161] It was a conservative, but majestic and proud, statement: the window consisted of a figure of St George in armour and a female Victory in armour holding a laurel wreath, with a lance by her side. A very clear sense of belonging and community was implicit; special permission had been granted to use the coat of arms of the City of London in the glass and the stained-glass borders displayed the badges of the ten great banking firms which had provided men for the battalion.[162] It was a massive reaffirmation of the meaning of the war: the defence of civilisation, epitomised in the commercial might of the British empire. The men of the Poplar and Stepney Rifles, 17th battalion London Regiment, erected a memorial organ in their church of St Stephen's, Bow. The battalion commemorated its 1,100 dead by ornamenting its own church.[163]

An alternative to a church memorial was one in the drill hall or headquarters. The City of London Rifles, known as the Cast Iron Sixth, chose this option. Their memorial was a true symbol of comradeship. It was designed by F. W. Hagall, an ex-rifleman of the battalion, the copper engraving and carpentry was carried out by the ex-servicemen themselves and the work was supervised by the father of one of the dead soldiers. Disaster nearly struck

---

157 GML, L92 MS 11,261, St Edmund, King and Martyr, PCC minutes, 24 Aug. 1923.
158 Ibid.
159 GML, L92 MS 18,319/52, St Michael's, Cornhill, faculty papers, 26 Oct. 1926.
160 Ibid.
161 GML, L92 MS 11,261, St Edmund, King and Martyr, PCC minutes, 24 Aug. 1923.
162 GML, L92 MS 18,319/44, St Edmund, King and Martyr, faculty papers, 13 Sept. 1923.
163 *ELA*, 5 Feb. 1921.

when the bank holding their funds folded, but their old brigadier, W. F. Mildren, stepped in to make up the deficit.[164] Mildren was then given the honour of unveiling the memorial at the Farringdon Road drill hall. He celebrated their special bonds: they were held together by their civilian jobs and that spirit that had inspired them to overcome the shortfalls in the Territorial Force system:

> it should never be forgotten that those men, drawn from workshop and warehouses in the City, who had displayed such fine qualities, had no great traditions or records, as men of other regiments had, to inspire them to bear the terrible stress and strain of a modern battlefield. They had nothing practically but the moral force of their own character, and the discipline learned at home in their spare time in a short training to fall back upon. Yet they acquitted themselves magnificently under the most trying conditions.[165]

It was not a speech designed for grieving parents; it was for ex-servicemen and celebrated their masculinity. Dr Leaf touched on a similar theme when he unveiled the London County, Westminster and Parrs Bank memorial. He, on the other hand, was more prosaic than the no-nonsense brigadier: 'They were inspired by that masculine energy which is the secret of the British Empire. They came forward and faced the Great Adventure with eager hearts.'[166]

Memorials also served as symbols of communal pride and self-glorification. The City seemed to take this process to extremes as war memorials were seen as the most recent symbols of a patriotic and glorious past. When the St Sepulchre war memorial was unveiled, it was likened to the ancient monuments already in the church. This became a favourite image. At St Olave's, the Trinity House memorial was compared 'to the memorials of great deeds and great men already preserved in that ancient shrine. It would lift up their hearts and encourage them to think that the path of sacrifice today was the same as old'.[167] When the St Giles, Cripplegate, memorial was unveiled the Revd B. G. Chandler made allusions to the glorious history of the church:

> The church was rich in tributes to great men. One was the name of John Milton on a slab over his resting-place. There was a memorial also of Martin Frobisher one of Drake's Captains. . . . Now once more a memorial tablet has been given to the church bearing the names of loved ones who had played their part in history no less than the great ones of long ago.[168]

---

[164] The men also endowed a bed at Bart's hospital which they named the Mildren Bed in his honour: Godfrey, *Cast-Iron Sixth*, 262. A similar event occured in Ilford where the ex-servicemen endowed a cot in the new war memorial children's ward (see ch. 5).
[165] *CP*, 3 Feb. 1923.
[166] Ibid. 12 June 1920.
[167] Ibid. 21 May 1921.
[168] GBL, St Giles, Cripplegate, parish magazine, Nov. 1919.

The dead had fulfilled the expectations placed upon them by their rich inheritance; the new memorial placed this mantle on the living. As a result the memorials were also reflecting a very specific form of pride and self-glorification. As part of a massive restoration programme, St Mary, Aldermary, erected a war memorial chapel which cost more than £3,000. The money was donated by City firms and in return their badges were displayed in the chapel. A similar scheme was instigated at St Helen's, Bishopsgate; 500 City firms raised over £4,200 for the project. The largesse and image of the firm and livery company had to be maintained at all times, with respect for the dead and self-advertisement going hand-in-hand. It was merely an extension of the traditional sponsorship of memorials and so put the war into a framework of history rather than outside time-honoured responses.[169] At St Mildred, Bread Street, Alderman Sir Charles Wakefield, a wartime Lord Mayor, took his role of civic leader and benefactor very seriously. He paid for a stained-glass window of Christ in majesty in memory of the parish dead. After the respectful inscription to the dead came the legend: 'This window was presented by Colonel and Alderman Sir Charles Wakefield, Bart, C.B.E. Anno Domini. 1920.' Its unveiling was covered in great detail by the *City Press* and included the unintentional irony of the archdeacon of London: 'deep down in human nature there was a longing to be remembered and they had responded to that today. Let us live such lives that we might, when we died, be worthy of being remembered'.[170] Sir Charles commemorated the dead and made sure that all would know it. In so doing he was merely following the traditions of the City he represented.

The evidence of the memorials suggests that religion still had an extremely important part to play in defining identity and was the natural place to turn to when in need of comfort and solace. The various churches and places of worship offered their leadership to their parishioners and provided a convenient channel for the emotions of the bereaved. But the extent to which it was the churches and their congregations or more particularly the clergy that took lead seems to have been determined by the class complexion of the district. Generally speaking, in middle-class areas, there was more proactive and expressive input from the congregation and community itself, while in working-class districts much of the organising appeared to rest directly with the vicar and a tighter collection of church members. In Poplar and Stepney, the Anglican Church managed to appeal on a broad ticket and passed off their schemes as civic projects. In reality the memorials were overtly Christian and Anglo-Catholic in taste. All the memorials exhibit traditional forms of ecclesiastical ornamentation, a combination of crosses, tablets, statues, panels and chapels. Even the Woodgrange Baptist church had a tablet to

[169] *CP*, 1 Mar. 1919, 29 Oct. 1921.
[170] GML, L92 MS 18,319/92, St Mildred, Bread Street, faculty papers, 25 March 1920; *CP*, 15 July 1922.

match its prize bibles and all the Jewish memorials relied on bronze, alabaster and marble work. This was only natural; the memorial was a substitute grave, so that names and words were paramount. An amazing degree of homogeneity of approach among the churches can be seen, which led in turn to a remarkable consensus on the meaning and value of the war. The memorials and the dedication services answered all doubts, not by providing new theories but by reaffirming wartime and pre-war values – which were, quite literally, set in stone by the process. Such a development (or rather lack of development) ensured that in the twenties Armistice Day inherited a strictly conformist nature. Memorials served many purposes and combined many emotions; they were symbols of both grief and pride; they were simultaneously both communal and individual. By defining their war dead, the sub-communities of these areas defined themselves. The value of each community to King and Country was displayed on the memorials; it was a standard of loyalty. At the same time the investment of so much emotion and cash in church memorials affected the nature, scale and form of borough and civic schemes.

4

The Alternative Bonds of Community:
War Memorials in Places of Work,
Schools, Colleges and Clubs

Although the bonds of residence and religion were clearly important in
defining identity and community, they were not the only forms of belonging.
Work and the workplace was (and still is) a vital institution in which certain
codes and beliefs were promoted and held in common. Walter Besant put it
into the specific geographical context of this study: 'East London is, to repeat,
essentially and above all things a city of the working-man.'[1] More recently,
the sociologists Willmott and Young studied attitudes to work in London and
stated that

> Whether or not labour is, in Marx's term, 'a commodity', it is a link with the
> collective life. Work also creates a time-ordering of the sort that is necessary
> not only to social structure. Routines in the way people organize their lives are
> indispensable to almost everyone.[2]

Work provided an extended family and the paternalist nature of some of the
East London firms such as the Thames Ironworks and the Gas Light and Coke
Company meant that a great deal of pride was felt in their shared achieve-
ments and endeavours.[3]

Schools, youth clubs and colleges were equally important elements in
forming bonds of identity and belonging. As 'rolling communities' constantly
taking in and losing members, the values each institution enshrined were the
only fixed points of reference and provided the framework and continuity
needed to give them stature and influence. The young were exposed to all
sorts of influences in these institutions, shaping them into patriotic, Christian and comformist citizens willing to do their bit for God, King and
Country in 1914.[4] The City and East London contained a great cross-section
of schools ranging from those of the City Guild Companies to the London
County Council elementary schools of Poplar and Stepney. Muscular Chris-

---

1 Besant, *East London*, 22.
2 M. Young and P. Willmott, *The symmetrical family: a study of work and leisure in the London region*, London 1973, 151.
3 For the history and nature of these companies see Korr, *West Ham United*, 1–6, and S. Everrard, *The history of the Gas Light and Coke Company, 1812–1949*, London 1949, 290–2.
4 See Springhall, *Youth, empire and society*, 18, 58–9, 101, 122.

tianity, a code of honour, chivalry and self-sacrifice, pervaded these institutions regardless of status. The 'lesser' schools always sought to ape the value systems of their 'superiors': schools like East Ham Technical College and Secondary School readily adopted the Officer Training Corps as a way of instilling such values.[5]

The workplace

The influence of a workplace over its community can be seen in the Gas Light and Coke Company works at Beckton. Beckton was a community almost entirely dominated by this one great employer. It was further defined as a district by virtue of its peculiar geography, cut off from East Ham by the railway line and Manor Road, both running from west to east. Such a situation led the community to resemble a medieval fiefdom. St Michael and All Angels' church, Beckton, was essentially a gas-workers church serving a gas community. Community, identity and work were utterly entwined in the area; the war memorial provides the proof of this. Although it was to include everyone in the parish, whether they were employed in the gas works or not, it was in effect a gas memorial: the works employees even offered to build it free of charge.[6] Thomas Goulden, chief engineer of the company, represented the board at the unveiling and a guard of honour was provided by the gas works company of the 12th battalion, London Regiment, the Rangers.[7]

The memorial within the works itself was the result of an initative taken and driven by the governor and board of directors. They voted for its erection and paid for it from company funds after brief consultation with the work force.[8] In this way the clear leaders of the work community imposed a decision without reference to any other interested party. There is no evidence of any protest or unease about this, it seems to have been accepted as part of the natural course of events.

The memorial in the works differed from those in the churches, and served a slightly different purpose. It is perhaps pride rather than grief that is the main message; they are just a little too formal to carry a genuinely personal message of mourning. A woman, writing in the *Co-Partners Magazine*, captured this atmosphere. Her pride at the works memorial (a gas eternal flame) was such that she was convinced that it had provided the model for

---

[5]   For the impact of war on public school tenets see P. Parker, *The old lie: the Great War and the public school ethos*, London 1987, 275–84. For general studies of the war memorials covered in this chapter see Boorman, *At the going down of the sun*, 14–33, and C. Kernot, *British public school war memorials*, London 1927.

[6]   NHL, East Ham parish magazine, Aug. 1920.

[7]   *Co-Part Magazine*, July 1922, 21.

[8]   Ibid.

the French unknown warrior's grave, even though the French had unveiled their memorial two years before the Gas Light and Coke Company:

> What makes our memorial unique, in this country at any rate, is its perpetual lamp, which according to the Governor's orders, will burn day and night as long as the Gas Light and Coke Company exists. It is a very beautiful thought and one which has been copied by the French in the grave of their unknown warrior at the Arc-de-Triomphe.
>
> As most of our readers know there are many visitors to Beckton, and in going round the works, whether by train or on foot, a halt is always made at the memorial and many have been the tributes paid . . .[9]

The memorials located in the offices of the City of London represented the work community in a slightly more varied way: they often commemorated not only the London-based workers (many of them from the East London area) but the provincial and even world and empire branches as well. Here the workplace served as a focal point for corporate pride and provided a sense of family. When A. C. Thompson, chairman of Prudential Assurance, unveiled the memorial at their Holborn Bars head office, he stressed the pride in 'the great Prudential family' and noted that

> We have come here remembering with thankfulness, not unmixed with lawful pride, the wonderful response made by *our colleagues*, men of the Prudential staff, who responded to the call addressed to them in the name of our country [emphasis added].[10]

A similar chord was struck at the London County, Westminster and Parrs Bank. According to Dr Leaf, the chairman, only their Lothbury head office was a suitable place for such a memorial:

> It is fitting also that here in London, the heart of the Empire; in the City, the heart of London; and in the heart of our own bank, we should feel and express the throb of gratitude to those who have, by their great sacrifice, done honour to their beloved England; to their fellows and to themselves.[11]

In the collective psyche of these institutions the British empire had been made and held together by the might of the City of London and their war memorials proved their allegiance to, and pride in, that empire.

A very specific set of workers and commuters erected their memorial at the Great Eastern Railway terminus of Liverpool Street. But it was not the memorial of a commercial community, but rather of a geographical one. The London Society of East Anglians advertised their role in the defence of the empire at 'their' entrance to the City. Its unveiling produced an exotic

[9] Ibid. Nov. 1925, 17.
[10] PB, Apr. 1922, 12.
[11] CP, 12 June 1920.

mixture of personalities: the society was joined by the Lord Mayor, the bishop of Norwich, representatives of the GER and Marshal Foch. Foch paid homage to the men: 'I have heard before of the valour of the men from the East of England. There is nothing more inspiring than details of the deeds you have performed.'[12] Pride, a sense of belonging and a complex set of allegiances were therefore at the heart of this memorial.

But some of the memorials did attempt to fulfil a wider function than the embodiment of corporate pride; the function of exorcising grief and providing reassurance was perceptible at times too. The London and Lancashire Insurance Company erected a pedestal surmounted by a bronze Britannia, 'holding in her right hand a wreath of laurel leaves and in her left a branch of palm, the pose of the figure being that of martial pride chastened by grief'. The conflict was seen as a war between the forces of light and dark, each man had imitated Christ in 'the most crucial test, to which mankind has been subjected since *Anno Domini* began'.[13] At the Guildhall, the bereaved were reassured with words from the dead: the Revd W. P. Besley confidently asserted that the dead would reaffirm their belief in God and empire:

'Do not grieve too much; remember that God gave us a chance. We took it; and there is no nobler death than to die for one's country and one's God.' [He concluded that] they met that day in thanksgiving to God that the good and proud and generous self-sacrificing spirit of England was still alive during the years of War, and that it still lived today.[14]

The message of comfort was therefore a two-fold one: the bereaved were assured that the dead had gone on to Paradise, and that the sacrifice had been for Christ and Country. The Revd J. Thomas of St Peter's, Mile End, made a similar point when he dedicated the Charrington's Brewery memorial. He stated that 'if there was one thing most certain, it was that they would meet their loved ones beyond the grave'.[15] When Sir Robert Rogers, proprietor of a shirt manufacturing company, unveiled the memorial at his warehouse, he spoke in grand terms, of a titanic struggle. Victory was clearly the difference between freedom and slavery:

Your dear ones can never be recalled, but may I venture to say that while time is the only healer of sorrow, you will at least be comforted by the reflection that these men gave their lives for King and Country, that you and I might enjoy the freedom of our home life. Except for their sacrifice we should have been under the 'iron heel of Germany' and under such a rule we should have become a downtrodden, vanquished nation, for Germany threatened we

---

12 NHL, *GERM*, Sept. 1920, 235. Foch was in Britain in order to attend the Russo-Polish war conference in Hythe. See *The Times*, 9 Aug. 1920.
13 GML, L75.1 MS 21,313, London and Lancashire Insurance Company, war memorial book, 31 Mar. 1922.
14 *CP*, 22 Jan. 1921.
15 *EEN*, 12 Nov. 1920.

should be 'bleached white'. It is to these men and their like that we owe this mighty respite.[16]

Wartime values and concepts were obviously still very much alive; the justification of the war was not an issue open to debate. The same message was imparted by T. Du Buisson of the London and Lancashire Insurance Company. He told the employees that:

the world's morality was at stake. The question had to be answered once and for all, whether all principle, all right and justice were to be irretrievably obliterated from the face of the earth, or whether they were still to be our stars to guide us. . . . It was that sublime cause for which these men fought.[17]

But the function of the memorials did not stop at reassuring the bereaved and enshrining the values for which the dead had fought. They were also used to set an example to younger workers and to future generations. Field Marshal Sir Henry Wilson unveiled the GER memorial at Liverpool Street. He believed that it would cause future generations to stop and think of 'those who died that we might live'.[18] The Great Eastern Railway Company was one of the great influences over the whole area and at Romford the men of the stores department erected their own memorial. It was designed to further the concept of community and teamwork as it took the form of a new athletics pavilion. The *Great Eastern Railway Company Magazine* noted that 'it was a pleasing thought that coupled the furtherance of the clean and wholesome activities of a young man's life with the memory of his departed colleagues, past participants in his sports, who gave their very lives that England might be saved'.[19] The bishop of Barking then unveiled the memorial plaque and spoke of 'sport as consistent with the teachings of Christ'.[20] It was clear that the best form of memorial was perceived to be one which would foster the same values among the new generation. It was certainly not a rejection of the ethics of the war. No lesser person than Lord Haig made this point when he unveiled the Carpenters' Livery Company memorial in the City. He stated that it was his prayer 'that it might ever remind those who looked upon it, not only of the debt they owed to the heroes commemorated but of *the splendid example set by the fallen* [emphasis added]'.[21] The young were promised an ironic world; allegedly freed from the menace of war, they were yet exhorted

---

16 CP, 19 June 1920
17 GML, L75.1 MS 21,313, London and Lancashire Insurance Company, war memorial book, 31 Mar. 1922.
18 NHL, GERM, July 1922, 174. The unveiling of this memorial was overshadowed by the assassination of Wilson at the hands of the IRA as he returned home. The GER later erected a plaque to his memory: ibid. Feb. 1923, 89. For his life and career see Major-General C. E. Callwell's two-volume biography, *Field Marshal Sir Henry Wilson*, London 1927.
19 NHL, GERM, Dec. 1921, 273.
20 Ibid.
21 CP, 31 July 1920.

Plate 5. Great Eastern Railway memorial, Liverpool Street Station

to emulate the dead if their world were threatened. Earl Balfour reinforced this idea when he unveiled the Stock Exchange memorial:

> These men in the hour of their country's danger rose to the height of the great occasion and if – as please God, will never happen – if again an equal necessity presses upon us or upon our children, we doubt not that we and they shall be found not unworthy of the great example set by the four hundred and eight heroes whose memory is enshrined in this Memorial.[22]

Earl Balfour's words were a clear injunction to be acted upon in the communities of the young.

Schools, colleges and clubs

War memorials in schools, colleges and clubs were also symbols of community and shared values. In the relatively new institutions of East London the memorial was the proof of its worth, the test of its values and the base on which to build a heritage. The East London College at Mile End certainly saw the unveiling of its memorial as a vital part of its development as a community. The college magazine stated of the unveiling service: 'Their common object was to honour the precious sacrifice of a band of heroes – a sacrifice which had served to knit and weld still closer together in bonds of comradeship the wide community of East London College.'[23] The dead on the memorial panel became the first saints of the college; they had shown the world the value of what they shared at the college and so became the inheritance of future generations. A tradition had been created for the institution to which the erection of the memorial was the fitting response, the *quid pro quo* for the sacrifice: 'Some things are unthinkable [said the principal, J. S. Hatton]. It would be unthinkable that there should be no memorial within the walls of the East London College to those of its old students who went forth for their Country and died in the Great War.'[24] That the unveiling ceremony was regarded as a great moment for the college can be seen in the magazine, which prefaced its report with the proviso that 'it is to a very great extent written for posterity'.[25]

The establishment of a tradition of service and honour and the great importance attached to a war memorial was shared by Ilford County High School. The school had been founded as recently as 1901 and so the war was its first great test. This in turn made the memorial its first great trophy, a fact reflected in the school journal: 'One of the most important events in the

---

22 GBL, SL64/6, Stock Exchange war memorial book, Apr. 1923.
23 *ELCM*, Mar. 1923, 23.
24 Ibid.
25 Ibid.

whole history of the school was the unveiling of our War Memorial.'[26] Exactly the same sentiment was felt at East Ham Technical College and Secondary School. The institute's magazine stressed the fact that as it was founded in 1905 few of its boys were of military age at the outbreak of war. That so many subsequently responded to their country's call was proof of the value of the school's teaching. Fifty-nine names of the fallen were on the roll and great pride sprang from that fact.[27]

Occasionally, the memorial was used to foster a wider aim or definition of community and its achievements. The Lord Mayor of London unveiled the plaque at the Freemen's Orphan School. He treated the children to a lecture on the liberal traditions of the British empire and compared it to the despotisms of the Greek, Roman, Carolingian and Napoleonic empires. He then emphasised the role of the City in English history: the London merchants' support for the American colonists in their struggle against oppression, the dedication of Henry Fitzailwyn, first mayor of London, the illustrious career of Richard Whittington.[28] History was also at the heart of the Merchant Taylors' School memorial. The plaques bearing the names of the dead were inscribed with lines from one of the greatest Old Taylorians, Edmund Spenser. This reinforced the sense of an all-embracing inheritance which no scholar could afford to ignore. The inscriptions included 'Faire branch of honor, flower of chivalrie, Joy have thou of thy noble victorie' and 'Nought is more honourable to a knight, Than to defend the feeble in their right.' Just as the British had defended gallant little Belgium in 1914.[29]

In many ways the most complicated use of a memorial aimed at the communities of the young were those erected for East End Jews. These memorials not only imposed an image of the Jewish community but also carried the views of the ascendant group within that community: Anglo-Jewry and its obsession with assimilation.[30] The leaders of the Jewish Lads' Brigade certainly intended that their memorial should make a grand impression on the British public. It was 'strongly felt that a West End hall should be secured for the [unveiling] ceremony in order to make the function as important as

---

[26] Ilford County High School, *CHSI Chronicles*, Spring 1921, 43.

[27] NHL, *EHTCSSM*, Apr. 1922, 3.

[28] *CP*, 8 May 1920.

[29] Kernot, *British public school war memorials*, 235. Christian chivalry was an important part of the public school ethos and it was also combined with the cult of games; that a true knight played the game was the message of the public schools: Parker, *The old lie*, 77–84, 99–105. Clifton College had set the standard for many school war memorials after the South African War when it erected a new gatehouse and a statue of St George; it embodied the spirit of Sir Henry Newbolt: Christie, *History of Clifton College*, 148–9.

[30] Walter Besant noted the desire of affluent Anglo-Jewry to impose assimilation on the poor, immigrant Eastern European Jews of the East End. 'I am informed, however, that the leaders of the people in London are persistent in their exhortations to the new-comers to make themselves English – to make themselves English as fast as possible; to send them to Board-schools, and to make them English. It is the wisest advice': *East London*, 195.

possible'.[31] The Anglo-Jewish hierarchy was imposing itself on the East End and manipulating it in order to present the nation with a trustworthy, integrated community. In the event the ceremony was held at the Brigade headquarters, Camperdown House, Aldgate, in a service which was hardly *froom* (Orthodox), thus avoiding any charges of non-integration.[32] The Jewish youth of the East End was presented with a highly controlled image of its own community via its war dead.

A whole set of didactic impositions came with memorials in schools and clubs: the community was defined by its shared values and the memorial was the glorious proof of their worth. These concepts were to be passed on to the successors of the dead. Duty was the key word. The dead had done their duty to God, King, Country and institution. The obligation to be ready to emulate that example if called upon to do so was placed upon their successors. The war to end war was therefore a flawed concept.[33] Paradoxical proof of this can found in the recollections of Jim Wolveridge, a Stepney schoolboy of the twenties:

> One of my first friends in the street was Abie Roberts. His father had fought in the war and was so shattered by his experiences he wouldn't allow the war mentioned in the house. Abie was a pretty bloodthirsty kid, just like the rest of us. He liked war films but he never got to see any. When his father got to hear there was a war film showing locally he docked Albie's pocket money.[34]

The potent combination of film, plus the repetition of certain values on Armistice Day allowed for few overt or totally pacifist views.

At Albert Road School, Romford, the headmaster assembled the children on Armistice Sunday 1919 in order to unveil the war memorial. The vellum scroll inscribed with the names of the dead bore the legend 'For England, Home and Duty'. In a stirring speech the headmaster exhorted the children to remember their obligations and spoke in terms laden with pride, pomp and circumstance. He said that the dead had given their lives

> to defend me from a cruel enemy and that their blood . . . [was] shed that you might grow up men and women in a free country. Boys, and girls, remember their blood was shed for you, not for your neighbour, but for you. . . . I clasped their hands, warm with the excitement of battle and with the blood of youth

---

[31] Jewish Lad's and Girls' Brigade Headquarters, South Woodford, Jewish Lads' Brigade, council meeting minutes, 15 Mar. 1920.

[32] Ibid. 7 Nov. 1921.

[33] This was a concept noted during the war. P. Buitenhuis has stated that 'The title [of H. G. Wells's pamphlet, *The war that will end war*] became an ironic catch phrase for subsequent generations. Even at the time it raised some ridicule. G. K. Chesterton sagely remarked "To tell a soldier defending his country that it is The War That Will End War is exactly like telling a workman, naturally rather reluctant to do his day's work, that it is The Work That Will End Work" ': *The Great War of words: literature as propaganda, 1914–1918 and after*, London 1989 edn, 120.

[34] J. Wolveridge, *'Aint it grand; or this was Stepney*, London 1981, 15.

rushing through their veins. They had no fear, for they felt they fought in a just and righteous cause.[35]

The young had a duty to remember what had been sacrificed on their behalf; the dead were to be remembered as role models. At the Freemen's Orphan School the Lord Mayor stated that 'Death came only when honour was lost. The flowers with which the memorial was for the moment decked would fade, but the scholars must see to it that the names inscribed therein never faded from the memory.'[36]

It was a message that Lord Mayors repeated each time a school memorial was unveiled. At St Luke's parochial school, for example, the children were asked 'never to forget those who had sacrificed so much for us. The noble example of the old scholars who had died for us should be an incentive to the present scholars to do their duty'.[37] The immortality of the heroes was the theme at the City of London School: 'It was well that their memory should be kept green. Death was not the end of life, but the beginning of something altogether higher.'[38] Children were given firm guidance as to their role models; the memorials proved that obedience and sacrifice freely given in a glorious, patriotic cause was the finest end any young citizen could aspire to. This was very much the lesson given at the Haberdashers' Aske's School. On 11 November 1922 Henry Allan, Worshipful Master of the Company, urged the boys to be ready to emulate the dead. He also admitted to a little disappointment at what had happened since the Armistice, a rare occurrence at such events:

> This memorial will serve to perpetuate the memory of their sacrifice and inspire future generations to rise to the same height of devotion if the occasion should unhappily arise. The Masters and Boys of our Public Schools were the first to volunteer for the Front. With such a sacrifice we deserved a better Peace.[39]

The bishop of London also allowed himself an extremely rare moment of doubt at a school war memorial unveiling. At the dedication of the Parmiter's School memorial, Bethnal Green, he stated that the years since the war had been disappointing as the spirit of unity had left Britain and had resulted in 'party and industrial strife, the game of grab, the unrest and reaction'.[40]

At East Ham Technical College and Secondary School the mathematics master, R. H. Gillender MC, unveiled the memorial. As a winner of the Military Cross Gillender was second only to E. K. Myles, an old boy who had won

---

35 *ET*, 15 Nov. 1919.
36 *CP*, 8 May 1920.
37 Ibid. 13 Mar. 1920.
38 Ibid. 9 Oct. 1920.
39 Kernot, *British public school war memorials*, 232.
40 *EP*, 15 Dec. 1920.

the Victoria Cross in Mesopotamia. Gillender was made a symbol of all the school's heroes and thus the living proof of the school codes:

> As he stood there, he was also the representative of that great number of boys who, as those whose names are on the tablets, bravely faced the foe. Some of them have returned scarred and maimed, others with little outward appearance of suffering though no-one can have gone to the firing line without suffering, they did their duty and we honour them as we remember.[41]

A teacher represented the community and the pride that community took in its achievements. It was a record of achievement that set targets for the pupils. The memorial was 'a reminder of duty nobly done and an inspiration to face the future with determination and courage'.[42] That the school was determined to heed the example can be seen in the fact that the Cadet Corps rolled on; it duly formed a guard of honour at the unveiling ceremony.

Duty and sacrifice were still valid concepts and were a vital part of remembering the dead. At Ilford County High School the boys were told of the value of self-sacrifice and service:

> The world is only a Great School, and it is in their present schools that boys and girls can learn to serve a community, can learn to understand the real interests of a corporate body, so that, having done their duty in 'House' affairs and in 'School' matters, they may pass out into the World to pursue the ideal of self-sacrifice for the common good. . . . Mr Franklin then spoke to the gathering in well chosen words of what the Memorial stood for, of the sacrifice made by those whose memories were perpetuated by that bronze, and of the sacrifices that must be made by those who were left that the former sacrifices might not be in vain.[43]

When the duke of York unveiled the Hay Currie School memorial in Poplar (he unveiled the St Michael and All Angels' memorial on the same day) he too gave the boys some advice. It was laden with concepts of sportsmanship, a real chip off the Newbolt block:

> he hoped they would live up to the traditions of the school. In the game of life he urged them to follow four rules which would assist them in becoming useful citizens. Don't play foul; don't chuck up the sponge; go all out to win; and play the game, not for self, but for the honour of the school.[44]

Earlier in the service the boys had been addressed by the chairman of the Old Boys' Association. He was clearly very proud of his old school and made a grand comparison, revealing the extent to which public school values permeated British youth: 'Mr Cole said it was often remarked that the playing fields

---

[41] NHL, *EHTCSSM*, Apr. 1922, 3.
[42] Ibid. 3.
[43] *CHSI Chronicles*, spring 1921, 47.
[44] *EEN*, 10 Dec. 1920.

of Eton and Harrow were the places where battles were won. That their old school was to them the Harrow of East London.'[45]

The members of Stepney Jewish Lads' Club were given a very particular duty and inspiration in their war memorial. Over 400 of the Club's members joined the services and forty-one were killed. Funds were collected for memorial scholarship prizes, thus reflecting the Anglo-Jewish interest in education as a means of breaking the chains of the ghetto. The duty of a member was to follow the dead by working to become a fully integrated citizen of Britain: 'These Memorial prizes will keep fresh the memory of those who were so devoted to the Club, and whose work had been a source of inspiration not only to those who were fortunate enough to be associated with them, but to many who have succeeded them.'[46]

An allegorical painting by Louis Conrad unambiguously entitled 'Hear, O Israel' was presented by the old boys of the Jewish Free School, Whitechapel, in 1917 as a memorial to the thirty-six scholars already fallen, seven missing, eighty-six wounded and four prisoners of war. Harry Barnett of the Old Boys' Committee addressed the school and stated that

> The title of the picture was a clarion call to racial consciousness and duty, and he trusted that it would carry its message to young Israel, inspiring their hearts. The old boys had subscribed with a readiness that made his task a pleasure. On their behalf he offered the picture to the School Committee in memory of those whose blood had been shed without a pang on the altar of faith and patriotism.[47]

The Jewish Lads' Brigade memorial also obliged its living members to promote a positive image of British Jewry. The *Jewish Chronicle* said that the memorial 'would inspire future generations of young Israelites and would stimulate them in the days of Peace to uphold the name of Anglo-Jewry in the face of all detractors'.[48]

Sacrifice was holy and it implied that each boy and young man would serve God, King and Country by upholding the spirit of their predecessors. Despite the mention of girls in the Ilford County High School magazine, the emphasis was almost entirely on boys. Occasionally, however, bizarre injunctions were made as at Albert Road School where the Revd J. L. Steer urged

---

[45] Ibid.

[46] THL, *Stepney Jewish Lads' Club, 1901–1926: a short history*, London [1926]. Two of the managers of the club were Denzil Myer and Gerald Samuel, both scions of Anglo-Jewry. They were involved in a great deal of community activity among East End Jews and therefore have a proliferation of memorials. As well as the Stepney Jewish Lads' Club memorial their names are also on those of the Jewish Lads' Brigade and St George's Jewish Settlement. Their parents and relatives also erected tablets in the East London Synagogue and established a communal kitchen for Stepney Jews: CP, 27 Oct. 1917; THL, St George's Jewish Settlement annual report 1919–20; JC, 2 July 1920, 6 May 1921.

[47] CP, 28 July 1917.

[48] JC, 6 May 1921.

both girls and boys 'to be worthy to stand beside the Albert Road School heroes by the practice of those true *manly* virtues of courage, courtesy, charity and chivalry [emphasis added]'.[49]

The pursuit and encouragement of true manly virtues was given extra weight when playing fields and sports facilities were incorporated into the war memorial schemes. This was a popular idea with many institutions: East Ham Technical College and Secondary School, Merchant Taylors', Haberdashers' Aske's and the City of London schools all erected sports pavilions.[50] Such memorials, serving the spirit of Muscular Christianity and the cult of games, reinforced the community of the school. By sporting achievement the living exalted the memory and exploits of the dead. Gillender stated at the unveiling of the East Ham Technical College and Secondary School pavilion that 'They were deeply thankful to those who had offered their lives, and he expressed the hope that through the instrumentality of the Club House wisely used, the memory of those who had made the supreme sacrifice would be remembered.'[51]

The City of London School followed suit: at both the stone-laying and formal unveiling ceremonies the Lord Mayor made speeches, both were models of the Muscular Christian ethos, with a dash of the history and traditions of the City thrown in:

Above all, a school was mostly judged by the proportion of fine characters it produced. Character was the most important result of a good schoolmaster's teaching, and character was often made and maintained by games especially those games which demanded unselfishness. . . . He left it to the boys of the City of London School, past, present, and future, to do honour to the memory of those Old Boys, who lost their lives in the Great War, in remembrance of whom the new War Memorial on the new athletic ground was being erected.[52]

And at the unveiling itself:

---

[49] *ET*, 15 Nov. 1919.
[50] Kernot, *British public school war memorials*, 232, 235.
[51] *EHE*, 6 Oct. 1933.
[52] *CP*, 8 Nov. 1924. As noted by Samuel Hynes (*A war imagined*, 442), R. C. Sherriff's play *Journey's end* (1929) captures exactly this spirit: 'There is one further element in *Journey's end* that makes it a canonical part of the Myth. That is the analogy that is drawn – unintentionally, one feels, but nonetheless persistently – between the world of the trenches and the world of the public schools. Stanhope, we are told, was skipper of rugger at his school, and kept wicket for the eleven; he is the schoolboy idol. Osborne, the wise older officer, tells young Raleigh that "rugger and cricket seem a long way from here", but in fact they don't. The company lives by a set of rules, unspecified but rigid, that are very like what public school seems to have been. . . . There is the same idolizing, the same adolescent emotionalism, the same team spirit and self-sacrifice, the same hovering note of homosexuality. That model of behaviour – so English, so male, so anachronistic – was killed on the Western Front. In Sherriff's play it was resurrected and sentimentalized.' Just as it was by war memorials and Armistice Day rituals.

It was a solemn as well as a joyous occasion – solemn because the minds of all went back to the dark days of the War; joyous because, in commemorating the memory of those champions of liberty, the living are to be trained and drilled, and be made worthy successors of those who fell.[53]

It seems that if the Battle of Waterloo was won on the playing fields of Eton, the Battle of the Somme had been won on those of the City of London School, and they were keen to start preparations for the next round. The pavilion was also the incarnation of the Prayer Book's dictum that 'in the midsts of life we are in death' as the tea room was decorated with panels illustrating 'the nobility of self-sacrifice'.[54]

The bishop of Stepney made the nobility of self-sacrifice the theme of his dedicatory address at the unveiling of Stepney's own public school, Coopers' Company and Coborn. He told the boys that the dead, whose names were inscribed on the memorial, had gone to glorious deaths for

> it was the greatest death a man could die, sacrificing himself on behalf of that which they considered was true and noble. What was needed to make this country great was to bring the spirit of the trenches into our social and industrial life. These old boys who had gone stood for three things: first the spirit of adventure which, in the past, had made England great; secondly, they stood for devotion to duty; and finally their names would always stand for faith in what they believed to be good and true.[55]

School memorials were mainly concerned with the maintenance of standards and traditions. That they did make an impression can be judged by the ease with which James Mee recalled the memorial in his Isle of Dogs school:

> At British Street school, Harbinger now, they used to have a big Roll of Honour for the soldiers that got killed in the First World War. Well, of course, I had two brothers killed in that, one was eighteen and one was nineteen, in the First World War, and they used to have the Roll of Honour in the hall. I always remember.[56]

---

53 *CP*, 18 July 1925. The printed history of the school refers to one other memorial, that of the 1917 Society. This was founded on the death in action on 23 July 1918 of James Hannan, one of the school's great sportsmen, by a group of his friends who had been at school with him in 1917. The aim of the society was 'to perpetuate the tradition of public spirit at the School in which many of them had been inspired by Hannan'. However the long-serving head porter and caretaker and a former history master of the City of London School stated that the society was rumoured to be involved in psychic activity and met in order to attempt to make contact with the spirit of Hannan. Interestingly, the author of the school history was a founder member of the society but he made no reference to this fact in his description of the society, not even to deny a long-standing school legend: A. E. Douglas-Smith, *City of London School*, Oxford 1965, 390.
54 *CP*, 18 July 1925.
55 *ELA*, 23 July 1921.
56 Quoted in Hostettler, *Childhood on the Isle of Dogs*, 34.

But did the memorials say anything about the nature or reasons for the war? A rather intriguing memorial was erected in Poplar commemorating eighteen children of Upper North Street School who were killed in a Zeppelin raid in June 1917 (*see* plate 6).[57] The tragedy caused a great deal of trauma and a memorial fund was started. The memorial was unveiled in 1919. Unlike any of the other memorials examined in this section, it commemorated children rather than men who had sprung from a community of the young. The memorial therefore made the justification for the war all the more apparent: it was a war between the forces of good and humanity against the evil brutality of Prussianism. The mayor of Poplar elevated the children to martyr status in his appeal for funds, but almost implied that they were legitimate targets as 'these little ones died as truly for their country as any of our gallant men who have fallen on the battlefield or on the High Seas'.[58] The importance of drink and pubs to East End culture can be seen in the mayor's special appeal to the publicans of Poplar, to enlist their help in fund-raising.[59] The unveiling ceremony allowed emotions to run free and an element of steely anger at the atrocity filled the day. That it was regarded as an important event can be seen in the fact the memorial was unveiled by Queen Alexandra, the king's mother. The *East London Advertiser* referred to the 'dastardly crimes' of the enemy and said that the children were 'victims of Hun savagery'; it was the work of German 'Apostles of Kultur'.[60] In form the memorial itself was of a very traditional, Victorian funerary type: a small, neo-Gothic obelisk topped by an angel made of Sicilian marble and Aberdeen granite.[61] The symbolism of the angel was obvious as it took the children into its protecting wings; it was thus a memorial of consolation and grief rather than of corporate identity and meaning. This also shows how children became symbols of everything England stood for and was fighting against. The novelty of death from the air was met by the solace of the traditional and conformist enshrined in the form of the memorial. The erection of the memorial was not the end of the matter, as each anniversary was marked by a service of remembrance. In 1934 the local branches of the British Legion took over the organisation of the service and thus, in some ways, claimed the deaths as military ones.[62]

People growing up in Poplar in the twenties recall that memorial and what lay behind it. Carrie Lumsden stated that:

---

[57] For a report of the raid see *ELO*, 23 June 1917.
[58] THL, Upper North Street School memorial, fund-raising circular.
[59] *EEN*, 22 Jan. 1918.
[60] *ELA*, 28 June 1919. Wartime propaganda had made the German word *kultur* a synonym for evil. Literally translated as *culture* it was used to describe the demonic German anti-civilisation of atrocity, irreligion and inhumanity and implied an innate racial defect in the German people: Buitenhuis, *The Great War of words*, 12.
[61] *ELA*, 28 June 1919.
[62] Ibid. 16 June 1934.

Plate 6. Memorial to children killed in a Zeppelin raid,
Upper North Street, Poplar

In the entrance to the playground there was a memorial to the children of Upper North Street school, nearly all infants of five years old, killed by a bomb during the First World War. The bomb passed right through the school to the ground floor.[63]

The contrast between England and Germany was also stressed by Lieutenant-General Sir Gerald Ellison when he unveiled the East London College memorial. He stated of the dead that:

> It was not merely England that they had to defend, but all that England stands for in the world. And think what that means. The men who made modern Germany were under no illusions as to the course they were steering. Bismarck, the statesman, Roon, the soldier, Treitschke, the historian and philospher, had thoroughly and conscientiously examined our ideals and deliberately rejected them.[64]

Germany had developed its own, unique *kultur*, distinct from the enlightened, civilised culture that England espoused. Ellison then elevated the conflict to a holy war as 'those who fought and died for England were crusaders even in a higher sense than their forefathers who sailed away to fight the infidel'. It was thoughts such as these that must 'be the truest consolation to those who have suffered and have lost their dearest ones'.[65] The East London College memorial justified the war as a fight against evil and offered consolation to the bereaved.

The memorials built in the communities of the young therefore played a different role to those in churches representing residential and religious communities. Their role as substitute grave or as a symbol of consolation was far less overt. Rather, these memorials emphasised the value of shared concepts, teamwork and leadership. The form and style of the memorial was imposed on the community and so the hierarchical system was buttressed. The young were presented with highly controlled images and emotions.

Jack Cornwell: boy hero

The ultimate example of controlled emotion was in the memorialising of the boy Victoria Cross winner, John Cornwell. The plaque and subsequent memorials to Cornwell display how the memory of one particular casualty was manipulated to fit the role of timeless hero. He was made into a twentieth-century legend, iconography carefully grafted onto a skeleton of reality. His death as a hero also did away with the need to grieve. Cornwell was revered and celebrated, his memorials were not conduits for grief.

[63] Lumsden, *My Poplar Eastenders*, 64.
[64] *ELCM*, Mar. 1923, 73.
[65] Ibid.

Jack Cornwell was fatally wounded at the battle of Jutland, remaining at his post when all around him were killed. After the battle he was taken to hospital but died a few days later aged only sixteen. Admiral Beatty commented on his bravery in his report of the battle and on 6 July Cornwell was gazetted with the Victoria Cross.[66] Not surprisingly this sparked a great deal of interest in East Ham and across the rest of the country.[67] The boys at his school in Walton Road, Manor Park, collected money for a plaque in his honour which was unveiled by Lady Jellicoe on 17 July 1917, a red letter day for the school. Cornwell was eulogised as a hero of and from the people. In a modern war of mass populations he was an important symbol of the ordinary person doing his bit. Paradoxically, however, he was presented in the manner of a saint devoid of mere human foibles. More particularly, as he died a boy seaman, he was used as an example to children throughout the empire. The headmaster certainly rammed home the message to the assembled school. He reminded the boys that he 'was a poor boy, a boy of the masses, who rose to heights of bravery and self-sacrifice'.[68] For the mayor, Cornwell was the apogee of everything an East Ham school instilled in its pupils:

> It was an illustration of what was being done every day, but it came all the more forceably to them because they knew the lad and grit that was in him. Their brass tablet would help to immortalise the connection of John Cornwell with that school and they would be able to look on Walton Road school as one that had produced a hero whose name had resounded through the lands of the English-speaking race. (Applause.)[69]

Jack therefore became part of the civic glory of East Ham – as did the dead on the borough war memorial when it was unveiled in 1921.

In October 1917 the education committee agreed to supply copies of Frank Salisbury's painting of Jack to each school in the borough. They were to be sold at 3d. each and all proceeds were put into a childrens' fund for a memorial on Cornwell's grave in Manor Park Cemetery.[70] In this way officials and teachers within East Ham ensured that the children were constantly aware of the example set. By 1920 there was enough money in the fund to pay for the memorial and it was unveiled by Dr Macnamara of the Admiralty and Navy League. Walton Road School children were marched to the grave where Macnamara began by reading the inscription. Like the headmaster three

---

66 *London Gazette*, 6 July 1916.
67 For a good discussion of the national cult see Sillars, *Art and survival*, 39–47.
68 *EHE*, 20 July 1917.
69. Ibid.
70 NHL, county borough of East Ham, education committee minutes and reports, 3 Oct. 1917. The painting by Salisbury was originally owned by the Admiralty but was later displayed in East Ham town hall. It showed a cherubic-looking Cornwell, steadfastly standing at his post, with no sign of injury. War and death were therefore sanitised. It gave the public a heroic death in a battle that provided disappointingly few great moments.

years earlier, it stressed Cornwell's ordinariness: 'It is not wealth or ancestry but honourable conduct and a noble disposition that make men great.' He then exhorted the pupils to follow Cornwell's example: 'Dying John Travers Cornwell touched to life the spirit of devotion to duty in the hearts of the youth of the British Empire, and his grave would be the birthplace of heroes.'[71] In 1929 Walton Road School was renamed Cornwell School. The headmaster addressed the pupils, emphasising the pride implicit in the new name:

> It is the custom in London and other big towns to name schools after famous people but it is not always the case that the famous person is an old boy. In our case it is so, and you boys have to live up to that name, and gain credit for the school in the future. (Applause.)[72]

Cornwell had also been a Scout and on 11 September 1916 Baden-Powell announced that a special medal was to be inaugurated in his memory. In 1919 he was further commemorated in *The Scouts book of heroes* and a detachment of East Ham Scouts were renamed in his honour.[73] In this way yet another group connected with Jack claimed his memory and used the legend for their own purposes.

The values that he embodied were constantly reiterated; as with the shrines, the pattern set in 1916 was followed in the post-war years. This is an important point, for the sheer weight of reassuring repetition prevented any questioning of the morality of the war or its conduct. Thus East Ham made its boys Cornwellites; the message of the war was still relevant, each boy had a duty to emulate and maintain Cornwell's reputation. Jack Cornwell's image was therefore frozen as the boy seaman, a paragon of determination and pluck, eternally at his post. He truly fulfilled the *zeitgeist* of inter-war remembrance; he did not grow old as those that were left grew old.

But that was not quite the end of the story, for the fate of Jack's surviving relatives was to become a national issue too. Jack's family became the epitome of the popular memory of the disillusioned twenties. In the spring of 1919 the poverty of Jack's mother was reported in the press. As was to be expected the *East Ham Echo* quickly picked up on the story. Jack's mother has been widowed in 1915, her husband – a veteran of the Egyptian and South African Wars – died from tuberculosis while serving in a local defence battalion on the Essex marshes. Her widow's pension was clearly not enough to live on, particularly as she had younger children to look after. She was found, working twelve hours a day, in a Stepney hostel. When asked about her state she refused to make any overt criticisms of the way she had been treated, but did feel that her son's memory had been let down: 'It seems odd . . . after all the

---

[71] *EHE*, 31 Dec. 1920.
[72] Ibid. 13 Dec. 1929.
[73] NHL, John Cornwell papers.

fuss they made over my poor son, that I should have to do this. I am not grumbling, but what I do mind is that no stone rests over the grave of my boy. After three years no tombstone.'[74]

The classic case of an ungrateful nation seemed to be in the offing. However that wrath was given a subtle emphasis, thus shifting it away from the state *per se*. Instead the blame was laid at the feet of the trustees of the various funds set up in memory of Jack. This led to 'a great outcry . . . against the alleged maladministration of the Navy League and East Ham Memorial Funds'.[75] In reply Sir John Bethell, Liberal MP for the constituency, stated that as the Cornwell family had moved out of the borough he had been unaware of their circumstances.

The case received a great deal of coverage from the *Daily News*. Its journalist, Ralph Whitfield, a resident of the nearby smart suburb of Wanstead, had been the first to break the story of the distress of the family. A few months after the initial report the *Daily News* sent one of its female reporters to interview Mrs Cornwell. The story was clearly meant to pull on the heartstrings for the journalist stated that she saw Mrs Cornwell come limping down the Commercial Road still wearing her mourning black. When asked about her limp she replied that it was because she had a job scrubbing floors: 'People say I ought not to work . . . that I am past the working age, but, really what am I to do? One of my two boys is out of work, and I have a daughter of thirteen to look after.'[76]

Such a pathetic account gave the editor of the *Daily News* a chance to thunder out against injustice:

When are the authorities going to deal with the sad case of Mrs Cornwell?. . . . It is curious that while everyone has been rejoicing and congratulating one another on peace, and people in high places have been talking about the heroes who made the peace possible, no one has communicated with the mother of one of the bravest lads England ever produced.[77]

And later he added: 'What will the millions of Jack Cornwell subscribers say when they hear of the fate of the widowed mother, who receives only 10s a week from the very large sum collected.'[78]

The problem became a national disgrace when Mrs Cornwell died suddenly on 31 October 1919. Worse still she died in such poverty that the funeral bills could not be met. T. C. MacCormack, a resident of Northampton who had written a book about Jack during the war and kept a close interest in the family, stepped into the breach. He later explained, in a private letter to

---

74 *EHE*, 4 Apr. 1919.
75 Ibid.
76 *Daily News*, 5 Aug. 1919.
77 Ibid. 21 July 1919.
78 Ibid. 5 Aug. 1919.

the editor of the *Westminster Gazette*, that when he arrived in London the day after Mrs Cornwell's death, he found 'that the undertaker would not go on with the funeral without some guarantee that the expense would be paid'.[79] MacCormack had tried to get the Navy League, the Royal Star and Garter Home and the East Ham trustees to take an interest in the case, but had never been able to achieve much. The line all three organisations took was that although they had raised money in Jack's name they had never agreed to present any of it to the family. The *Westminster Gazette* noted that as the money raised, some £22,000 in Navy League coffers, was 'for the relief of disabled soldiers and sailors, the Charity Commissioners had no power to allow any part to be diverted'.[80] Thus the Cornwell family found that service to God, King and Country might mean the memory lionised in public but the survivors neglected in private.

After the death of Mrs Cornwell the story went quiet for a few years, until the winter of 1923 in fact. Once again it was left to MacCormack to help the family in their moment of need, for the surviving members had decided to emigrate to Canada. Writing in the *Northampton Independent*, MacCormack told his fellow townsfolk that he had been asked to say a few words when the memorial over Jack's grave had been unveiled. But he declined for:

> if I said anything I would smite them hip and thigh for cadging all the money for that memorial from the School Kiddies of East Ham district, while they had over £6,000 with added interest from 1916 untouched, and I am sure that the mothers of East Ham would be only too glad to get those pennies back and buy bread for their needy children at the present time. But I had better finish as my wrath usually rises when I review the past in connection with the name of Jack Cornwell, V. C.[81]

By implying large-scale want and deprivation in East Ham, MacCormack had certainly pushed the debate towards taking a political complexion. This was not lost on other campaigners for the Cornwell family. James Whittle of Manchester had urged his local paper to set up a new fund to help the family and wrote to C. F. G. Masterman, former Liberal MP for West Ham, on the subject. The fact that a resident of Manchester had become involved with the case shows how great Jack's image was as a national icon. Whittle did not mince words in his letter to Masterman and hinted at a dark future for them all if something was not done swiftly:

> Up to now it has been nothing short of a public scandal that homes and hospitals should fill their funds as a memorial while the hero's mother dies also the sister starves. Can you wonder they are working towards a Labour Govern-

---

[79] NHL John Cornwell papers, letter dated 14 Nov. 1923.
[80] *Westminster Gazette*, 14 Nov. 1923.
[81] *Northampton Independent*, 19 Nov. 1923.

ment. God save us from such but we have only our present method of adminis-
tration to thank for it.[82]

The Cornwells therefore went to Canada, during the 1923 Armistice
commemorations, with controversy surrounding their treatment.
Northampton, which had adopted the Cornwell family, treated the story to
full coverage. The *Northampton Independent* carried a photograph of
MacCormack bidding farewell to the family at Waterloo. They noted that it
was a scene to 'make every Briton blush with shame', a statement echoed in a
letter to the editor, stating that the whole affair 'makes one blush with shame
to call themselves British'.[83]

With this the Cornwell family slipped out of public eye. But Jack's image
was never to erode for he had become an institution in himself. The resilience of the Cornwell legend can be seen in the fact that after the Second
World War Manor Park saw the erection of a John Cornwell VC House, Jack
Cornwell Road, a new Cornwell school and, in 1970, a pub named 'The
Victoria Cross'. Each June the British Legion still parade at his grave. Thus a
highly embellished icon still survives, a hero of self-sacrifice in a war that
supposedly instituted a new, all-pervasive sense of irony into the world.[84]

War memorials in these communities played a different role to those in
churches and places of worship. The role of surrogate headstone was not vital,
and thus lessened the element of grief invested in them. Instead pride and
sheer numbers were far more important: the greater the sacrifice, the greater
the pride, the greater the glory of the institution. The war memorial was a
definition of the values the institution promoted and held dear; and it was a
constant reminder to the living and the successors of the dead. Grief certainly
did enter the equation at times and the bereaved seemed to find some comfort
in this type of memorial. When the Corporation of the City of London
erected a plaque commemorating its fallen staff, David Coates, father of one
of the dead, wrote to the town clerk and stated that 'I can assure you that
both my wife and myself feel very grateful, and appreciate this thoughtful act
on the part of the Corporation.'[85] But the thoughts and feelings of the bereaved always appear to be at a slight variant to the true significance of the
school and work memorial. When the headmaster of the Hay Currie School
addressed the audience at the unveiling of the memorial, he noted that 'they
joined in the sorrow of the parents and relatives, but they also looked with
great pride at the honour done to the school'.[86] The Parmiter's School memo-

---

[82] James Whittle to C. F. G. Masterman, Nov. 1923, John Cornwell papers.
[83] *Northampton Independent*, 17 Nov. 1923.
[84] John Cornwell papers; *Evening Standard*, 15 Sept. 1970.
[85] CoLRO, file Misc MSS 18.34, David Coates to the town clerk of City of London, 20 Feb.
1920.
[86] *EEN*, 10 Dec. 1920.

rial was also defined as an inspiration first and foremost and not a substitute grave. The chairman of the governors expressed the opinion that 'the memorial – at once beautiful and permanent – would be to the whole of the school, past, present and future an inspiration for all time, and it was hoped would be a solace to the relatives of the lads who had laid down their lives'.[87]

[87] *EP*, 15 Dec. 1920.

5

Civic War Memorials:
Public Pride and Private Grief

The City of London

The City of London erected two great military memorials, one for the Royal Regiment of Fusiliers and one in memory of all the London Troops. The latter was instigated by the Lord Mayor, Sir Horace Brooks Marshall, in May 1919 and as such can be seen as the official civic response of the City. Brooks Marshall was maintaining the City's role as leader of the capital; further, by suggesting the space in front of the Royal Exchange as the site for the memorial, he chose the economic heart of the empire as the fitting place to honour the men of the capital.[1] Sir Aston Webb was invited to design a suitable memorial and in June 1919 he presented his original plans. He advocated two 75ft flag masts for flying the Royal Standard and the City pennant. The flag bases themselves were to be engraved with figures of Victory and Peace. Webb mixed the practical with the truly monumental:

> It was felt that no finer site could be found for such a memorial in London, and the form chosen was selected because the ground space occupied by such a memorial is sufficiently small to offer little or no obstruction to the traffic here, while however crowded the space in front of the Exchange may be, this memorial, owing to its height, will always be visible and easily distinguished from any other memorial in London, as a reminder of the great deeds of the men of the London Regiments.[2]

It was a peculiarly apt design for the City for was copying a great trading empire of the past: Leopardi executed three flag masts for St Mark's Square, Venice in 1505.[3]

The Royal Fusiliers also broached the subject of a war memorial in June 1919. A number of practical schemes were suggested, but the Regimental War Memorial Committee decided 'that it is not possible at the present time, when so many deserving institutions such as hospitals, are in serious monetary difficulties, to raise sufficient funds to found and endow a club or similar institution'. Eventually they accepted the advice of the sculptor Sir George

---

1 CoLRO, file 605A–6C, 1920/9A, Lord Mayor's correspondence, 15, 16 May 1919.
2 Ibid. Webb's memo, 19 June 1919.
3 *Rough guide to Venice*, London 1989, 34.

Plate 7. London Troops' memorial, Royal Exchange

Frampton and approached his ex-pupil, Albert Toft, who was duly commissioned to design a suitable memorial.[4]

Both schemes then ran into difficulties. The court of common council declined to give Webb permission to erect his memorial according to the design submitted.[5] He submitted a new design which consisted of a stone, panelled pillar surmounted by a lion supporting shields bearing the arms of the City and county of London. The pillar was to be flanked by statues of men of the London Regiment 'standing on pedestals to keep the statues well above the heads of the crowd' (*see* plate 7).[6] Common council duly agreed to this scheme on 18 September.[7] No reasons were recorded in the minutes as to why the original plans were considered unsuitable. The main reason may well have been its subtlety. It simply was not grand enough, it did not scream out its purpose and was therefore not quite what the common council wanted, whereas the new design was far more obvious and far less metaphysical. It must be stressed that no clear evidence can be found to support this claim other than the aldermens' reluctance to explain their actions.[8] A similar problem affected the Royal Fusiliers. This time, however, it was not Toft's design that worried them but the location. They had approached many people for a suitable site, but had not gained satisfaction. They were reluctantly forced to choose their main depot in the obscure suburb of Hounslow, outside the county of London.[9] In November 1919, Major-General Sir Geoffrey Barton, colonel of the City of London Regiment, Royal Fusiliers, wrote to the Lord Mayor asking him to provide a site. He clearly felt that the Royal Fusiliers needed to show its war record to maximum advantage:

After the South African War of 1899–1902, a monument to the memory of those members of the Regiment who fell in that campaign, including Regulars, Militia and Volunteers, was placed in the Guildhall; but it is the *general opinion that a more conspicuous site is preferable on this occasion; in order to commemorate the sacrifice of those who gave their lives for King and Country, to bring home to the public the great services rendered by the City during the War, and as an incentive for citizens of all times to patriotism and national duty.* . . . The Royal Fusiliers is the only Regular Corps of the British Army connected with the City of London;

4 *Royal Fusiliers Chronicle*, Sept. 1920.
5 CoLRO, minutes of the court of common council, 26 June 1919.
6 CoLRO, file 605A–6C, 1920/9A, Webb's memo to the town clerk, 28 Aug. 1919. In some ways it resembled the Temple Bar memorial. The original Temple Bar arched entrance to the City was taken down in 1878 as it obstructed traffic. It was replaced by a plinth designed by Horace Jones and was surmounted by a griffin designed by C. B. Birch, holding the arms of the City: E. Gleichen, *London's outdoor statuary*, London 1928, 139–40.
7 CoLRO, minutes of the court of common council, 18 Sept. 1919.
8 One English city, Sheffield, did adopt a flag mast as its memorial. The huge bronze base was placed at the traditional meeting point of the city, Baker's Port, and unveiled in 1925: Boorman, *At the going down of the sun*, 132–3.
9 *Royal Fusiliers Chronicle*, Sept. 1920.

and it seems therefore appropriate that our memorial should find a place within the City [emphasis added].[10]

It obviously took a great deal of time for this request to filter through the system, for it was not until 14 February 1922 that the streets committee offered a site on the City's western boundary at Holborn Bars.[11] This would give the memorial a particular power, as was noted at its unveiling: 'It stood at the City boundary, in the midst of one of the busiest thoroughfares of the City of London, where it could be seen daily by many thousands of the fellow-citizens of the gallant men whom it commemorated.'[12]

Both monuments were therefore carefully placed and designed in order to have maximum public impact. A certain amount of ambiguity was built into this process however; the memorials do not appear to have one, simple function. The London Troops' memorial at the Royal Exchange listed all the battalions of the London Regiment and its battle honours, but it was also agreed that the names of all the wartime Lord Mayors should be inscribed there too, with the legend: 'Raised by public subscription at the Mansion House in the Peace Year 1919 during the mayoralty of Col. Right Hon. Sir Horace Brooks Marshall' on the base.[13] Brooks Marshall was rather keen on advertising his own beneficence as well as the memory of the glorious dead. When the war memorial at his own legal firm at Temple House was unveiled, the *City Press* noted that it bore an inscription at the bottom stating that 'this tablet was erected by the Rt. Hon. Sir Horace Brooks Marshall KCVO LL.D. Lord Mayor of London 1918–1919'.[14] Another wartime Lord Mayor, Sir Charles Wakefield, was, of course, equally keen to record his role in the erection of the St Mildred, Bread Street, memorial.

The unveiling was performed by the duke of York on 12 November 1920. A huge crowd assembled around the Royal Exchange. The *City Press* emphasised the fact that it was an event specific to London: 'a typical London fog hung around like a pall, as if to accentuate the metropolitan significance of the occasion'.[15] Brooks Marshall honoured the London dead but he seemed to bestow an equal honour on those who had recognised the need for a memorial in the first place: 'Today we pay both to the dead and the living our grateful and lasting tribute in setting up this enduring proof of the affectionate remembrance in which the London men in the Great War are held by their fellow citizens for all time.'[16]

---

[10] CoLRO, file 605A–6C, 1920/9A, Maj.-Gen. Sir Geoffrey Barton to the Lord Mayor of London, 21 Nov. 1919.
[11] Memo from the town clerk, ibid.
[12] *Daily Telegraph*, 6 Nov. 1922.
[13] CoLRO, minutes of the court of common council, 4 Nov. 1920; C. S. Cooper, *Outdoor monuments of London*, London 1928, 62.
[14] *CP*, 21 Jan. 1921.
[15] Ibid. 20 Nov. 1920.
[16] Ibid.

In 1923 the City presented bronze plaques, embossed with the design of the memorial, to the battalions of the London Regiment in a ceremony at the Mansion House. Alderman (and by this time Lord) Brooks Marshall spoke of the enduring quality of the Royal Exchange memorial. He believed that it would inspire generations yet to come:

> whatever changes may take place, that memorial, sacred to Londoners, will never be removed. From generation to generation it will stand to speak in praise of famous men of the City and County of London, who, by great sacrifice, gave proof of the quality of their patriotism in the gravest crisis in the Empire's history. (Hear, hear.)[17]

The City had met the obligations its illustrious history placed upon it, namely its duty to mark the greatest war in the nation's existence and to prove its role in that conflict. Grief and consolation played second fiddle to the pride of the regiment. But an Ilford man wrote to his local paper stating that his wife felt happiest laying a wreath to their son at the London Troops' memorial as he had served in the London Regiment. For some place of residence was not the strongest bond in the community of the bereaved.[18]

The Royal Fusiliers' memorial was not unveiled until 4 November 1922. Glory and masculinity were an implicit part of this monument. Toft's design was of a stone pillar surmounted by a bronze fusilier 'in fighting dress, grasping in his right hand a rifle with fixed bayonet, in an attitude of victory, and thus, figuratively, guarding the entrance to the City of London' (see frontispiece).[19] Ambiguity also pervaded certain aspects of this unveiling service. Instructions issued to the guard of honour stated that its object was 'not only to pay respect to the Lord Mayor, but also to do honour to the memory of 22,000 of all ranks of the Regiment'.[20] The honour of the City seems to have slightly overshadowed the memory of the dead.

But the nobility of the cause did provide the bereaved with some comfort. The Lord Mayor told the 'immense crowd' that the memorial 'would remind the thousands who passed by of the immense body of men of that City Regiment who served in the War, and especially of the 22,000 who gave their lives in the sacred cause of right, justice and humanity'.[21] The colonel of the regiment, Major-General Colin Donald, then spoke of the example inherent in the memorial:

> Let us hope . . . that when they look upon it it may act as an inspiration to them, and that if at any time they should be called upon to fight for their

[17] Ibid. 12 May 1923.
[18] *IR*, 15 Sept. 1922.
[19] RFM, file M23, unveiling ceremony order of service, 4 Nov. 1922.
[20] Ibid. Instructions for unveiling, 10 Oct. 1922.
[21] *CP*, 11 Nov. 1922.

country, they will do so with the same courage, loyalty and devotion as these splendid men who died that this glorious old England of ours might live.[22]

As military memorials bearing bronze soldiers, both these monuments were infused with a distinct masculine quality and both attracted a feminine response. The female clerks of the City became the chief mourners and guardians of the memory of the dead. In May 1922 the *Daily Graphic* noted that

> Even the Cenotaph itself is not as well attended as the London soldiers' war memorial in front of the Royal Exchange. The wreaths there are always in place, and the little bunches of flowers have the water in their vases renewed daily.
> The women clerks of the Bank of England months ago undertook this care, and the memorial yesterday – this is a great week in the war records of London's citizen soldiers – showed how truly they maintained their trust.[23]

In May 1915 the 1st City of London Regiment, Royal Fusiliers, made their debut on the Western Front at the battle of Aubers Ridge; a few weeks later the 47th (London) Territorial division took part in its first action, the battle of Festubert, and that September the battle of Loos. This made mid-May and late September mini-remembrance days in the City.[24] The example of the lady clerks of the Bank of England was followed at Holborn Bar by those of Prudential Assurance who volunteered to ensure a fresh supply of flowers and to arrange the wreaths at the Royal Fusiliers' memorial.[25] It was the ultimate reaffirmation of the meaning of the war: the men had died to save British women from the Germans, the women displayed their heart-felt gratitude and grief in a simple act of continued remembrance.

East and West Ham

The residential areas of East London also embarked upon civic memorial projects. It will be possible to see whether a memorial erected to commemorate the dead from an entire borough was invested with a different table of meanings and significance from that set up in place of worship and thus representing a smaller community.

In both East and West Ham the main inspirations behind the war memorial schemes were men in positions of influence and responsibility, just as on a lesser scale the memorial erected in a place of worship was the result of local notables providing leadership and expertise. For example, Banks-Martin,

[22] *Daily Telegraph*, 6 Nov. 1922.
[23] *Daily Graphic*, 15 May 1922.
[24] A. H. Maude (ed.), *The 47th (London) Division, 1914–1919*, London 1922, 11–23, 25–36; J. E. Edmonds, *Military operations France and Belgium, 1915*, ii, London 1928, 29–37.
[25] CoLRO, file 605A–6C, 1920/9A, clerk of public health department to the town clerk, 21 Nov. 1922.

mayor of East Ham, called a public meeting to discuss memorial projects. His audience consisted of those who were in positions of influence or who had the time, interest and money to become involved in such schemes. The *East Ham Echo* noted the presence of 'ladies who have taken a prominent part in war work and other influential residents'; they went on to form a committee representing all sections of the borough; 'the mayor said the idea was not sectional representation, but to combine all those citizens, irrespective of class or creed, who were willing to help'.[26] Whatever the mayor may have thought about sectional representation in effect the committee was a model of just that; it consisted of representatives of all churches, schools, councillors and certain places of trade and industry, and it seems likely that the same people were involved in the war shrines and church memorial schemes. In this sense East Ham was the sum of its sub-communities. West Ham's scheme was also instigated by the mayor (and Labour MP for West Ham South) Will Thorne. A nine-man executive committee was formed after a public meeting, its secretary was a local JP and it included the governors of Queen Mary's Hospital for the East End as well as union, council and trade representatives.[27] Once again the local hierarchical ladder, a scale determined mainly by wealth, was seen as the most effective way of handling the project.

The next stage was to decide upon a suitable memorial, but this was a question that fuelled markedly little debate as both boroughs accepted the solutions proposed by their mayors. Banks-Martin, in East Ham, may have been partly motivated by his own dreams; he was an architect and laid his own designs before the committee. He believed an aesthetic memorial was the finest tribute and one which could not be confused with any purpose other than the commemoration of the dead:

> The money it might be urged could be spent on a more practical object than a monument; but it would be impossible for them to do anything that would be of service to a large body of individuals. A monument, placed in a conspicuous position, could be made an ornament to the borough; and taking everything into consideration, he had come definitely to the conclusion that such a memorial would meet the case better than anything else.[28]

None of the committee members disagreed with this and Banks-Martin's obelisk was duly adopted. But there was opposition from other quarters. A letter printed in the *Echo* claimed that only a practical memorial was fitting: the correspondent stated that 'our gratitude should take some permanent and useful form'.[29] In fact, a group of East Ham residents had decided to instigate a practical memorial plan, but were in no way influenced by public pressure: the governors of East Ham Cottage Hospital (and in particular Sir John

---

[26] *EHE*, 19 Oct. 1917.
[27] *SE*, 4 May 1918.
[28] *EHE*, 19 Oct. 1917.
[29] Ibid. 2 Aug. 1918.

Bethell, who had lost his eldest son at Loos) had taken the decision to erect a new war memorial hospital. Like the borough scheme, however, it was a decision reached by a relatively small group without reference to the borough as a whole.[30]

In West Ham, Will Thorne's idea was also connected with a hospital. He floated the idea of an extension to Queen Mary's Hospital for the East End.[31] A number of factors may have made West Ham more likely to adopt a practical scheme, than East Ham. The Queen Mary hospital was in many ways the pride of the borough and was an important war hospital for wounded soldiers; it was therefore a natural focus of public attention and emotion.[32] West Ham also had the economic power needed to finance such a scheme, unlike the less industrialised East Ham. Lastly, as a borough with a Labour tradition the idea of extending a hospital was attractive. By the same token Labour politics could also obstruct such schemes: a union member of the executive committee noted that in his opinion it was the government's duty to support hospitals, although he agreed to support the plan nevertheless.[33] Leo Lyle, one of the governors of the hospital, summed up their position: 'no war memorial could be more worthy to perpetuate the remembrance of their sacrifice in war than one which would carry on in peace the work of helping others to live'.[34]

Both boroughs were led by their local elites, although East Ham perhaps displayed a little more of its bourgeois psyche. Clearly, the schemes were on a large scale and involved the raising of considerable sums. To a certain extent the realisation of sufficient funds was the acid test of public acceptance of the plans; if the targets were quickly and easily reached the plan had obviously struck a public chord.

In East Ham the funds were raised in traditional manner: house-to-house collections, 'leave your change' boxes in shops and other events such as concerts at the town hall.[35] By April 1918 the committee had collected the sum of £1,168 9s. 2d.[36] Then in the winter of 1918 the scheme suddenly and inexplicably ground to a halt, and was not resurrected until July 1919.[37] It is impossible to discover why this hiatus occured. The cause may well lie in the members of the committee who, as leaders of their sub-communities, were drawn back as a result of the Armistice into co-ordinating the local war memorial efforts in their churches, schools and clubs. Once these schemes were up and running they could afford to return to the borough project. This

---

[30] NHL, East Ham Hospital, annual report, 1919.
[31] NHL, West Ham Hospital, general committee minute book 5, 14 Apr. 1918.
[32] See J. Parsons, *A short history of Queen Mary's Hospital for the East End*, London 1962.
[33] *SE*, 4 May 1918.
[34] Ibid. 11 May 1918.
[35] *EHE*, 19 Oct. 1917, 9 May 1919.
[36] Ibid. 12 Apr. 1918.
[37] Ibid. 18 July 1919.

is a plausible explanation, given the explosion of small-scale memorial activity in the winter of 1918–19.

In West Ham, on the other hand, fund-raising reflected the borough's industrial importance. Abram Lyle, the sugar manufacturer, promised £1,000 if nine other firms did the same. At the same time, Will Thorne suggested that the largest firms in the borough give £500 apiece.[38] In the meantime the committee agreed to contact every firm and business in order to ask for donations. A local employer agreed to donate 5s. for every 1s. given by his workers and suggested that all employers adopt this plan.[39] By November 1919 the total stood at £31,633 10s., a truly colossal amount.[40] The subscription lists printed in the *Express* revealed donations from all the major firms in the borough. West Ham also capitalised on the peculiar development of industry in the district where many of the firms straddled the boundary with East Ham.[41] After November 1919, however, the effort slowed down and became more reliant on smaller-scale donations and charity events.

What cannot be denied is the fact that much of the success was due to the sheer power of Thorne's personality. He had staunchly supported the war, during which he had lost his eldest son at Passchendaele. It also cost him West Ham South as the ILP and BSP forced him out in December 1918. He then stood for Plaistow and won. He wrote in his autobiography:

> It was no easy job to collect such a large sum as £40,000. I am afraid I made myself somewhat of a nuisance doing it. I visited all the managers, managing directors, and shareholders of the big factories, breweries, and other large works in the borough, and asked them for their contributions, and although they were opposed to my politics they subscribed very generously.
>
> Many of them were surprised to see me; they told me they had heard and read a lot about me and thought I was very dangerous man; but I explained to them that I was not nearly the ferocious animal some people made me out to be.[42]

West Ham's total easily dwarfed that of East Ham but the latter was still collecting for its new war memorial hospital. It might also be said that West Ham managed to raise money from sources that strictly speaking ought to have been shared with East Ham. To an extent, it is amazing that so much was collected, given the amount of war memorial activity within the boroughs and the onset of economic depression. It surely reflects a desire to memorialise at all levels.

As these memorials were erected on a large scale and as the result of combined action by different groups, it is worth examining the values they

38 *SE*, 4 May 1918.
39 Ibid. 15 May 1918.
40 Ibid.
41 Ibid. 16 Nov. 1918, 1 Feb., 22 Nov. 1919.
42 W. Thorne, *My life's battles*, London 1989 edn, 50, 181–2.

actually represented. The strangest memorial by far was the new East Ham hospital. Aside from the original claim that it was to be a war memorial the instigators rarely referred to this function. A further confusion arises as the original cottage hospital was built as a memorial to Queen Victoria and much of the literature refers to the memorial hospital, but never uses the term 'war memorial'.[43] When the foundation stone was laid in 1926 the *Echo* gave the event due coverage but there was not a single reference to the war dead.[44] This may have provoked the subscribers into a response: a letter appeared in the *Echo* in which fears were expressed that the title 'war memorial' was not to be included in the name of the hospital; the correspondent said it would be 'a very big and serious mistake' if it were omitted.[45] It was not until 1928 that an unambiguous statement was made in the annual report: 'The names of over 2,000 local men who gave their lives in the Great War, are publicly recorded in the Entrance Hall of this Hospital. It is impossible to conceive a more fitting manner in which to perpetuate their memory.'[46] But when the hospital was formally opened by Queen Mary, the *Echo* again completely ignored its memorial purpose.[47]

Indeed it was civic glory that dominated the occasion, a sentiment that seemed to permeate the whole gestation of the hospital. When the scheme was first announced in the *Echo*, it was noted that both West Ham and Woolwich had decided to erect war memorial hospitals. In an atmosphere of civic rivalry it noted that 'other boroughs are actively working on similar projects, and it is not to be expected that East Ham will fail to respond to such an appeal as is now being made'.[48] The new hospital was not, therefore, an expression of grief, nor even of grateful and proud remembrance, rather it was a jewel in the civic crown.

East Ham's main memorial, Banks-Martin's obelisk, was erected in the aptly named Central Park. Banks-Martin had conceived it as a symbol of communal unity; he reaffirmed this at the unveiling but included the memory of the dead as well:

> Let them trust it might be the means of always keeping their memory green, that it might be the means of bringing before them at all times the sacrifices they had made and the sacrifices their friends and relatives had made in parting with these men. Let them never forget – and he prayed that the memorial

43 NHL: examples occur in the annual reports for 1921, 1922, 1923 and 1924.
44 *EHE*, 29 Oct. 1926.
45 Ibid. 19 Nov. 1926.
46 NHL, East Ham Hospital, annual report, 1928, 36.
47 *EHE*, 26 July 1929.
48 Ibid. 22 Nov. 1918. Although Woolwich was south of the Thames a tiny part of it lay on the north bank, dividing East Ham's riverside boundary, an ancient anomaly creating 'Kent in Essex'. It made East Ham very aware of the activities of Woolwich: VCH, *Essex*, vi. 8. This traditional interest was cemented in 1889 when the Woolwich Free Ferry was opened. 'It was the first successful attempt to provide additional means of communication across the Thames for eastern districts': Weinreb and Hibbert, *London encyclopaedia*, 99.

would always bring it back to them – the deeds which they had done on behalf of their country and which commanded their undying gratitude.[49]

For the *Echo*, the whole event was a glorious chapter in the history of the borough; the unveiling was compared with the erection of the town hall, technical college and the King George V dock.[50] The memorial was not really a substitute grave, rather it was a civic monument, it glorified East Ham's war record. Only at the end of the ceremony did the memorial actually perform the role of a cenotaph, when wreaths were piled up at the base. Even this action had a communal nature as several wreaths 'were from the inhabitants of whole streets'.[51] The division between the grandeur of the official ceremony and the more personal element of remembrance was symbolised on the following day when a large crowd gathered to lay wreaths and read the messages. Ilford saw a similar impromptu pilgrimage on the day following the unveiling of its memorial.

When the foundation stone was laid for the war memorial out-patients department at Queen Mary's hospital, an atmosphere of civic glory was equally apparent. The dead were hardly mentioned during the course of the ceremony. Instead, the manager of West Ham United FC was invited so the borough could wish the team well in the forthcoming Cup Final at the new Empire Stadium, Wembley. It also gave Thorne the chance to re-establish his socialist credentials; he spoke on the futility of war:

> It was a wicked waste of money and a wicked waste of life, and if people only had the common sense they ought to have, the millions spent on building armaments would be devoted to social purposes and bettering the conditions of workers.[52]

The extension was formally unveiled on Armistice Day 1924. It was a purple moment in the history of the borough; the *Express* emphasised this fact in its coverage of the event. The size and cost were constantly referred to, heights of hyperbole were reached and the odd fact or two was ignored: 'It is the largest war memorial in Great Britain, and certainly none that may be erected in the future will perform a greater service for humanity.'[53]

West Ham was elevated above all others:

> In many towns and cities huge blocks of granite bear tribute to the dead, but in West Ham service to the living is to be the town's memorial to the fallen . . . the war memorial was part of a triple plan that has now been completed at the cost of over £100,000.[54]

49 *EHE*, 15 July 1921.
50 Ibid.
51 Ibid.
52 *SE*, 18 Apr. 1923.
53 Ibid. 15 Nov. 1924.
54 Ibid. A maternity home and X-Ray department had also been built.

Significantly, the plaque in the entrance hall saluted civic achievement first and foremost: '1914 – To the Honour of the Borough and the Glory of the Dead – 1918.' Civic achievement was the touchstone of Prince Henry's address. His words matched the pride of West Ham: 'One hundred thousand men from West Ham answered the call. They went to every branch of the services, both on land and sea and in the air. They served in every theatre of war and upon the seas, both in the Navy and in the Mercantile Marine.'[55] A touch of genuine pathos and grief did tinge the day; the sobs of a woman broke the two minutes' silence.[56] But the over-riding impression is of pride replacing grief and community replacing individuality. It was a fitting memorial for the borough, but served to emphasise the complementary importance of the more personal memorials in the churches.

There was one element the borough memorials shared with those of the sub-communities, the education of the young. By displaying the war record so publicly and bathed in such glory, the young were left in no doubt as to their duty. East Ham's memorial was unveiled by General Lord Horne who stated his belief that 'the memorial would serve as a call to duty, alike to the citizens of the present and the future'.[57] It was not a belief confined to the great and the good: an address was given by an ex-sailor of HMS *Queen Mary*:

> [He believed that the] memorial should stand, not only in remembrance of those who had gone, but as an inspiration to their young folk to follow their footsteps and be ready, should the occasion demand, to take arms for their country's honour and to fight for right against might.[58]

Such sentiments were part of the Cornwell cult and the meaning of many other memorials. They ensured that the young, and indeed the survivors, were given no grounds on which to question the war; all the issues were neatly sidestepped and emotional barriers of rhetoric were maintained.

The borough memorials reflected the sub-community memorials in some ways, insofar as relatively small groups imposed a decision on those beneath them. But unlike the smaller units these memorials did not find space to reflect individual grief. The scale was simply too large. Instead, the boroughs proved that the people respected their dead by erecting glorious monuments to their memory, but achieved it at the risk of forgetting the objective altogether. However both boroughs reacted in a highly traditional manner: they

---

[55] Ibid. These words seemed to find an ironic echo years later when Joan Littlewood first staged *Oh! What a lovely war* at the Theatre Royal, Stratford East: 'M.C.: Ladies and gentlemen, when the Conscription Act was passed, 51,000 able-bodied men left home without leaving any forwarding address . . . / GIRLS: Shame!/ M.C.: . . . and that's in West Ham alone': Theatre Workshop and Charles Chilton, *Oh! What a lovely war*, London 1984 edn, 56.

[56] Ibid.

[57] *EHE*, 15 July 1921. Horne had commanded the First Army on the Western Front and ended the war with a considerable reputation: Terraine, *Douglas Haig*, 423.

[58] Ibid.

followed the Victorian pattern of public and/or utilitarian monuments.[59] Thorne believed he was following a tradition when he compared his scheme with the plans for the Albert Memorial.[60] The only difference to the established tradition lay in the fact that these memorials commemorated ordinary men elevated to hero status, rather than a great individual or occasion.

Ilford

The Ilford war memorial scheme reflected the problems of balancing civic pride and aspirations with the wishes and finances of the residents. It achieved success of a sort, although it was forced to modify its grand plans to a more modest scheme. However, even this qualified degree of success was greater than the cases which follow. Ilford is therefore worth looking at in some detail as it provides an insight into the overall gestation of a civic war memorial.

The Ilford war memorial committee was formed in November 1918 by the chairman of the urban district council, W. H. Stevens. He was joined by a host of the town's worthies including three bank managers, a company director, a schoolmaster, a representative of the local hospital, Ilford's stationmaster, an undertaker, a representative of the Anglican churches and one woman. In some ways the strangest member was the Revd H. Dunnico, a Baptist minister and committed pacifist who had attended anti-war demonstrations throughout the conflict.[61]

The relatively swift formation of this committee should have given it a head start in the race for funds against the church schemes. But the committee took a long time to decide upon a scheme: the first public meeting was held in January 1919, the *Recorder* reporting that 'there was a large attendance'. It was a slightly odd meeting insofar as the issue of the form of the memorial itself was deferred, to be decided by plebiscite, but a fund-raising target of £20,000 was fixed.[62] Adopting a budget before deciding on a project looked a little like putting the cart before the horse. The meeting's actions certainly reveal the great confidence of the committee: West Ham set itself a target of £40,000 but had a population more than three times the size of Ilford

---

[59] In 1917 a town-planning journal wrote favourably on a sewage system built as a memorial to Queen Victoria: quoted in J. Curl, *A celebration of death: an introduction to some of the buildings, monuments, and settings of funerary architecture in the western European tradition*, London 1980, 315.

[60] *SE*, 4 May 1918.

[61] *IR*, 29 Nov. 1918. Sylvia Pankhurst noted Dunnico's work for the Peace Society in her book about the East End during the war: *The home front*, London 1987 edn, 69, 328. Dunnico later became an MP and suggested a World Fellowship Day to replace Armistice Day: Graves and Hodge, *The long weekend*, 215–16.

[62] *IR*, 24 Jan. 1919.

Plate 8. Ilford Urban District war memorial

and an industrial infrastructure. Another meeting was held in March but 'attendance [was] not so large as it should have been'.[63] Still no firm decisions were reached which served to provoke a letter to the *Recorder* complaining that the figure set was too high. A week later another correspondent criticised this stance, stating that 'it was the bodies of our dead heroes which made the rampart between destruction and this town'.[64] In April an ex-serviceman added his voice to the argument, complaining of 'the shameful indecision' of the committee.[65] The following week the *Recorder* announced that the plebiscite cards were being distributed to the 45,000 registered voters in Ilford. Although this was probably the easiest way of organising the vote, it does imply that only those people who were fully qualified citizens were entitled to a say in the nature of the town's memorial.[66] When the result was declared the committee's preferred option of a children's hospital was the majority decision with over 14,000 votes in favour. This leaves a key question unanswered, namely just how many people voted for alternative schemes?[67] The committee, however, took this as their mandate to continue with the scheme.

There had been debate over the form and nature of the scheme and the various alternatives proposed. The question of what form the main civic war memorial should take had been posed as early as 1916 when it was suggested that a bungalow estate be built, primarily for returning ex-servicemen. Another man was obviously more interested in the reputation of the town as he proposed a permanent shrine at the corner of Ley Street and Balfour Road so that visitors coming out of the railway station could not miss it: this also inadvertently reveals the importance of the Great Eastern Railway to the town.[68] Nothing came of either of these suggestions and it was not until October 1918 that the question was raised again, provoked by a local proposal to erect a memorial in the outlying ward of Barkingside. The editor of the *Recorder* responded with his own views:

> This opens up the larger questions of a memorial for Ilford, which composes, of course, the whole of the seven wards, one of which is Barkingside village. What is our policy in the matter? Are we to set up one memorial, or are we to leave the several areas included in the civil parish to inaugurate their own? Ought not this question be settled first of all? It appears to me that the Urban Council should consider the subject in all its bearings, and, if necessary, call a town meeting to deal with it.
>
> If district memorials are to be the rule, then mention may be made of a proposal that comes from a ratepayer that the strip of wooded land near the

---

63 Ibid. 7 Mar. 1919.
64 Ibid. 21, 28 Mar. 1919.
65 Ibid. 4 Apr. 1919.
66 Ibid. 11 Apr. 1919.
67 Ibid. 9 May 1919.
68 Ibid. 22 Dec. 1916.

'Wash' should be purchased by subscription . . . and equipped with an obelisk or something of that kind, upon which should be engraved the names of all the men who have been killed in the war, from the two adjacent wards of Park and Cranbrook. Other propositions of a similar restricted character will no doubt soon be forthcoming from Seven Kings, Goodmayes, Clementswood and Loxford.[69]

This provoked a flurry of correspondence. Some readers believed that the old clock tower in the High Street should be renovated and used as a memorial. Another reader wanted a great carillon tower built in Newbury Park, the geographical centre of Ilford: the tower should have seven sides, one for each ward with corresponding memorial plaques. The implication of civic awareness, identity and localism in a new community is very clear in this suggestion.[70] It was also proposed that the air-raid siren should be kept as a memorial and sounded every Sunday morning, calling people to church in order to remember the dead. This would have made every Sunday a day of remembrance and thanksgiving for the sacrifice.[71]

All these suggestions were for aesthetic memorials; not one of the correspondents urged a memorial of practical utility. This immediately put them at odds with the council, as at one of its meetings in December a children's hospital was suggested and then put forward at the first war memorial committee meeting.[72] This meeting saw this scheme discussed alongside the suggestion that a YMCA centre or some sort of boys institute be built as a memorial. No decision was reached on that occasion.[73]

The debate rumbled on into the next meeting, reflecting the varying views on what function a civic memorial should serve. Edwin Hodnett, the ecclesiastical architect for the parish, spoke in favour of a children's hospital. His comments displayed a clear sense of civic duty and a wider obligation to England and empire: 'it was our bounden duty to replace the lives that had been lost, and every child saved in this hospital would be a valuable asset to the town and the nation'.[74] Another man spoke in favour of a sports institute, expressing sentiments which exactly mirrored those put forward at the

---

[69] Ibid. 11 Oct. 1918.

[70] Ibid. 18 Oct. 1918.

[71] Ibid. 6 Dec. 1918. This suggestion also shows that Adrian Gregory is not quite accurate in stating that sirens signalled the first Armistice silence 'only where such devices were available, coastal communities, such as Devon and Cornwall fishing villages, at the port of Yarmouth, and in mining and quarrying communities. Some large port cities such as Newcastle and Swansea also made use of harbour sirens': *Silence of memory*, 31. The Zeppelin threat to south-east England meant that by 1917 sirens were installed at major civic buildings across London and in 1919 they were used to signal the Silence and became a permanent feature of Armistice Day observance. See below and A. Rawlinson, *The defence of London, 1915–1918*, London 1923, 23, 227, for air raid precautions in the capital.

[72] *IR*, 22 Dec. 1918, 24 Jan. 1919.

[73] Ibid. 24 Jan. 1919.

[74] Ibid. 7 Mar. 1919.

unveilings of school memorials: 'Waterloo, Wellington said, was won on the playing fields of Eton. We were told before the war that sport had killed us as a nation. He did not think any of us would say today that the war was lost because we were sportsmen. (Applause.)' This was supported by a regular Anglican communicant who said that the young men who did not go to church would find their moral guidance through the club. In this way the memory of the dead would help to shape the citizens of the future.[75]

But there was still a strong current of opinion against utilitarian schemes. Mrs Harvey George argued for an aesthetic memorial and had earlier written to the *Recorder* urging 'the erection of a beautiful monument, bearing the names of the fallen'.[76] This judgement was echoed by others present: Mr Fredrickson spoke in favour of an extravagant memorial and said that the principle the men had fought and died for 'would outlive a thousand Pyramids'. When Rudyard Kipling wrote on the work of the Imperial War Graves Commission he made a similar comment. Comparing the commission's achievements with that of the ancient Egyptians, he stated that it was 'the biggest single bit of work since any of the Pharoahs . . . and they only worked in their own country'.[77] Whether in the Great War or in the commemoration of that war, the British were making a monumental effort. The dichotomy between the views was summed up by Mr Porter when he made a speech which encapsulated the meaning of a war memorial as a surrogate grave and headstone for the bereaved to focus upon: he supported 'a marble monument which would typify to the bereaved a tombstone such as they would like to place on the graves of their dead'.[78] It might be said that the church schemes were really fulfilling this role and a town memorial by sheer virtue of its scale was bound to represent something slightly different from a substitute grave. Some of the bereaved did support the idea of a practical memorial. A widowed mother, who had lost both her sons in the war, said her boys would have liked to see their mother cared for. She therefore suggested memorial cottages for people like her. The editor of the *Recorder* also threw his weight behind a practical scheme, stating that the memorial should serve to improve 'the social condition of the town in which we live'.[79]

The result of the plebiscite did not completely resolve the debate. In September 1922 Mr T. Baker wrote a stinging letter to the *Recorder* in which he stated that the hospital scheme was merely a plot to boost the civic profile of Ilford rather than a genuine attempt to commemorate the dead. He added that the committee was 'filled with vanity, they should outface all other towns!' and further accused them of having 'an axe of their own to grind [so]

---

[75] Ibid. The concept that sport had killed the nation was discussed by Kipling in his 1902 poem 'The islanders': *Rudyard Kipling's verse*, 301–4.
[76] *IR*, 24 Jan. 1919.
[77] Ibid. 7 Mar. 1919; F. Ware, *The immortal heritage*, Cambridge 1937, 56–8.
[78] *IR*, 7 Mar. 1919.
[79] Ibid. 21 Mar. 1919.

they exploited our boys'.[80] But the scheme did make provision for an aesthetic memorial to stand beside the hospital: £3,000 out of the £20,000 had been earmarked for its erection.[81] Land was purchased at Hatch Lane, Newbury Park, next to the existing emergency hospital and it was planned that the new hospital and the memorial should be built on this site.[82] But this decision still did not resolve the controversy; instead it threw up a variant, an argument over the location, in which the nature of civic pride and development clashed with individual sensibilities.

The winter of 1921 was marked by more letters to the *Recorder*. For many the proposed location was not a fitting or dignified place; the civic heart of the town was not a field at Newbury Park.[83] Mr Dillon stated that most town memorials were sited on the High Road and, significantly, he compared Ilford's scheme with those of similar communities, quoting examples at Romford, Wood Green, Enfield, Crouch End, Chiswick and Turnham Green. William Manning of St Alban's Road, Seven Kings, not surprisingly believed 'a garden space outside Seven Kings station' would be preferable to the proposed site. 'A Parent of One of the Fallen' wrote a letter which serves to emphasise the attraction of the parish schemes:

> I sincerely trust the committee have not definitely decided to erect the monument in Hatch Lane on the plot largely used as a cabbage ground, where it would be hidden out of sight, quite away from the town. Many poor mothers would find it a difficult task to get there. . . . Why have our committee chosen such an 'inglorious' position for ours (right away from the town?) I would suggest that we have it in the main road, where all who pass by may be reminded of the great sacrifice our brave men made for us.[84]

There was obviously some sort of gap in the information chain as the purchase of the Hatch Lane site was one of the earliest actions of the committee.

The January 1922 annual general meeting of the war memorial committee attempted to answer the questions regarding location. They stated that the building of the new arterial – the A12 Eastern Avenue – on the old Hatch Lane would turn it into the main civic thoroughfare. In short a war memorial to tell the future generations of the bravery of the men of Ilford had to be in the prospective heart of the town not its old centre. The logic was inescapable, 'the monument was not only for today – it was being placed there for the future'. This was followed up with the sly observation that a memorial in Valentines Park would be convenient for some but not 'in the future for a

---

80 Baker's letter also included the references to laying wreaths at the county of London memorial mentioned in the section on the City of London: *IR*, 15 Sept. 1922.
81 Ibid. 24 Jan. 1919.
82 Ibid. 7 Nov. 1919.
83 Ibid. 25 Nov. 1921.
84 Ibid. 2 Dec. 1921.

great many people in the town, particularly those at Goodmayes and Chadwell Heath'. However, the committee did not hold a united position. J. S. Parker, for example, buttressed the concept of the memorial as a substitute grave. He said that the site was too inaccessible and added that relatives would not only want to visit the memorial on Armistice Day, but also on the anniversary of the deaths of their loved ones.[85] Again this was a concept the churches had already grasped, as the Revd A. W. Ottaway of St Clement's, Great Ilford, wrote in his parish magazine:

> [He referred to] the vases that have been supplied with flowers week by week by the relatives of those whose names are recorded on our Roll of Honour. It has been a labour of love, which many of them will wish to repeat as the anniversaries they will not cease to observe come round.[86]

At the same meeting the winning design for the sculptural memorial was announced. The memorial itself was to consist of a celtic cross 27ft high. On a pedestal in front of the cross was a private soldier, cast in bronze, in full field service marching order presenting arms. On a tablet on the pedestal the inscription: 'To the glory of God and in memory of the men who gave their lives in the Great War 1914–1918. Their name liveth for evermore.' The sculpture was by Newbury Trent and is a fine example of the sentinel soldier memorial common to towns the size of Ilford.[87]

Not everyone accepted this without reservation. A letter opposing the location was even included in the edition of the *Recorder* which covered the unveiling of the sculptural memorial in 1922. 'Homage', a bereaved mother, overturned all the arguments on the future growth of the town and identified its true, spiritual centre:

> Why should our memorial soldier be hidden away in the drab surroundings of Hatch Lane? Surely he is put up for the present and rising generations as a remembrance and as a witness to the glory of sacrifice. He should be placed in beautiful surroundings, and there is no more beautiful place than Valentines Park. Thoughtless youth on its way to play would learn to love his steady face. Quiet strollers would utter a voiceless prayer of thanksgiving for all he typifies.[88]

---

85 Ibid. 6 Jan. 1922.
86 St Clement's, Great Ilford, parish magazine, Oct. 1920.
87 Sentinel soldiers were also erected in such towns as Streatham, Elland, Enniskillen, Dumfries and Thornton Cleveleys: Boorman, *At the going down of the sun*, 78–114. However, Trent used this particular design on only one other occasion, at Tredegar, some years later.
88 *IR*, 17 Nov. 1922. In using the term 'his steady face' the correspondent reveals the way in which figurative memorials were invested with life by the bereaved. Catherine Moriarty has noted that 'the bereaved spectator engage[d]' with the figures. In turn the figures hide the reality of modern war. She states that 'The soldiers, being whole and unmaimed, diverted attention from the horror of war and the tragedy of death and injury. They represented a pure race unsullied by foreign blood. The splendid physiques belied the reality of pre- and post-war poverty, malnutrition and disease. . . . Thus, the figurative sculpture of First World

She suggested that if it were placed in Valentines Park a rota of ladies, like the lady clerks of the City, would keep the flowers fresh and maintain the flower beds around the memorial.

But nothing would have happened had not the funds been raised and donations made in the first place. In some ways, the fund-raising was hampered by the initial decision to set a figure without presenting the public with a vision of the memorial; effectively people were being asked to part with money without knowing how it would be spent. Fund-raising started with a series of whist drives which immediately incurred the disapproval of Eardley-Willmott (of the shrines controversy) and the bishop of Chelmsford, both of whom condemned any form of gambling as a way of raising funds in a sacred cause.[89] In November the committee voted to form seven sub-committees to arrange fund-raising in each ward. They also followed the example of St Clement's by adopting a collecting card system.[90] Many events were arranged including concerts and fetes. After one of these a letter was sent to the *Recorder* expressing displeasure at the sale of German goods: 'What bitter irony that German manufactured articles should be given as prizes at a fete organised for erecting a memorial to those who fell fighting that country.'[91] The importance of the Great Eastern Railway was also demonstrated by the stationmaster, A. Cadman. Along with his fellow stationmasters at Seven Kings, Goodmayes and Chadwell Heath he devised a system of collecting from the 20,000 commuters that went through the station each weekday. He aimed to raise £1,000 and in January 1920 he reported contributions from 10,040 passengers.[92] An equally innovative idea was the launching of the *Ilford War Memorial Gazette* in February 1920. This magazine appears to have been unique to Ilford for no other organisation in Britain seems to have had a publication devoted to a war memorial fund.[93] Edited by W. H. Stevens, it carried potted histories of the war, subscription lists, biographies and photo-

War memorials provided one complete symbolic body which replaced the many absent, fragmented corpses which were, at this time, still being salvaged from the battlefields, reinterred and, if possible identified. Never before had a single body represented so many who had "passed out of the sight of men". The dead's very absence facilitated the process of idealisation, of whom they had been as people and the circumstances of their death. The sculpted body shaped private personal memory as well as creating public myths. By avoiding any reference to physical and social fragmentation it engendered a literal and metaphorical remembering': 'The absent dead and figurative First World War memorials', *Transactions of the Ancient Monuments Society* i (1995), 19–21, 37.

[89] *IR*, 28 Mar. 1919.

[90] Ibid. 7 Nov. 1919.

[91] Ibid. 26 May, 23 June 1922. The 'Made in Germany' debate stretched back to before the war and continued after it. The import of German toys caused particular concern and was commented on by *The Times* on 20 November 1920.

[92] Ibid. 30 Jan. 1920.

[93] RHL, *Ilford War Memorial Gazette*, no. 1 (Feb. 1920). Catherine Moriarty, former co-ordinator of the National Inventory of War Memorials at the Imperial War Museum, has stated that she saw no record of any similar publication.

graphs of the fallen, appeals for information, details of the fund-raising and the roll of honour.[94]

But the fund ran into problems, mainly of the committee's own making. It missed a great opportunity to appeal and collect donations by not organising anything to coincide with the Peace Day celebrations in Valentines Park.[95] In fact the committee did little in regard to collecting throughout the summer of 1919, when the major charity event was the annual emergency hospital fete.[96] At this point an understandable element of confusion entered the proceedings and seems to have dogged the fund until the very end. The committee's purchasing of land next to the emergency hospital appears to have started the trouble. At the next committee meeting J. S. Parker stated that many people had confused the emergency hospital fund with that of the war memorial. It was also well known in the town that the hospital had wanted a children's ward for some years. The fact that the war memorial fund was for a children's hospital must have encouraged the belief that the two funds were in fact one and the same.[97]

At the same meeting Mr Hustwayte, a churchwarden at St Alban's made an extremely pertinent point. He noted 'another thing that militated against this fund was that most churches in the neighbourhood were arranging, or had arranged for their own memorial'.[98] People could not afford to contribute to all the charitable causes put before them and the ones that meant most were the ones physically and emotionally closest to them. In 1922, just prior to the war memorial fete, this problem was still haunting the fund. The editor of the *Recorder* noted that donations stood at 15s. per head of population in Ilford (it is not known how he reached this figure); he believed that it would have been a lot higher had it not been for the other worthy causes vying for the available cash.[99] At the previous annual general meeting of the fund in January, J. S. Parker perfectly analysed the problem. He said that the first six months of a fund were the most crucial time and as it had not reached a healthy sum within that time it was doubtful whether the scheme would ever reach its target.[100] Parker was merely reiterating what he had said in 1919, that 'it seemed to him . . . that the apathy of the people of Ilford was such that it appeared like whipping a dead horse'.[101]

---

94   The magazine was not issued at regular intervals: in total it ran to eight numbers as follows: 1 (Feb. 1920); 2 (June 1920); 3 (Dec. 1920); 4 (May 1921); 5 (special edition for Armistice Day, Nov. 1921); 6 (special edition for unveiling of war memorial, Nov. 1922); 7 (special edition for laying foundation stone of children's war memorial ward, Nov. 1926); 8 (special edition for unveiling of children's war memorial ward, June 1927).
95   *IR*, 25 July 1919.
96   Ibid. 8 Aug. 1919.
97   Ibid. 7 Nov. 1919.
98   Ibid.
99   Ibid. 26 May 1922.
100   Ibid. 6 Jan. 1922.
101   Ibid. 7 Nov. 1919.

As the fund did not achieve the heights that the committee had at first believed possible, the atmosphere turned sour. In October 1921 the local branch of the British Legion called for the fund to be wound up as it was unlikely ever to achieve its target.[102] Paranoia seemed to infect the war memorial committee, for the annual general meeting in January 1922 was restricted to those who could provide proof of having contributed. This led to a heated debate in the *Recorder* and at the last moment the committee climbed down. It was, however, too late to matter and consequently it was 'a rather small attendance'.[103] At the same time people were starting to discuss another problem, namely who would pay for the upkeep of the hospital if and when it was ever built.

This effectively turned the whole matter into a rating row. Anxious councillors had demanded an investigation of the finances of the committee in the winter of 1920 and an acrimonious atmosphere festered from that point.[104] The committee was interviewed by the council in October 1921 and it was suggested that the fund be merged with that of the emergency hospital trust, thus removing the question of a hospital on the rates.[105] The following December Arthur Gilderson, an influential Ilford undertaker and member of the committee, openly admitted at the annual general meeting that it was now a 'question of rating and not of a memorial to the fallen'.[106] Two sets of banner headlines from the *Recorder* can be used as evidence to show that interest in the scheme continued, but in the mutated form of local government funding obligations. Both examples come from January 1926:

When – Oh When?/Still Wrangling over Childrens Hospital/Scheme/ Special Meeting to Hear Grievance/Objectors Ask for Inquiry/Grave Warning by Adam Partington.

Ilford War Memorial Sensation/Scheme of Amalgamation Rejected/ Counc. Taylor Refuses to State Objections/Committee Described as 'Quiet as Little Lambs'/Chairman Complains of Delayed Support/Question Referred to Charity Commissioners.[107]

Eventually, the committee acknowledged that they could not raise enough for a separate hospital, and even if they could the council would not then support it on the rates. They were forced to amalgamate their scheme with the plans of the emergency hospital and the result was a scaled-down project in the form of a war memorial children's wing, although wrangles continued until November 1926 when its foundation stone was laid. When the children's wing was finally opened by Lady Patricia Ramsey in June 1927 just over

102 Ibid. 28 Oct. 1921.
103 Ibid. 23, 30 Dec. 1921, 6 Jan. 1922.
104 Ibid. 24 Dec. 1920.
105 Ibid. 28 Oct. 1921.
106 Ibid. 15 Dec. 1922.
107 Ibid. 15, 29 Jan. 1926.

£10,000 had been collected. W. H. Stevens issued his final issue of the *Gazette* and even he had to admit that 'money had not come in so fast as was anticipated'.[108]

It is possible to draw some conclusions on the exact nature of the fund-raising campaign and the personalities involved. The subscription lists reveal that virtually every trader in Ilford made some form of contribution. It was of course only to be expected that local businesses should respond; demands of local prestige and kudos alone were enough of an inducement. All the churches and schools also made collections, as did the sports clubs and political parties. But the real interest is in the motivation of the personal contributors. For some, like Lord Rowallan or the Griggs family, it was partly the need to maintain an image of *largesse* and the same can be said of the donations of councillors. From the five subscriptions lists produced for the *War Memorial Gazette* some statistics can be derived. They reveal only 369 individual contributors, thirty-three of whom made more than one contribution. This excludes W. H. Stevens and his family, the many Misses Stevens and his other relatives, all of whom made contributions with a religious zeal and regularity. Of the multiple contributors, five donated on three occasions and one made four separate appearances on the varied lists. The state of the fund in November 1922, when the last subscriptions list appeared, was £8,100 in net income. This implies that the bulk of the money collected came, instead, through collections made by the various social, religious, educational and employment groups in Ilford. By cross-reference with the roll of honour, the *Ilford Recorder*, and *Kelly's directory of Ilford* it is also possible to deduce that many of the contributors were related and further were related to men who had served and died in the war. One example serves to highlight this point. Sidney G. Templar, killed in action during the war, was the son of Mr and Mrs W. G. Templar; the subscriptions list reveals that Mr and Mrs Templar contributed twice, their daughter once, and Sidney's three brothers once each. It is also interesting to note that a number of contributors had already given money for parish war memorials. James Cockburn, who lost both his sons, contributed to the Presbyterian memorial and the Ilford fund; C. W. Scotcher, who lost his son, contributed to the St Clement's fund and the Ilford scheme. Indeed the parishioners of St Clement's provided many dual contributors including Mrs Aldridge, A. W. Green, Mr and Mrs Stuart A. Russell, Mrs Jeffry and Mrs Lee. As the richest parish in Ilford this is not surprising, but the overwhelming conclusion is that the weight of the fund-raising fell on the shoulders of a relatively small group of people who were already active in various parish affairs. It is also clear that if people did not contribute in the first six months of collecting they invariably did not contribute at all until the last great effort of the late summer of 1922. The last pattern to emerge from the list is the intriguing imbalance in the locality of

---

[108] RHL, *Ilford War Memorial Gazette*, no. 8 (June 1927), 4.

the contributors. It has not been possible to trace the addresses of all the individual contributors, but those that have been traced, largely through reference to *Kelly's directory*, show a majority resident in Seven Kings, in particular in Aldborough Road. This may reflect the fact that both Stevens and Parker lived in Aldborough Road and so organised a more systematic collection scheme. It may also reflect the strong sense of community that was felt to be so marked a characteristic of Seven Kings. After Seven Kings, most of the contributors were resident on the estates around Valentines Park, and dominated by St Clement's. Goodmayes also provided a cluster of contributors; again a relatively new district anxious to find some sort of identity.

The memorial was clearly handicapped by appearing on the scene at a fairly late stage. The plebiscite on what form it was to take was not organised until the spring of 1919, by which time many other committees had been formed on a lower and more intimate level. The work of fund-raising and contribution also appears to have fallen on a relatively small number of people. In many instances these were people who were already involved in other war memorial schemes or were active in their own locality in another capacity. This situation was never properly remedied and led to some terrible breakdowns of communication, most notably the confusion between the emergency hospital fund and the war memorial scheme. Some of the blame for this must rest with the committee for not approaching the emergency hospital earlier: a pooling of funds might well have provided the cash a great deal more quickly. People were well aware of emergency hospital events and a formal merger at an earlier stage would have avoided clashes over who could appeal and when. The second issue the committee never really addressed was the location of the memorial; until the last moment people were complaining and in ignorance of the fact that the site had not only been proposed, but had already been bought and designated. The argument that Eastern Avenue was to become the main artery of the town clearly held little sway, particulary with the affluent residents around Valentines Park. Some element of inter-district rivalry is perhaps discernible as the site chosen was within walking distance of Aldborough Road and parts of Seven Kings. The imbalance in favour of Seven Kings residence in the organisation and funding of the memorial is a bit double-edged however, as the Seven Kings Ratepayers' Association subjected the committee to a veritable inquisition over their plans for the maintenance of the hospital.[109]

Finally it is important to look at the services of unveiling and dedication at these memorials. In May 1921, the *Recorder* announced an open-air memorial service in aid of the fund, to be held in the presence of the bishop of Chelmsford, at the Hatch Lane site.[110]

---

[109] Information drawn from the subscriptions lists printed ibid. nos 1 (Feb. 1920), 4; 2 (June 1920), 5–6; 3 (Dec. 1920), 6; 4 (May 1921), 5; 6 (Nov. 1922) 8; *Kelly's directory of Ilford* [1922]; *IR*, 9 Dec. 1921.
[110] *IR*, 20 May 1921.

The *Recorder's* coverage of the service reveals the complexity of the situation and the fact that the state of the fund cannot be regarded as the only barometer of interest. The report gives the impression of history-in-the-making, a moment of civic pride. This is most clearly seen in the statement that 'there was an assembling of people such as has never been known in the history of Ilford'. The crowd was estimated as 'not short of seven to eight thousand, while it is probable that the numbers reached as high as ten thousand, or even more'.[111]

A temporary granite cross had been erected, courtesy of Gilderson, behind which another cross was marked out on the grass, measuring 75ft by 45ft and in the centre of this yet another cross 20ft by 12ft made entirely out of floral tributes. It was obviously meant to be a service of consolation. The *Recorder* made much of the widows with their fatherless children and the bereaved parents:

> But perhaps the most pathetic of all those who showed evidence of their loss was the widowed wife without child or parent to share her sorrow. There were many such on the field that memorable afternoon . . . much sympathy of heart . . . went out to them, as it did also to every other bereaved father, mother, wife or child present.[112]

The bishop of Chelmsford led the united service: he reminded the congregation that the decision to erect a children's hospital was a parable of the war as the men had gone to war to preserve the lives of others.[113] But amongst the now standard platitudes on sacrifice the bishop used the occasion to make some wider points. He said that the war had distorted and jumbled the lives of millions of men; the sudden coming of peace meant that men had 'plunged back into light' after emerging from the 'dark room' of the war and that it was a bewildering and disturbing experience. He implied that it led to new ideas like socialism and communism, but fortunately the recent coal strike had shown that the British were still a peaceful race, unwilling to descend into chaos. The overtone of the address was the reinforcement of a conservative message and once again the reaffirmation of traditional values; the Anglo-Saxon Christian morality that had sent Britain to war was still valid. The bishop also repeated his story, told at St Edward's, Romford, about the war being valueless in terms of pounds, shillings and pence but invaluable in the timeless spiritual terms of freedom, righteousness and justice. His sermon to the people of Ilford was reassuring by virtue of its sheer lack of genuine substance, vague references to a perfect world that was still visible and perceptible in spite of the desolation caused by the war.[114] The service ended

111 Ibid. 10 June 1921.
112 Ibid.
113 Ibid.
114 Ibid. For the career of the bishop of Chelmsford see E. N. Gowing, *John Edwin Watts-Ditchfield*, London 1926.

with a collection that raised £120, but much more important was the display of genuine interest and emotion that appears to have renewed the resolve of the committee.[115]

The unveiling of the aesthetic memorial on Armistice Day 1922 was certainly the grandest day so far in the history of Ilford. Stevens issued a special edition of the *Gazette*: he mixed civic pride with solemn dignity, writing that the loss of Ilford men was 'far above the average, being considerably more than the one-thousandth part of the total losses of the British Empire'. In total more than 10,000 Ilford men had joined the forces and 1,170 men fell.[116] He believed that the memorial would provide the 'sacred spot to which we can go on particular "days of remembrance" and place a few flowers'.[117] The soldier symbolises the effort of the town and he guards not only his dead comrades, but the honour of Ilford as well. A citizen-soldier was a fitting monument for the town.

The council turned out *en masse* for the unveiling, seemingly unaware of the paradox of their position: their intransigence over accepting any commitment to fund the hospital was effectively blocking any development of that part of the scheme. Lord Lambourne, lord lieutenant of Essex, escorted Princess Louise to the memorial. The bishop of Chelmsford and the Revd A. W. Ottaway shared the task of dedicating it. There does not appear to have been a representative of any other church, and Anglicanism dominated this particular day. A huge marquee was filled with relatives of the dead; Scouts, Guides, the British Legion and soldiers of the 4th battalion, Essex Regiment formed a guard of honour. Virtually every service, club and society in Ilford was represented including the Ilford Psychical Research Society.[118] The *Recorder* captured the mixture of sorrow and pride: 'In the grey atmosphere of a chill November day, in keeping with the solemn occasion, Ilford paid homage to her glorious dead, on Saturday, the fourth anniversary of the signing of the armistice by the unveiling of the town's war memorial monument.'[119]

After the service a special luncheon was provided for the princess at the town hall. The report of the service itself is actually a little sterile and strangely unmoving: perhaps it was a little too formal for those present as well, for the *Recorder* noted that on the next day, a Sunday, a massive and impromptu pilgrimage to the memorial took place with many wreaths laid. In the light of some of the squabbles it is not surprising that the ceremony seemed a little hollow. It is also intriguing to note that a large crowd gathered outside the town hall on Armistice Day at 11.00 a.m., expecting a repeat of

---

115 Ibid.
116 RHL, *Ilford War Memorial Gazette*, no. 6 (Nov. 1922), 3; no. 8 (June 1927), 5.
117 Ibid.
118 Spiritualism had received a huge boost thanks to the war (see chs 6, 7). The Church was not at all well-disposed towards it and it must be assumed that the bishop of Chelmsford had no knowledge of their presence at the unveiling.
119 *IR*, 17 Nov. 1922.

the bugle call and silence marked by a short service that had become customary. The *Recorder* noted that the people who gathered maintained the silence in impeccable fashion but were disappointed that the council had not arranged any form of service, an episode which demonstrates that people were anxious to show their respects and honour the dead but also implies widespread ignorance of the events at Hatch Lane which had been widely publicised well in advance of that date.[120]

A special service took place four years later, when, on 26 November 1926, the foundation stone of the children's ward was laid. Stevens and Lady Wise, wife of the Sir Fredric, laid the stones. Ottaway conducted the prayers, reminding the crowd of their debt to those who had sacrificed everything for King and Country. The Revd F. C. Barton, the Wesleyan superintendent minister, then made a speech in which he displayed how rich a crust of iconographic clichés had attached itself to the war dead. He did not speak with the tone of a disillusioned or cynical age; instead he recommitted all those present to a life of service. He stated that

> They must interpret life, not in terms of self-interest, but in terms of service. In every church in the land they found tablets – made of wood, marble, bronze, or brass – with the names upon them of the men who had died – the flower of their youth – for England.[121]

He then highlighted the common post-war theme of the gap in society: 'These memorials were not momentoes of our military genius – they were momentoes of a missing generation.'[122] However, the message is not one of a wasted generation, but men who went missing fulfilling an honourable cause. Barton said that the message of the memorial was 'to measure life by loss not by gain, not by the wine drunk, but by the wine poured forth'.[123] The imagery is unmistakable and archaic. Rupert Brooke's 'The Dead' is the obvious reference point: 'These laid the world away; poured out the red/Sweet wine of youth.'[124] The constant incongruity was that the new, Christian world bought by the sacrifice of the men was to be made out of the old values that are English and timeless. The ceremony, like the unveiling of the memorial, was also a moment of civic chest-beating. Sir Fredric Wise said that the hospital would be 'the soul of Ilford' and Cadman was proud that 'Ilford had risen to the occasion'.[125] Stevens then concluded by fulfilling the prophecy made by A. W. Green at the meeting in March 1919: 'Their memory would remain not only so long as they themselves remained but to their children and their

---

120 Ibid.
121 Ibid.
122 Ibid.
123 Ibid.
124 R. Brooke, *The complete poetical works of Rupert Brooke*, London 1918, 7.
125 *IR*, 12 Nov. 1926.

children's children, that children's hospital would be an ever present reminder of what had gone before.'[126]

On 25 June 1927 the wing was formally opened by Lady Patricia Ramsey and the *Ilford Recorder* proclaimed: 'After Eight Years!/Ilford's War Memorial Finished/At Last.'[127] The gardens surrounding it were described as 'sacred ground': in the absence of a grave the land surrounding a memorial thus became consecrated turf, just as the locations where British soldiers fought and fell were often referred to in reverential terms. (In 1920 a book was published with the title *Ypres: the holy ground of British arms*.[128]) A. W. Green, a member of the board of the emergency hospital, accepted the ward on its behalf. He revealed how far the war dead were used to support other values; he said that England had a tradition of voluntary hospitals and he was proud to accept such a fine addition and maintain it in memory of the dead.[129] These, then, were the values for which the men went to fight.

The ex-servicemen of Ilford donated their share from the United Services Fund to pay for a cot in the ward and thus symbolised the lives to be saved through the sacrifices made in the war.[130] Tablets were unveiled in the entrance hall and revealed the roll of honour; it contained a message of dignity and grief: 'In Loving Memory of the Ilford Men who died in the Great War 1914–1918. These are dead. They died that we might live life more abundantly. Greater love hath no man than this, that a man lay down his life for his friends.'[131] The inscription shows the desire to achieve a balance between homely, personal sentiments, as might be found on any family gravestone – 'In Loving Memory' – and the need to show pride and dignified mourning as demonstrated in the second half of the inscription. It was therefore a little different from West Ham's decision to put civic pride first on its inscribed roll of the dead. The iconographic escalation of the dead to a unique place of honour in the fabric of Ilford was achieved.

Ilford thus eventually completed its war memorial scheme. Stevens believed that Ilford had 'one of the finest Memorials for a long way around'.[132] It was certainly grander than Romford's, but it could not compare with those of East and West Ham. Ilford managed to salvage a scheme from what appeared to be a disastrous position. Even as the debate degenerated and mutated into an argument about the limits of the ratepayers obligations, the *Recorder* still showed the genuine interest and concern of many that a fitting war memorial be erected. Indeed the most ironic thing about the whole scheme was the constant level of interest but low level of monetary imput.

---

[126] Ibid.
[127] Ibid. 1 July 1927.
[128] See Lieutenant-Colonel H. Beckles-Willson, *Ypres: the holy ground of British arms*, London 1920.
[129] *IR*, 1 July 1927.
[130] RHL, *Ilford War Memorial Gazette*, no. 8 (June 1927), 4.
[131] Ibid.
[132] Ibid.

The vast crowds present at the special service of remembrance, at the unveiling, at the laying of the foundation stone, and the pilgrimage, all point to a very genuine and heart-felt desire to remember the dead. Even the many complaints show that people were not apathetic; instead they aired their views because of very real concern. The downturn in the economic situation no doubt played a major role in drawing off funds, but the crucial fact is that most people contributed to other schemes first. In the end, despite the interest in the main war memorial, it was still the nearest one that was felt to be the most fitting place to lay a wreath and say a prayer.

Romford and Bethnal Green

Romford and Bethnal Green have been juxtaposed as both districts encountered similar problems and made similar mistakes. It thus becomes possible to determine which factors made a scheme a success or a failure. However, like is not (quite) compared with like: Bethnal Green was a metropolitan borough with a large population and a considerable degree of poverty, whereas Romford Urban District was a much less densely populated suburb, sedate and genteel in character.[133]

The gestation and development of Romford's war memorial was fraught with every conceivable difficulty and problem; it also became a byzantine puzzle of competing ideals and concepts, civic pride and pretension conflicting with the finite nature of civic funds.

Romford's problems started with an inability to settle on one particular scheme. The initial moves towards a war memorial began in the winter of 1916. In December 1916 a meeting was called at St Edward's in order to discuss the matter; it was 'representative of the town in its official, religious and industrial capacity'.[134] The Revd G. M. Bell of St Edward's chaired the meeting but he believed that 'it would be a great mistake if the Church, or any other section of the community took up as their business what obviously was the town's business'.[135] The Anglican Church therefore initiated but subsequently refrained from taking the lead. Bell himself suggested three options: a stone memorial, a practical scheme such as a library or a benefit scheme for soldiers and their dependants. Views were expressed in favour of aesthetic and practical schemes, but no decisions were actually reached.[136] The editor of the *Essex Times* came down in favour of a library, as he believed that it would be the best way to perpetuate the names of the dead:

---

133 See ch. 1 for full descriptions.
134 *ET*, 9 Dec. 1916.
135 Ibid.
136 Ibid.

A memorial of public utility would be of far greater advantage than one that would speedily become commonplace. The fundamental principle in deciding the form of the war memorial should be to perpetuate the names on Romford's 'Roll of Honour'. This would be more effectively done inside a public building used by all. A public monument would soon cease to attract local attention, and would have no very great interest for the passing stranger.[137]

When the council finally discussed the matter in 1919, it suggested three different options with which to commemorate 'Romford's fallen heroes': a park, a children's playground or a YMCA centre.[138] At this point matters started to degenerate, for although the YMCA idea seemed to gain acceptance among the councillors and negotiations were started with the YMCA no decision was reached. Debate went on and little was decided until suddenly a statue was suggested as an alternative.[139] But that was not the end of the matter, as in July the library scheme made a comeback and the council spoke of approaching the Carnegie Trust. The editor of the *Essex Times* welcomed this news claiming the town's long-standing support for the idea.[140] None the less nothing more was done and in January 1920, when the council discussed the memorial again, it voted to put the matter off for six months.[141] Councillor Goulden asked about the war memorial committee in April but the clerk told him that it no longer existed because 'it could not and did not deal with anything'.[142] Finally, the matter was taken out of council hands thanks to the intervention of a resident, C. M. Dyer, who offered to organise a scheme on behalf of the town, an offer which the council accepted. Dyer's profession is not known but he lived in Gresham Lodge, one of the grand houses near the Gidea Park estate.[143]

Meanwhile, in Bethnal Green during the corresponding phase, a special meeting of the council took place on 15 January 1919 in order to discuss a war memorial; a public meeting was duly fixed for 4 February. In many ways the writing was already on the wall as the *Hackney and Kingsland Gazette* reported that only about fifty people were present,[144] although among them was the bishop of Stepney and the borough's two MPs. Various suggestions as to the form of the memorial were put forward; they included a clock tower, an ex-service institute, homes for ex-servicemen, a memorial hall connected to a library and a huge cross.[145] Many of these suggestions were also aired in Ilford and Romford, and as in Ilford and Romford, no decision was taken at this

---

137 Ibid. 20 Jan. 1917.
138 HHL, RUDC minutes, 7 Jan. 1919.
139 Ibid. 17 Feb., 24 Apr., 12 May 1919.
140 Ibid. 29 July 1919; *ET*, 2 Aug. 1919.
141 HHL, RUDC minutes, 6 Jan. 1920.
142 *ET*, 24 Apr. 1920.
143 HHL, RUDC minutes, 3 May 1920.
144 *HKG*, 5 Feb. 1919.
145 Ibid.

initial meeting. Instead, a committee was formed on 12 February, repre-senting every section and interest in the borough.[146]

The committee met on 1 May and discussed the options. A grand memo-rial hall to function as a men's club was suggested. The borough surveyor esti-mated the cost at £35,000. It was then decided that it was too close to the plans of the National Federation of Discharged and Demobilised Sailors and Soldiers to erect their own hall and was therefore rejected. The Oxford House Settlement put forward a scheme to convert the Excelsior Baths, leased by the council from the Settlement, into a war memorial project. This idea was well-received but again no decision was made and the matter was held over until the next meeting.[147] Such delays caused nothing but harm as the public were not given anything to focus on. When the committee met again the baths scheme was also rejected as too expensive. They then indulged in the NFDDSS idea of building a maternity hospital. Practical common sense was alternating with moments of grand imagination. Finally, it was noted that the borough still needed to complete its library and £5,000 was needed. The secretary suggested that this money be raised and used to provide a war memorial library. It was agreed to contact the public libraries committee and report back at the next meeting.[148]

Mr J. Radcliffe, the borough librarian, duly addressed the next committee meeting on 17 June. Radcliffe believed that a library was the best way of commemorating the dead, especially if the money was used to build a chil-dren's section. The men had gone to war to protect their homes and make the world safe for their children and so the education of those children was truly a noble monument; a similar sentiment to that of Ilford. It was also a scheme influenced by the Victorian belief in charitable foundations to reform the manners (and therefore provide the salvation) of the young. Such a scheme was also a monument to self-improvement.[149] Radcliffe stated with evangel-ical zeal:

> It has become more and more recognised that the future prosperity and safety of the world, depends in the main upon the education of the people. It may be claimed, without exaggeration that the foundation and structure of education is built upon the accumulated literature of the ages as expressing and recording

[146] THL, BGWMC minutes, 12 Feb. 1919.
[147] Ibid. 1 May 1919.
[148] Ibid. 22 May 1919.
[149] Walter Besant wrote of the value of East London's free libraries and perfectly encapsu-lated this atmosphere: 'There are six or seven free libraries in East London. Who was the benefactor to humanity who first invented or discovered the free library?... By means of the free library we actually give to every person, however poor, – we *give* him, as a free gift, – the whole literature of the world. If he were a millionaire he could not acquire a greater gift that the poorest lad enjoys who lives near a good free library ... since none but good and worthy literature should be admitted to the free library the readers cannot use its treasures without forming, purifying, and elevating their taste': *East London*, 338.

experience. Carlyle was of the opinion 'that the true University is a collection of books'.

Recognising the value of a library of carefully chosen books as such a medium, I can conceive of no more appropriate proposition for a War Memorial, than the dedication of a suitable proportion of the proposed Public Library as a department – consisting of a Lending Library and Reading Room – for the exclusive use of the children of the Borough under the age of sixteen years [He went on to describe the children's department] Frescoes, pictures and a Roll of Honour could be arranged round the walls and everything practicable done to make the Memorial at once useful, bright and cheerful, and a perpetual reminder – at any rate to the more thoughtful – of the years during which their relatives and countrymen fought to preserve our ideals and the world's freedom.[150]

This scheme was finally adopted on 10 July and a target of £10,000 was set.[151]

Romford, on the other hand, was taking a very long time to reach a firm decision. Money was at the heart of the problem; the initial meeting with the YMCA had seen a figure of £10,000 mentioned, to be raised by public subscription, but the agreement allowed both sides to withdraw if the funds were not forthcoming.[152] A council meeting on 6 May 1919 degenerated into a slanging match over the principle of a rate rise to fund the memorial. Councillor Franklin stated that 'if the proposals were the measure of their gratitude for what had been done to keep the Germans away, then God help Romford'. He further said that if the memorial eventually cost £50,000 it should be paid for by 8d. extra on the rates. In the furore that followed Councillor Ward began a running feud by stating that 'it was all very well for people who had stayed at home and made money to talk of an 8d rate for a war memorial'.[153] It all made for exciting reading, but it is difficult to tell how far the debate centred on the question of public finances or was merely an undignified personal squabble.

During all this the people of Romford played a largely subdued and anonymous role. At the start of activity, during the winter of 1916–17, the editor of the *Essex Times* noted that:

Not much general interest is yet being shown in the movement to decide upon what form the permanent memorial of the war shall take in Romford. Many people appear to think that there need be no hurry to decide upon a war memorial and that the great thing to concentrate all efforts upon at the present time is the bringing of the war to a victorious end.[154]

---

150 THL, BGWMC minutes, 17 June 1919.
151 Ibid. 10 July 1919.
152 HHL, RUDC minutes, 17 Feb., 12 May 1919.
153 *ET*, 10 May 1919.
154 Ibid. 20 Jan. 1917.

This attitude prevailed at a second meeting on the question when Bell stated his disappointment at the low turn-out, A letter from Sir Montague Turner, director of the P&O shipping line and a prominent Romfordian, was read in which he stated that he was 'rather at a loss to understand why it is necessary to consider the question of a war memorial at this present stage. Peace may not come yet awhile. Much may happen before that much-desired day. I should be in favour of postponing the question for the present'.[155] Nevertheless at the cessation of hostilities interest was still not aroused. In January 1919 Romford Men's Meeting distributed 2–3,000 leaflets calling for suggestions as to a war memorial; twelve replies were received.[156] At this point the council entered the fray, but hardly as a *deus ex machina*. Indeed, the council seemed to stifle the situation still further as no public announcements were made of their intentions. When it finally agreed to a public meeting the resolution was rescinded a few days later.[157]

Dyer then seemed to be taking quite a risk when he offered to organise the scheme, but he obviously had a clear plan of attack. He quickly erected a model of his proposed war memorial in Laurie Gardens, an open space at the top of the High Road and Market Place; it was a simple Celtic Cross on a large base.[158] He then called a meeting, which was very well attended, and said all the schemes so far floated had little to do with the memory of the dead, whereas his 'would form a memorial which the widows, children and other relatives of the fallen could look upon as having been definitely and permanently erected to the memory of their dear ones'.[159] This was a clear expression of the need for an alternative grave, a place to lay flowers and remember. The cost of the memorial was estimated at £500. Messrs Ind Coope and Company then displayed their largesse by making the first donation, of fifty guineas. But the disastrous lack of co-ordination that had haunted earlier efforts seemed to rise upon again when a completely separate committee was set up in order to resurrect the YMCA scheme. Fortunately, this scheme never got off the ground as any division of the public attention, just as it had something to focus on, would have been damaging.[160]

By late July £210 7s. 9d. was in the kitty. It was noted that there had been little criticism of the design and there was a great interest in inspecting the full-scale model in Laurie Gardens. The children of Mawney Road School were singled out for particular praise as they had made repeated donations; it is interesting to speculate on whether the children of the Mawney estate had a heightened awareness of the war due to the still prominent shrine. The fund-raising campaign also revealed the power of cinema as a special, illus-

---

155 Ibid. 27 Jan. 1917.
156 Ibid. 25 Jan. 1919.
157 HHL, RUDC minutes, 12 May 1919.
158 *ET*, 22 May 1920.
159 Ibid. 5 June 1920.
160 Ibid. 12 June 1920.

trated appeal was put on at the Laurie Cinema.[161] In September the work was put out to contract and Banks-Martin of East Ham was successful, the same Banks-Martin who had designed the East Ham memorial and ensured its acceptance during his term as mayor of the county borough.[162]

Although Bethnal Green appears to have got its act together once a project was finally adopted, the scheme was still dogged by a lack of dynamism. Instead of immediately forging ahead with fund-raising the committee attempted to discuss the matter with local clergy, traders and teachers. There was little response, except from teachers and the only effect was to delay the appeal.[163] Enthusiasm for the project obviously waned as nothing was done in the autumn and the committee did not meet again until January 1920. After nine meetings in six months they had now gone to the other extreme. The meeting opened in a depressing atmosphere as nineteen resignations from the committee were reported. However fund-raising schemes were discussed and it was proposed that collections should be made in pubs, places of worship, social clubs, local shops and house-to-house. Mystifyingly, these ideas were not acted upon; instead a series of sub-committees were formed in order to target specific groups. Committees for appeals, canvassing, schools and finance were established. This was, no doubt, a good idea, designed to maximise efficiency and publicity, but it should have happened much earlier.[164]

The sub-committees agreed to distribute appeals to every house in the borough. Businesses were to be interviewed by members of the committee: they were obviously aware of the local hierarchy as they also decided to 'compile a list of the prominent people in the Borough, who will be personally interviewed by members of the committee'. School children were especially targeted with the novelty scheme of buying 'My Brick' tickets.[165] By April 35,000 copies of the general appeal had been printed along with 2,500 copies of the special appeal to go to local trades and 'to persons interested in, but not resident in the borough'.[166]

At this point things quite obviously came to a dramatic halt for the next meeting did not take place until 4 July 1922. Unsurprisingly, it turned into a *post mortem* on the failure of the scheme. The total amount collected stood at £354 10s. 6d., which after the necessary deductions was only £282 13s. 5d. Radcliffe reported what he perceived to be the reasons for the failure:

(1) The impossibility of obtaining sufficient number of collectors.
(2) The coincident [sic] raising of funds for the local Church Memorials and other bodies.

---

161 Ibid. 24 July 1920.
162 Ibid. 18 Sept. 1920; HHL, RUDC minutes, 3 Nov. 1920.
163 THL, BGWMC minutes, 16 July 1919.
164 Ibid. 6, 23 Jan. 1920.
165 Ibid. 16, 18 Feb. 1920.
166 Ibid. 14 Apr. 1920.

(3) The special appeal for the [London and Bethnal Green] Hospital which was being made at the same time through the schools.

(4) The economic situation, with its terrible distress so keenly felt in this district.

This latter [sic] being the most serious obstacle in the way of a really successful appeal.

I am also of the opinion that the Appeal was issued too late to achieve real success.[167]

His analysis rings true on all counts. The church schemes were never short of collectors or canvassers, although (or because) they were only working at the parish and not the borough level. Many churches and other institutions also devised war memorial schemes while the fighting was still going on, which placed schemes launched a considerable time after the Armistice at a disadvantage. The economic situation was clearly a terrible problem and in this context the fund entered the public eye at the wrong time. People were attracted to the most immediate projects first; Bethnal Green had sixteen Anglican parishes alone and their war memorial schemes were operative long before the council got into gear. The contributions made can be broken down: £183 9s. 4d. was raised by direct donation. After this came the school children with £101 0s. 3d. from the sale of 'My Brick' tickets.[168] The teachers of Bethnal Green were obviously well aware of the sacrifice and ensured that the children responded to the call.

It was therefore agreed that the fund should be wound up, and the balance spent on providing a war memorial stained-glass window at the head of the staircase leading to the library reference department. It was also agreed to place a roll of honour in a glass case with a bronze plaque

There was one further flurry of controversy in Romford in the spring of 1921 as the council procrastinated over whether to help pay for the foundations of its memorial.[169] In a final snub to the council, Dyer arranged the unveiling and informed the council that Lord Lambourne, lord lieutenant of the county, would attend. The dignity and authority of the council had been completely outflanked by one influential resident.[170] None the less the council turned out for the unveiling unhampered by a sense of irony. Lord Lambourne stressed the holy nature of the war; he told the large crowd that God had led the British armies and victory was the reward to the truly religious nation.[171] The Revd G. M. Bell dedicated the memorial: in his address the bonds of belonging and community were obvious; he took pride in their

---

[167] Ibid. 4 July 1922.
[168] Ibid.
[169] HHL, RUDC minutes, 19 Jan. 1921; *ET*, 19 Mar. 1921.
[170] HHL, RUDC minutes, 20 July 1921.
[171] *ET*, 24 Sept. 1921.

achievements and consoled the grieving by reminding them that the dead had sacrificed themselves in a noble cause:

> The names of those men on the cabinets round the memorial represented their own men who were born there and had been taught in the local schools there with their families all their lives. They were men like themselves; men with human feelings just as they had. They went out when their country called them and they fought and died for England. They had died that England might live. Their names were written in the Book of Life, which was a roll of honour more permanent than wood or stone, because it was a roll of God's Saints.[172]

But the matter was not quite finished for in December 1921 the council formally took charge of the memorial. Councillor Jones proposed a letter of thanks to Dyer; in reply Councillor Philpott said that 'he thought they had had enough of the war memorial, so far as the Council was concerned (Hear, hear). It would be best to let the matter drop otherwise they would only stir up the mud'. Councillor Rudkin supported Philpott 'for once' but other councillors then started to discuss the fiasco. As the atmosphere turned ominous the chairman called the meeting to order and they moved on.[173] The war memorial was evidently the subject of lingering bitterness and controversy among the councillors. Paradoxically they wanted to forget a monument to those that liveth for evermore.

Romford Urban District therefore erected a memorial but not before a tortuous drama had been played out. The memory of the dead had little to do with it. Rather it was a debate about local finances with an unpleasant additional edge of personal animosity. An alternative leader came forward in Dyer and despite the fact that nearly two years had passed since the Armistice his bold and clear decision to erect a full-scale model gave the public a focus and provided some sense of impetus in the town. However, it must be said that only some £800 was raised in total, hardly a massive sum, only Bethnal Green raising less for its memorial. Romford fulfilled its duty to its dead, but only just; an alternative grave was unveiled in order to show the world Romford's pride in its sons and its grief at their loss, but it was not quite the response envisaged in the early days.

Bethnal Green unveiled its war memorial on 17 March 1923. The service lived up to the near farcical gestation: it was a day marred by controversy. The former mayor led a protest against the fact that ex-servicemen and the parents and relatives of the dead had not been invited. The invited guests no doubt reflected the local hierarchy. During the service a large crowd of ex-servicemen gathered outside and held their own impromptu gathering. Such an incident also helped to create the 'us and them' divide between those who fought and those who did not; it also throws up the question of what the

[172] Ibid.
[173] Ibid. 10 Dec. 1921.

memorial really enshrined.[174] The ceremony in the library itself was interrupted by a protest about the allocation of tickets 'but it subsided when two bereaved women expressed their gratitude at receiving invitations, in response to their requests to be present'.[175] The memorial, consisting of three stained-glass windows representing Manhood, Peace and Womanhood, was unveiled by the mayor. The bishop of London then dedicated it in an address buttressing the *status quo*. After referring to the difficulties of unemployment, he stated his hope that 'municipally and politically, [they] would try to remember that it was the Christian spirit they wanted at home and abroad, a brotherhood between class and classes and all nations of the world'.[176] The gathering outside the library, however, displayed different concepts of remembrance.

Poplar and Stepney

Neither Poplar nor Stepney erected a war memorial. Stepney made tentative movements and then abruptly stopped, but nothing at all happened in Poplar. Nor do the council minutes of either borough refer to any memorial plans, though Stepney did erect a tablet for council workers lost in the war.[177] It is not clear why this happened, but suggestions may be advanced. Both boroughs were hardly wealthy and both were chronically short of the major requirement for any sort of public monument – open space or parkland. Both boroughs were quite literally collections of Tower Hamlets as the dock basins, canals, railways and industries of the area divided every part of it into self-contained communities poorly linked to their neighbours. Lastly the councillors of Poplar may have found themselves deflected from thoughts of a memorial by virtue of the fact that they were in prison over the rates and relief controversy.[178]

All the local government districts examined, with the exception of Poplar and Stepney, erected some sort of official war memorial. Many factors influenced the development and success of these schemes. The relative size and wealth of the population was important, as in the case of West Ham where large corporate donations provided the great bulk of the funding. But it was equally important to decide upon a scheme swiftly and efficiently and then embark on a campaign of vigorous fund-raising. The first six months of each

174 *HKG*, 19 Mar. 1923.
175 Ibid.
176 Ibid.
177 *ELA*, 5 Apr., 16 Aug. 1919; THL, metropolitan borough of Stepney council minutes, 1918–22: see 2 July 1919 for the decision to erect a memorial; metropolitan borough of Poplar council minutes, 1918–24.
178 See Branson, *Poplarism, 1919–1925*, 61–80.

of these projects determined whether they would progress smoothly or radically otherwise. The middle-class wealth of Ilford and Romford gave both boroughs far more potential for success than areas like Bethnal Green, but in the event both erected civic memorials that really only hinted at the grandeur they thought was theirs. These failures were partly the result of not getting on with the job, of constant debating and niggling. Once the residents felt that the task was never going to get underway it became far more difficult to infuse it with life. Morevoer, the churches tended to snap up all the most enthusiastic campaigners and as their smaller-scale projects seemed to be far more realistic the momentum could be maintained and results achieved much more quickly.

Once in existence the central memorials carried a wider meaning than simply to provide a focus for the emotions of the bereaved. They were shining symbols of civic pride, fully displaying the largesse and loyalty of the community. In many ways the bereaved reclaimed these memorials via the annual Armistice Day ceremonies; civic backslapping was not part of the 11 November observance. Indeed the greatest service the central memorials came to provide was an easily recognisable focus for the Armistice Day observance. The individual found his/her solace in the churches, but expressed communal emotion around the central memorial. It is the nature of Armistice Day between 1919 and 1939 that must now be examined.

PART II

ARMISTICE DAY, 1919–1939

6

Laying the Foundations, 1919–1921

The Great War ended on 11 November 1918, the news was greeted with a day of wild, unrestrained rejoicing.[1] How, then, did the anniversary of the Armistice take on a sombre, respectable form, observed with religious zeal and dedication? Did Armistice Day have any direct antecedents?

Even before the end of the conflict there was speculation on how to commemorate the dead. Throughout the war the anniversary of Britain's entry into the conflict, 4 August, had been treated as a day of solemn prayer and reflection. In August 1918 the City of London journal, the *City Press*, stated its belief that the date would remain important long after victory had been achieved. The editor assured his readers that 'a Day of Remembrance there will always be'.[2]

But it was the unforgetable poignancy of the eleventh hour of the eleventh day of the eleventh month that was to stick in people's minds. The commemoration of the first anniversary of the Armistice, in 1919, was largely at the instigation of King George V. His secretary told him that South Africa had observed a daily two minutes silence since 1916. This idea caught the king's imagination and he requested such a silence on 11 November.[3]

It was enthusiastically received in the City, where reaction was the most crucial: if the demands of business were subdued once, and a popular desire to remember expressed, then a potent precedent would be established. Proof that the captains of commerce were willing to acquiesce in marking the anniversary can be seen in the reaction of the general purposes committee of the Stock Exchange. This met on 10 November 1919 and noted that the king had suggested a silence at eleven o'clock. It was agreed that a gong would be sounded in the main hall at eleven and at two minutes past the assembled crowd would sing the National Anthem.[4]

On the day itself the response of the public was overwhelming. The *Daily Chronicle* recorded the effect of the silence on the boys of the City of London School:

---

[1] See Siegfried Sassoon's diary entry for 11 Nov.: R. Hart-Davis (ed.), *Siegfried Sassoon diaries, 1915–1918*, London 1983, 282.
[2] CP, 4 Aug. 1918.
[3] For the full story of the gestation of the first Armistice commemoration see Gregory, *Silence of memory*, 8–12.
[4] GML, L64.6 MS 14,600, London Stock Exchange Company, general purposes committee book, no. 106, 10 Nov. 1919.

simultaneously in this temple of learning on the Embankment all instruction ceased. In 22 class rooms 22 masters a moment before had been imparting knowledge to 730 boys. Now pens no longer scratched, youthful brows unpuckered as problems were thrust aside, and the voice of authority stopped abruptly.

All rose to their feet, and intense silence ensued upon the scraping of feet – a silence emphasised by the ticking of clocks telling off the memorable two minutes.[5]

A massive crowd gathered at the main City crossroads between the Bank of England, the Royal Exchange and the Mansion House. The Lord Mayor addressed the crowd, stating: 'It was wonderful – the silence and the solemnity – the spectacle of all manner of men obeying a common impulse. It was a time for great thoughts.'[6]

The great thoughts of the first Armistice anniversary in the City revolved around the certainty of life after death. At St Vedast-alias-Foster the bishop of London 'dwelt upon the reality of the future life, and said that mothers should pray for their sons who had made the Supreme Sacrifice. In that other world, those who had passed away were still serving, and learning, and growing'.[7] An employee of Brooks Marshall's firm wrote, 'it is because I know that the heartache of millions would be relieved if they believed with certainty that their sons were living, I ask for your valuable space to say that I know that my son Rupert Wynn is alive. . . . He is happy. He is near me'.[8] The bishop was keen to stress the futility of spiritualism; only the Christian version of the after-life was certain. He said that 'mothers would find no satisfaction in spiritualism and mediums'.[9] When he spoke at the London Rifle Brigade's service it was noted that 'he warned mourning relatives and friends against spiritualism, being convinced after five years' study, that necromancy did nothing but harm'.[10] A similar message was put forward at All Hallows', East India Dock, where the rector warned his congregation that

There is much talk nowadays of 'Spiritualism' so called, as a means of communion with the dead. It may be, but the Communion it gives is a very poor thing, and the spiritual life it reveals, according to those who dabble in it, is a wretched substitute for what we Catholics hold about the Communion of the Saints.[11]

In Ilford the start of the silence was heralded by the maroons at the police station and the hooter of the *Ilford Recorder* works. The *Recorder* noted that

5 *Daily Chronicle*, 12 Nov. 1919.
6 CP, 15 Nov. 1919.
7 Ibid.
8 Ibid.
9 Ibid.
10 LRB Record, Dec. 1919, 15.
11 THL, All Hallows', East India Dock, parish magazine, Dec. 1919.

'most people were in the streets or at their doors awaiting the stroke of eleven'[12] This is an important point as it reveals that the silence was perceived as an active and communal event, not something to be done at home, but a public expression. The silence was perfectly observed and described as 'awesome beyond words'.[13] The foundation of Armistice Day traditions in East and West Ham can also be seen in the year 1919. It was a slightly strange experience as a genuine desire to commemorate the dead cast around for solid points of reference. Both boroughs saw the silence spontaneously observed; neither council had made any plans formally to mark the occasion. The *East Ham Echo* noted the fact that 'in the streets men reverently bared their heads; others stood rigidly to attention'.[14] Stratford saw a similar tribute: the *Stratford Express* reported it as an extraordinary, but pious, phenomenon:

> At 11 o'clock on Tuesday morning the sound of maroons crashed out warning of the Armistice anniversary, and there followed a scene unprecedented in the annals of the Country. . . . In Stratford Broadway the scene was a memorable one. Hundreds of people stood in silence, the men bareheaded, paying reverent homage to the memory of the fallen . . . and the silence was accentuated by the faint purring of a motor engine and a child's cry.[15]

By referring to a child's cry the *Express* had initiated one of the great clichés of Armistice Day.

The East London press responded with remarkable consistency. The *Ilford Recorder* stated that 'All the manifold activities of a busy, bustling community suddenly surceased as though under the potent spell of a magician's wand.'[16] In Romford the silence and the public response was equally striking: 'The streets were unusually animated at the time the signal was given, but immediately a profound silence prevailed, all traffic and work stopped, and everybody was standing silently in their places in reverent attitude.'[17]

There was obviously some confusion over the Armistice anniversary as many churches had arranged special All Souls' and All Saints' Day services for 1 and 2 November in order to pray for the war dead. The Church of England had in essence reinstated prayers for the dead in 1914 in order to meet the demand to mark the sacrifices.[18] In the High Church, Anglo-Catholic parishes of Poplar and Stepney 1 November was particularly important. The church of All Hallows', East India Dock, arranged prayers for the

---

12 *IR*, 14 Nov. 1919.
13 Ibid.
14 *EHE*, 14 Nov. 1919.
15 *SE*, 12 Nov. 1919.
16 *IR*, 4 Nov. 1919.
17 *ET*, 15 Nov. 1919.
18 See Wilkinson, *The Church and the war*, 176.

war dead, as did St Anne's, Limehouse.[19] In Romford the vicar of St Edward's organised a complete roll-call of the dead on 1 November.[20]

Ben Thomas, a schoolboy in Limehouse in 1919, recorded his memories of that time in his autobiography, *Ben's Limehouse*:

> Another big event at Northey Street School was the 11th of November, which was Armistice Day in honour of all those killed in the 1914–1918 War. I remember the very first one. It was a cold, dull day, and as we waited around the flag mast with the Union Jack at half-mast, there was a loud gun fire, a fraction after which there were many others, and then complete silence. It was so uncanny to me, those two minutes silence seemed to last for so long I thought they would never end. Then the loud bang of the gun fire let us know that the two minutes were over. Then we began to sing, 'Oh Valiant Hearts'.[21]

Despite the mass public response, some elements of doubt over the permanence of the Silence were expressed. Sir Charles Wakefield, Lord Mayor of London, wrote to the *City Press* and stated that 'It will probably not be possible to repeat this formal commemoration at succeeding anniversaries of this historic day, and, in any case, the idea is one which would suffer by being stereotyped as an annual ceremony.'[22]

On the second anniversary of the Armistice a correspondent to the East Ham parish magazine, upset at the lack of an Armistice Day service in 1920, urged the Church to take a positive lead. He asked

> why, during the heart-stirring times and the spiritual emotions aroused during the Armistice celebrations, nothing was done to stimulate the people of East Ham to join again in a hearty service of praise to God?
> Surely it was an occasion to have one, and I believe there are many who would have welcomed the opportunity. [He spoke of the war encouraging Christian sentiment and added] surely it must be for good to encourage and stimulate that feeling by arranging a service where the opportunity should be given of expressing that relief and joy? It was not only in 1918 when people experienced these emotions, and I am sure there are very many who, as the time comes round, have vivid memories of the great moment – so I say it should be a duty to keep alive the feeling of that eventful time – Lest We Forget.[23]

This also reveals how far churchgoers at least saw the Church as a natural leader and expected the day to have a Christian connotation: the Church was

---

19 THL, All Hallows', East India Dock, parish magazine, Nov. 1919; St Anne's, Limehouse, parish magazine, Dec. 1919.

20 *ET*, 15 Nov. 1919.

21 Thomas, *Ben's Limehouse*, 54.

22 *CP*, 3 Jan. 1920.

23 NHL, East Ham parish magazine, Dec. 1920. This also reflected the wider feeling that the Church could have used the war to promote a greater awareness of Christianity: Wilkinson, *The Church and the war*, 72–90.

equipped with a language of consolation, hope and even had a day of the dead in the same month as the Armistice, so it was in the best position to interpret the meaning of the sacrifice and reaffirm its worth. This fact can clearly be seen in the parish of All Hallows', East India Dock, where the rector noted

> Remember November. It is the month of Remembrance. It has been for centuries the month for Remembrance of the Faithful Departed, who await the final coming of our Lord, the Holy Souls with whom we have such sweet communion at the Altar. And the past November has been a special month of Remembrance for millions, who except as it touched themselves, never before thought much of their state.[24]

The ancient significance of November as a month of the dead was equally evident at St Michael and All Angels', Bromley-by-Bow. The parish magazine stated that:

> November is sometimes called the 'Month of the Dead'. But we thank God that there are no dead, and that those who have passed from our company in this world are alive, in the safe keeping of the Father.
>
> The Anniversary of the signing of the Armistice naturally brings to our minds the thoughts of those who have given their lives for us, and we should remember them with thankfulness before God, praying that all that yet is wanting to complete their happiness may be granted to them. We should all make an effort to be present at Mass, on All Souls' Day, and at other Requiems through the month, when our prayers for the peace and happiness of our dear ones may go up in union with the Pleading of the Great Sacrifice.[25]

As Christian theology had given the churches the leadership of the war memorial movement, the same reason gave them domination over Armistice Day; this was especially true in the absence of borough war memorials in the immediate post-war years. War memorial unveilings between 1919 and 1921 gave the churches blueprints for remembrance services: the language of Armistice Day was formulated during dedication services. It has been possible to identify the unveiling and dedication of some twenty-six memorials in East and West Ham between January 1919 and Armistice Day 1921, forty-one in the City, twenty-two in Tower Hamlets, ten in Ilford and three in Romford. An example is the parish of St Clement's, Great Ilford. The church war memorial windows were unveiled and dedicated in November 1919; the following November the oak panels containing the roll of honour were fitted and dedicated. Armistice Day 1921 was therefore the first one with the

---

[24] THL, All Hallows', East India Dock, parish magazine, Dec. 1920.
[25] THL, St Michael and All Angels', Bromley-by-Bow, parish magazine, Nov. 1920. The general cultural connection between November and death can be seen in the last lines of Thomas Hood's (1799–1845) poem 'No!': 'No shade, no shine, no butterflies, no bees/No fruits, no flowers, no leaves, no birds – November!': W. Jerrold (ed.), *The complete poetical works of Thomas Hood*, Oxford 1911, 364.

complete memorial. Ottaway arranged two special services, one for Sunday 6 November and one for 11 November. He obviously expected a great response from the parishioners; he appealed for the floral offerings to be brought to the church on the afternoon of Saturday 5 November in order for them to be arranged around the memorial for the Sunday service. He then conducted his Armistice services in a manner very similar to his memorial unveiling ceremonies and wrote 'how deeply stirring are those sacred memories created by the years of war'.[26] This gave the day a ritual status which provided the bereaved with a sense of reassuring solidity; Wilkinson has written on the subject:

> In situations that are totally new and bewildering, rituals can supply boundaries and signposts, so reducing the sense of chaotic novelty; through the familiar rituals a sense of solidarity is established with both 'normal' life beyond the emergency, and with previous generations. Rituals can 'contain' feelings too overwhelming or perplexing to be otherwise expressed.[27]

1920 was also a key year as it saw the burial of the Unknown Warrior and the unveiling of the permanent Cenotaph; a tradition of war remembrance was evoked at a stroke.[28] The effect of these events on East London was obvious: the significance of the Unknown Warrior lay in his sheer universality; he was all things to all people. The rector of St Giles, Cripplegate, suggested two reasons for his power. First, the ability to appeal to an ancient, subconscious instinct:

> How easily we 'revert to type'. Tens of thousands of people have gone on pilgrimage to the grave of the 'Unknown Warrior'. And that is how tens of thousands of people used to go, in olden days, on pilgrimage to the shrine of St Edward in the self same Abbey, or to the shrine of St Thomas a Becket at Canterbury.[29]

He then made him an ordinary man, with all the ties of an ordinary man:

> Unknown today; yet then dear in some home, and the centre of some grouping of love and affection and hope. Some mother's darling; someone's friend. Today the sovereign of an Empire follows the unknown body to its resting place.[30]

W. H. Stevens wrote in similar terms in the *Ilford War Memorial Gazette*. He

---

[26] St Clement's, Great Ilford, parish magazine, Nov. 1919, Nov. 1920, Oct., Nov. 1921.
[27] Wilkinson, *The Church and the war*, 133–4.
[28] See David Cannadine's essay 'War and death, grief and mourning in modern Britain', in J. Whaley (ed.), *Mirrors of mortality: studies in the social history of death*, London 1981, 187–252.
[29] GBL, St Giles, Cripplegate, parish magazine, Dec. 1920.
[30] CP, 13 Nov. 1920.

stressed the role of the king and the importance of the warrior to women in particular:

> In that moment the King-Emperor steps out, a solitary modest figure in the khaki service dress of war. He stands, comrade to greet comrade, mourner to reverence the dead that was so great, back to the Cenotaph. . . . Would you know who lies in state? That shall never be. Just one and all who died that we shall live. Your son and our brother. . . . Of all the scenes of this memorable occasion that which followed was the most poignant. It was the march past of the bereaved. Aged mothers and youthful widows, women whose garb betrayed their poverty and others of obvious means and station, but sisters alike in their sorrow, walked by with streaming eyes.[31]

At All Hallows', East India Dock, the vicar made the Unknown Warrior the subject of his monthly letter in the parish magazine:

> The Unknown Warrior lies there a symbol of the highest ideal, not of the common ruck who did not care. His grave is the glorious tomb of every lad who understood what England in her most exalted and unselfish mood stood and stands for.[32]

It was a simple reminder to duty and service and thus confirmed the ideals that sent the men to war. In Romford Scoutmaster Ashby addressed the Church of England's Men's Meeting; he too spoke on the subject of the self-less Unknown Warrior and compared him to 'Our Boys' and 'the youths who were filling the ranks of the fallen'.[33] In short, the youth of Romford could find no better role model than that contained in the hagiography of the Unknown Warrior. When the bishop of London unveiled the Parmiter's School memorial he too referred the boys to the example of the Unknown Warrior and linked him to their own dead:

> He had been privileged to walk behind the body of the Unknown Warrior, and he said that he knew of no more glorious event than that burial. They gloried in those boys' splendid sacrifice. Those boys had gone to a fuller and far more joyous life than they had had at home or at Parmiter's. Christ was making those boys happy in Paradise.[34]

He was also the comrade of every ex-serviceman. The London Rifle Brigade provided a pall bearer, who recalled his thoughts as he carried the casket: 'I saw again faces that I had not seen for years; scenes of war came back to me, but purged of their horror in the light of that sacrifice.'[35] From the medieval saint to the mother's son, the warrior filled all hearts. Westminster and

---

[31] RHL, *Ilford War Memorial Gazette*, no. 3 (Dec. 1920), 2.
[32] THL, All Hallows', East India Dock, parish magazine, Dec. 1920.
[33] *ET*, 20 Nov. 1920.
[34] *IR*, 17 Dec. 1920.
[35] *LRB Record*, Dec. 1920, 11.

Whitehall, the administrative heart of the empire, made their great gesture; the City of London, the commercial heart of the empire, also came to a halt in order to salute the glorious dead. There was such a popular desire to take part in the second anniversary that the church of St Catherine Coleman, closed for more than two years, was forced to re-open to admit City workers who wanted to observe the silence.[36]

The tradition was set and was further confirmed in 1921. At the Mansion House crowds gathered; the Corporation laid wreaths at the London Troops' memorial and then the crowds were addressed. Sir Charles Wakefield stated that they should not be too down-hearted at what had happened since the war, an admission that perhaps the world was not quite in a utopian condition. It did not stop people keeping the already seemingly ancient Armistice traditions. Armistice Day took on a mantle similar to Christmas and Easter insofar as it induced the most reluctant Christian into church:

> The people poured in like an avalanche. The Churchwardens, and members of the Men's Committee, were taxed to the uttermost in finding accommodation for the enormous crowd. We filled every seat, and the choir stalls, and then hundreds stood. It was not the crowd that was impressive. It was their deeply reverent demeanour, and the way in which so many were evidently touched.[37]

The sentiments expressed on Armistice Day thus mirrored those demonstrated during dedication services. Belonging was an important component: in 1919 the *East Ham Echo* spoke of 'the dignity of silence consecrated to the memory of *"Our Boys"* ' [emphasis added].[38] Consolation was offered to the bereaved: at Plaistow Congregational church the dead were described as 'new crusaders'.[39] Use of this image reassured the bereaved that their loved ones had died in a holy war, purifying the world, and like the original crusaders the dead could expect Paradise as a right. It was also a time to reaffirm the reasons for the conflict: the *Express* wrote of 'the re-establishment of humanity's tenets in a bloodsoaked continent'. In the magistrates' court, a JP told the court that 'German power was a threat to the world; and the world recognised it.'[40] But perhaps the most potent message came in the *West Ham Central Secondary School Magazine*. The glory of the sacrifice was described in purple prose:

> 'We died for England' – yes, for the land which fought in the European War because she had never realised that it could be possible for any nation to throw aside solemn promises. This was the land for which so many men and boys

36 *CP*, 13 Nov. 1920. The universality of the Unknown Warrior was perfectly captured by C. F. G. Masterman who wrote: 'We were burying every boy's father, and every woman's lover, and every Mother's child': quoted in Wilkinson, *The Church and the war*, 299.
37 GBL, St Giles, Cripplegate, parish magazine, Dec. 1921.
38 *EHE*, 14 Nov. 1919.
39 *SE*, 13 Nov. 1920.
40 Ibid. 12 Nov. 1919.

made the Great Sacrifice in the Great War, that her traditions and reputations might remain untarnished.[41]

Big Words indeed. Remembrance of the dead reminded the young of their duty to protect England and all she stood for, just as their predecessors had done.

But Armistice Day was not only used to promote a common purpose in schools. In the peculiar atmosphere of the East End it was also seen as a moment when racial barriers disappeared. An article on Armistice Day in the Mile End Road appeared in the *East London Observer* in 1921. It covered many themes and included a note on the Jewish community, describing an incident when a Jewish and a Christian boy imitated soldiers in the moments leading up to the silence:

> A band of children passes by – the pavement is wide and allows them to 'form fours'. At their head is a chubby faced Jewish boy, while his lieutenant is clearly a Christian. Both wear paper cocked hats. Their 'army' has no uniform as yet; but it does not seem to worry them, for they are singing at the top of their voices 'It's a long, long way to Tipperary'. A policeman sees them, and looks the other way. Who knows but what they are the Haigs and Beattys of the future?[42]

Haig and Beatty were obviously the men who had won the war and were therefore glorious heroes, fitting subjects for the boys, unified by nationality, to follow.

Unity was also at a premium at the works of C. and E. Morton in Millwall. The firm unveiled its war memorial on Armistice Day 1920; the management gave ex-servicemen pride of place in the factory yard in an act of humility and respect. An occasion of communal remembrance was used by the directors to subtly reinforce the hierarchy for a moment by inverting it.[43]

But Armistice Day was also used to highlight social and economic problems in the East End. In 1921 the radical borough of Poplar voted to 'assist in every possible way the demonstration which is being organised for the unemployed on Armistice Day, as a protest against the proposals of the Government in limiting wages to 75 per cent of current rates, and to demand provision of work'.[44]

The potent symbol of the poppy entered Armistice Day symbolism in these years. Poppies were first sold in 1921 by the Royal British Legion which had been formed earlier that year as the result of the merger of most of the different bodies representing ex-servicemen. The Legion promoted contributions to the poppy appeal as a way of helping the living, while showing

41 NHL, *West Ham Central Secondary School Magazine*, Winter 1920, 43.
42 *ELO*, 12 Nov. 1921.
43 *EEN*, 16 Nov. 1920.
44 THL, metropolitan borough of Poplar, council minutes, 27 Oct. 1921.

respect for the dead. The idea had actually originated in America, but soon crossed over to Britain. Its appeal was twofold. It already had a firm connection with the battlefields of France and Flanders, immortalised in John McCrae's poem 'In Flanders Fields'; further it had ancient connections with sleep and restfulness. Such a combination ensured that the poppy appeal would strike a chord with the British public.[45]

The first appeal in Ilford was organised by Councillor and Mrs J. Waters. As Adrian Gregory has noted, 'selling poppies was a female prerogative',[46] and this was certainly true of Ilford where it soon became the work of a few highly dedicated women. The response was phenomenal; the original batch of poppies was sold out by the late evening of Thursday 10 November. Mrs Waters managed to obtain 5,000 more but these were gone long before 11.00 a.m. on the eleventh. In the true spirit of British improvisation the ladies bought a supply of red ribbon and made their own poppies, but even these ran out before the silence. The total collected was £450 3s. 4d., an amazing amount when compared to the agonies of the local war memorial fund. The poppies had an enviable advantage in that the campaign had received national media coverage. Nevertheless it also shows the deep seated desire to actively remember the dead and to be seen to be doing so.[47]

Women therefore had a crucial role in the observance of Armistice Day. The first Armistice silence in Ilford was marked by the fact that the Ilford Women's War Help Society had purchased a wreath inscribed 'A tribute of love and gratitude to the memory of our noble boys, who passed to the great Beyond, 1914–1918.' This was displayed in the High Road and then taken to Whitehall and laid at the foot of the temporary Cenotaph.[48] A year later it was once again the women of Ilford who were in the vanguard. The War Help Society again purchased a wreath, this time in conjunction with the Ilford Housewives Union and the Liberal War Workers, which was placed against the clock tower in the High Road and then taken to the Cenotaph.[49] The rector of St Giles, Cripplegate, had implied the peculiar significance of the Unknown Warrior to women when he referred to him as 'some mother's darling'. Stevens seemed to be making the same point in the *Ilford War Memorial Gazette*, when he mentioned a woman who 'could not control her sobs' and further that 'The "Unknown Warrior" is the symbol of every "husband", "son", "brother" or "loved one" who fell in the Great War. About his glorious tomb will centre the sorrows of the bereaved, and in the imperishable beauty of his fate they will find solace.'[50] In 1921 a Miss Y. M.

---

[45] For the full story of the British Legion and the origins of the poppy appeal see G. Wootton, *The official history of the British Legion*, London 1956, 37–41, 142–3.
[46] Gregory, *Silence of memory*, 101.
[47] IR, 18 Nov. 1921.
[48] Ibid. 14 Nov. 1919.
[49] Ibid. 12 Nov. 1920.
[50] RHL, *Ilford War Memorial Gazette*, no. 3 (Dec. 1920), 2.

Alexander submitted a piece to the *East London Observer* on Armistice Day in the Mile End Road. She mentioned a woman falling to her knees in prayer and grief at the stroke of eleven.[51] The day was thus connected with the bereaved and the female bereaved in particular, over and above the responses of ex-servicemen.[52]

Armistice Day was shaped in the years 1919–21: those three years saw the day establish itself in the public imagination and take on all the attributes that were to distinguish it for the following twenty years. A desire to do something was clear, but it needed the guidance of local leaders to transform the day into a tangible and consoling exercise. The City, a great impresario of pageants and public spectacles, took on the Armistice tradition by combining its own elements of stage management with the very obvious public desire to uphold the anniversary. Other districts reacted by establishing their own Armistice traditions. But like the war memorials, Armistice Day performed more than one function. It was not just an occasion of grief and consolation; it was also a day of pride and of re-dedication to a set of ideals. The years 1922–9 saw Armistice Day reach maturity, a rich tapestry of symbols developing around it.

[51] *ELO*, 12 Nov. 1921.
[52] Adrian Gregory explores the general connection of women with Armistice Day but although he mentions the significance of the Unknown Warrior to bereaved women he implies that it was not until the late twenties that women were specifically linked with the day: 'By the late 1920s perception was being channelled through rhetorical constructions, one of which was the association of the bereaved with women. . . . A language had grown up around Armistice Day, for which the bereaved, usually pictured as women, were the main subjects': *Silence of memory*, 31–43. Although the connection certainly did become stronger the material examined for this study implies a special link between women, those mourning and Armistice Day from its inception.

7

The Years Rich in Imagery, 1922–1929

The years between 1922 and 1929 saw Armistice Day come to full maturity. The elements laid down between 1919 and 1921 were expanded upon and as the war memorial process tailed off towards the mid-twenties the day became the major focal point of remembrance. Deep reverence and a high level of public interest were the touchstones throughout these years as Armistice Day took on an aspect of seriousness and reflection by confining itself to the values enshrined in the war memorials. The annual act of remembrance was therefore also a catharsis as it provided a comforting reminder of exactly why men had fought and died.

The values of Armistice and the establishment of 'Armistice Sunday'

Sacrifice, duty and patriotism were the concepts reiterated each 11 November. The *Prudential Bulletin* reminded all its workers of the glory of sacrifice and devotion to duty:

> when we cease from our work at the historic eleventh hour and meditate upon its significance, our thoughts will lead us back through the avenue of years and recall to us those who proved by their sacrifice to what heights of loyalty, devotion, and greatness of service the sons of men may rise.[1]

The amazing thing about Armistice Day in the years from 1922 to 1929 was its consistency; the atmosphere of the occasion was remarkably solid and reassuring. When Ben Thomas vividly recalls the Armistice observations of his youth, the clarity of his recollection is surely – in part – due to the sheer repetition of certain images:

> I was in the main road at the time of the two minutes silence, at eleven o'clock. All the traffic came to a standstill, and most of it was horse traffic at that time. People on the pavement all stood still, and as you can guess, the trams and buses also came to a standstill. People stood at their street doors or leaned out of their windows, and some factories let their employees stand at the factory gates. The war memorials in parishes and villages had a good congregation around them, and many beautiful wreaths laid around them. The war memorial in Limehouse Church park used to get a big congregation

---

1 PB, Nov. 1924, 32.

around it on November 11th, and many beautiful wreaths were laid at its foot.[2]

If anything the day became increasingly respectable and reverential. In the early years it had retained some elements of frivolous triumphalism, as noted by Canon T. G. Rogers in his Armistice service of 1923, but by 1925 the *Stratford Express* reported that

> Hitherto it was looked upon as quite the proper thing to spend at least the evening of Armistice Day in social pleasantries and trivialities thereby effectively robbing the day of its true significance. As a day of remembrance it ran the risk of being obliterated or reduced to travesty. This year, however, efforts were made in good time to ensure a higher conception of the day's meaning.[3]

The growing solemnity of Armistice Day was also noted in Ilford and the City. In 1923 it fell on a Sunday and this was generally perceived as the main factor behind the more sombre reaction to the day. It was a day on which the City was usually deserted, but such was the interest in the event that a large crowd gathered at the London Troops' memorial; at St Botolph, Bishopsgate, 'the church was filled to overflowing, and many came in from the streets to stand for the solemn silence'.[4] The parish magazine of St Clement's, Great Ilford, noted that

> The observance of the 'Day of Remembrance' was marked everywhere by a more religious spirit, and Ilford was a conspicuous example of the more excellent way of keeping Armistice Day. It is fitting that it should be so on the first occasion since the War on which the 'Day of Remembrance' has fallen on a Sunday. . . . It is a most hopeful sign that calls for thanksgiving and for renewed effort to retain the same spirit as we pass into the 'Great Silence' year by year.[5]

The rector of St Giles, Cripplegate, concurred with these statements and believed that the Armistice Day falling on a Sunday was the ideal chance for people fully to comprehend the meaning of remembrance:

> Armistice Day falling on a Sunday will give people plenty of time to THINK, and a little quiet thought is worth a great deal of sensationalism.
> If our words can influence anyone, this is what we appeal for: to mark the day as a day of quiet thought and remembrance.[6]

The connection of Armistice Day with the religious observances of the Christian sabbath was extremely important; the holy aura surrounding the

---

2 Thomas, *Ben's Limehouse*, 54.
3 *SE*, 14 Nov. 1923, 14 Nov. 1925.
4 *CP*, 17 Nov. 1923.
5 St Clement's, Great Ilford, parish magazine, Dec. 1923.
6 GBL, St Giles, Cripplegate, parish magazine, Nov. 1923.

Plate 9. Armistice Day 1928, Poplar Central Methodist Hall

day was effectively sealed by this juxtaposition. In Ilford the Church had been very quick to seize on the connection and had established a 'Remembrance Sunday' as opposed to an Armistice Day as early as 1922. The vicar of Ilford, Ottaway of St Clement's, organised two special remembrance services on Sunday 5 November and invited the district council and the British Legion to attend.[7] In some ways the interest in Remembrance services on the Sunday nearest Armistice Day was natural in Ilford. Of all the areas studied, its war memorial was the most remote from its residential centre (and heavily criticised for the fact) which meant that attendance there was almost impossible when Armistice Day fell on a weekday. The silence in Ilford was therefore usually observed at the town hall in the High Road. As the Armistice fell on a Sunday in 1923 a civic service was held at the memorial; it was greeted with massive public interest. The *Ilford Recorder* noted 'the vast multitude of people stretching along the roadway far to the left and right, *among them many whose business on previous Armistice Days had made it impossible for them to be near their own, local memorial* [emphasis added]'.[8] The *Recorder* had recognised the vital fact that only on a Sunday could the day be a truly communal, civic event, especially when the war memorial was relatively difficult to reach. Ilford Urban District Council appeared to take note of the public

7 St Clement's, Great Ilford, parish magazine, Nov. 1922.
8 *IR*, 16 Nov. 1923.

response: in 1924 the official service at the memorial took place on the Sunday nearest to Armistice Day. No other district covered in this survey took such a step. But it did not quite suit everyone as people gathered outside the town hall on the 11th only to find that nothing had been arranged. Undeterred, the crowd spontaneously kept the silence and sang the National Anthem at its conclusion.[9] Matters were finally resolved a year later when two official ceremonies took place, one at the town hall on the 11th and the second at the war memorial on the Sunday nearest the 11th. Ilford had effectively recognised the importance of both Remembrance Sunday and the exact Armistice anniversary in the lives of the people.[10]

This shift gave the day an added element of solidity and reverence. By the mid-twenties the effect was generally felt throughout the City and East London. In 1925 the rector of St Giles, Cripplegate, noted that 'the intense reverence was all that could be desired' and 'prayer and seriousness are more appropriate for today than revelry and forgetfulness'.[11] These sentiments were echoed by the Revd Havelock Davidson of All Saints', Goodmayes:

> There is evidence on all sides that the Armistice was better observed this year, in every respect, than in any year since 1918. There was less of the gala spirit, and more of the re-dedication to the tasks that lie before us. That is all to the good, for I am sure that unless the keeping of Armistice is going to make for the inspiration to us all to nobler endeavour and higher ideals of personal and national life, then it had far better be dropped altogether. If anyone wants to see how an anniversary of mere exultant rejoicing will degenerate they have only to look around on Guy Fawkes' Day. We certainly don't want a repetition of that in connection with the Armistice, for apart from its stupidity, it would only tend to keep open the wounds of war among the nations, wounds which every man of good will must want to see healed.[12]

This perception arrived a little later in Poplar and Stepney but it was felt nevertheless. In 1927 the *East London Observer* stated that 'It has been generally observed that the ninth anniversary of the signing of the Armistice at the end of the Great War has been more marked in acceptance and reverence than any preceding anniversary.'[13]

Such an action (or indeed reaction) had also been debated in the national press. The morality of Armistice balls and concerts had been a theme of contention between the *Daily Express* and the *Daily Mail*. The *Mail* objected to such trivial events whereas the *Express* defended the right to party on Armistice night.[14] The controversy also opened up the question of whom

9   Ibid. 14 Nov. 1924.
10   Ibid. 13 Nov. 1925. For a general study of the Armistice Day/Remembrance Sunday debate in the twenties and thirties see Gregory, *Silence of memory*, 188–9.
11   GBL, St Giles, Cripplegate, parish magazine, Dec. 1925; *CP*, 14 Nov. 1925.
12   All Saints', Goodmayes, parish magazine, Dec. 1925.
13   *ELO*, 19 Nov. 1927.
14   For a fuller analysis of this debate see Gregory, *Silence of memory*, 74–7. The Ypres League

Armistice Day served – the bereaved or the ex-servicemen? It was the ex-service community that most enjoyed a good sing-song and indeed General Sir Ian Hamilton defended the old soldiers' right to enjoy themselves when he addressed the North West Ham branch of the British Legion during Armistice Week 1925.[15] In Ilford the difference between those who served and those who did not was graphically demonstrated during the Armistice of 1923. The Revd F. C. Barton of Cranbrook Wesleyan church addressed his congregation and recounted his experiences on the Western Front. He spoke of the horror of war and the glory of comradeship and expressed his firm desire that the War should truly be the War to end war. He quoted Abraham Lincoln's famous words from the Gettysburg Address:

> The memory of the great wastage of life – of which at least 95 per cent should have been with us today – ought to spur every humane being and ought to be a command to those who profess to act in the spirit of Christ, not to rest until the foul practice of war, unclean and inglorious in its general ethics, no matter how fine the personal courage of soldiers may be, has been swept from the earth.[16]

At exactly the same moment the Revd H. V. Eardley-Wilmot was taking the Territorial Army service at the battalion drill hall. He spoke of those who answered 'the call of God, King and Country' and urged them to remember the 'dauntless courage, the glorious heroism, the steadfast endurance, the ready sacrifice of those who died that we might live'. His patriotic, glorious paean was then also given extra gravity with Abraham Lincoln's words: 'We here highly resolve that these dead shall not have died in vain.'[17] Two clergymen, both quoting from the same source, offered differing interpretations of the war: the key to their divergent approaches to Armistice Day lay in the fact that one was an ex-serviceman whilst the other had never seen the Western Front.

Armistice Day therefore increasingly saw ex-servicemen retreat into their own world, holding their own services and indulging in their own particular brand of memories. In Poplar and Stepney the Old Comrades' Association of the 17th London Regiment, the Poplar and Stepney Rifles, met at their battalion church of St Stephen's, Bow, each Armistice Day. Their chaplain, the Revd G. H. Lancaster, always took the service. In 1924 the Revd C. C. T. Wood, also a chaplain in the 47th London Division, joined him in leading

---

was condemned for holding a grand ball at the Royal Albert Hall on 30 November 1922: *Ypres Times: Journal of the Ypres League*, Apr. 1923, 9.

[15] *SE*, 19 Nov. 1925. Hamilton had commanded the ill-fated Gallipoli expedition but retained his dashing reputation. He became president of the London Area British Legion after the war. See his autobiography, *Listening for the drums*, London 1944.

[16] *IR*, 15 Nov. 1923.

[17] Ibid.

the service.[18] The sermons were tailored to suit the audience and both men drew together a number of themes inspired by their own joint war experiences.[19] During Armistice week 1923 the *East London Advertiser* carried a piece on the British Legion by a correspondent named 'Poppy'. Unsurprisingly, it was virtually an advertisement for the Legion but it contained the ironic exhortation to ex-servicemen to claim 'their place in the sun'.[20]

As the ex-servicemen retreated the bereaved slowly became the real owners of Armistice Day. Their hold was clearly illustrated by the *Prudential Bulletin* in 1923. Despite the firm's close association with the London Territorial battalions, the day was perceived as primarily an expression of bereavement rather than a tribute to the company's ex-servicemen:

> On this day of commemoration our thoughts turn first to those who by the sacrifice of their lives made Victory possible; our grief is still keen, but their memory is fragrant and our gratitude is deep.
>
> We rejoice with those who came through the fiery trial unscathed and were spared to return to their homes with strength and energy unimpaired; we would also remember with affectionate sympathy those in our midst who were scarred, injured, and broken in the fight.[21]

The desire to impose a sombre atmosphere on the whole day may partly have been triggered by guilt. In the early twenties the residents of East and West Ham were reminded of their neglect of ex-servicemen. When he unveiled the East Ham memorial, Lord Horne spoke of their obligations to the survivors; the Territorial Army service in West Ham Park, for Armistice 1923, saw the clergyman refer to ex-servicemen and unemployment; the Revd J. Merrin spoke on the same subject in Stratford church, also in 1923.[22] A sense of guilt, this time over the deaths, was very clear in a short story entitled 'The Cenotaph' which appeared in the St Matthew's, Manor Park, Men's Meeting magazine. The story was set in 1970 and centred around a government minister who is forced to sacrifice his son in order to avoid war with Germany. With his son dead the minister agonises over what he has done. Finally, he resolves 'I would not have given them my son, except for the sake of Humanity.' Then the story concludes on a reassuring, if solemn, note:

---

[18] The 47th Division was a Territorial Force formation which included the Poplar and Stepney Rifles: Maude, *47th (London) Division*, 227, 242.

[19] *ELA*, 15 Nov. 1924.

[20] Ibid. 24 Nov. 1923. The phrase was ironic: it had been used by the German Count von Bulow in the Reichstag in 1897 to justify Germany's plans for an empire: *Oxford dictionary of quotations*, London 1982 edn, 106.

[21] *PB*, Nov. 1922, 16. For the company war record see H. E. Boisseau, *The Prudential staff and the Great War*, London 1938.

[22] *EHE*, 15 July 1921; *SE*, 14 Nov. 1923; NHL, Stratford church parish magazine, Nov. 1923.

In the moonlight, as in the sunlight, the Minister's head was bowed and bared. He walked slowly along Whitehall until he reached the Cenotaph, and placed a wreath at the foot of it. For a few moments he stood motionless. Big Ben boomed the hour as he passed on, heedless of the indicative light in St Stephen's tower, passing on – but to return to Duty.[23]

A story such as this provided many reassuring messages to parents or widows struck by guilt over the deaths of their loved ones or in doubt as to the value of the sacrifice. By using a man in authority, equality of sacrifice was introduced; no group had been spared loss, and the loss was glorious as it was for the good of humanity.

Consolation and reassurance were an integral part of the Armistice Day observance, just as it was in the war memorial movement.

Christian imagery and Armistice Day

Christianity was the main source of comfort and Christian images permeated the language of the day. No death had been in vain, all sacrifice was worthy and pleasing to God; such a message was a great comfort to the bereaved. The Revd A. E. Wilkinson, chaplain to the 'Cast Iron Sixth', addressed this theme in 1929. He took into account the fact that over ten years had elapsed since the Armistice:

> It was true to say that every family that had suffered the loss of a father, a brother, or a son was, in a sense, the richer for it, since the memory of the lost one raised the quality of their thoughts and reminded them continually of one of the noblest Christian values. If this were so, and he believed it was, then there had been, in a sense, no waste.
>
> There had been a great but gradual change in people's attitude to the dead. No longer did we mourn with that intensity that marked our first inexpressible grief. That had given place to feelings of proud and grateful remembrance.[24]

The slow dulling of the pain of grief was another strand of the Armistice celebrations in the twenties. No one dared to suggest that the grief would ever totally pass away, only that it would be balanced by a deeper sense of gratitude

---

[23] NHL, St Matthew's, Manor Road, Men's Meeting magazine, *The Steeple*, Nov. 1923. Stanley Baldwin recognised the guilt of those too old to have served in the war. He knew that they needed a positive aim in life in order to overcome this feeling. In 1925 he told the Leeds Luncheon Club that 'There is nothing in the first twenty years after the war that can make good to this country the loss of so many men of that age. And that was an additional reason why we men who were middle-aged already when the war began should have banded ourselves together by the time the war ended under a vow to our better selves that we would give for the rest of our lives, as a thank-offering to the dead, nothing but the best services we could render to our country': S. Baldwin, *On England*, Glasgow 1926, 64. In other words they too had 'to return to Duty'.

[24] *City of London Rifles Quarterly Journal*, Dec. 1929.

and remembrance. In December 1923 it was noted that 'the passage of time may dull the sharp edge of grief . . . but ever the dear remembrance is with us of our pride in those Glorious Dead'.[25] The *Ilford Recorder* caught this spirit perfectly and implied that it was the parents of the dead who were most deeply hurt by the loss:

> We renew today our sympathy with the bereaved. Time, the great healer, has done much, but Time will never really heal the wounds, will never fill the void in the love and affection of the bereaved. Only eternity can do that. Our hearts go out to those who are now going down the hill of life, without the comfort and support of those they loved and tended from birth.[26]

Armistice Day had a tremendous power and was one of the few occasions when a genuine spiritual brotherhood linked people. The Revd H. C. Robins, vicar of Romford, told his congregation that

> The season was for the man and woman in the street who were largely out of touch with organised religion, the greatest spiritual opportunity of the whole year. It was their act of remembrance and dedication; an act of remembrance; first and foremost of their fallen brethren, those who, like Jesus Christ, gave their all and, like Him, passed to that fuller life which was theirs today.[27]

Beckton celebrated Armistice Day in the carpenter's shop of the Gas Light and Coke Company; it provoked a rich thread of allusions from the editor of the firm's magazine:

> Never shall I forget that silence. It seemed that great crowd of men and women bowed their heads as one and almost ceased to breathe. I do not know what were the thoughts of those people, mine did not at that moment go to our Glorious Dead. I pictured that Great yet lowly Carpenter of Nazareth looking down upon that great gathering in what would be to Him the familiar surroundings of a Carpenter's shop . . . and it seemed that He was there, giving peace and comfort to those who were mourning their lost ones.[28]

Christ was there, with the bereaved, but the Churches offered more than that. Christ took the dead soldiers to Him. The relationship between Christ and the soldiers was a much-repeated Armistice Day image. The Revd H. C. Robins reminded his congregation that Christ was 'the great Elder Brother of all who tried to live comradely and with sacrifice'.[29] Archdeacon Bayne

25 *PB*, Dec. 1923, 12.
26 *IR*, 16 Nov. 1928.
27 *ET*, 16 Nov. 1929.
28 *Co-Part. Magazine*, Dec. 1927, 25. According to Christian iconography Christ spent his childhood in the carpentry shop of his earthly father, Joseph. A much-loved painting in Victorian Britain was the Pre-Raphaelite John Millais's 'Christ in the house of his parents' (1850), showing the infant Christ, Mary and Joseph standing around a carpenter's bench: W. Shaw Sparrow (ed.), *The Gospels in art*, London 1904, 46, 110.
29 *ET*, 14 Nov. 1925.

stressed this bond and stated that 'Christ is their elder brother still, and so we thank God as we think of them on his day of remembrance'.[30] In 1932 Rutherford Lane told the East Ham Brotherhood that during the war he found a deeper faith in Christ as the 'Great Comrade'.[31] The soldiers had followed Christ and trod their own *via dolorosa* in Flanders. In 1923 the *East London Observer's* correspondent 'Wayfarer' used a potent phrase when he wrote that 'Saint Tommy Atkins' had watered the poppies of the Western Front with his own blood. He filled his piece with images reminiscent of Tennyson's 'Idylls of the king' and the quest for the Holy Grail in particular. He noted that 'Here is our great thin red line – the poppy path from Nieuport to Bapaume – the line that none can ever break.'[32] The Revd H. W. Booth of St John's, Romford, linked the act of Holy Communion to the sacrifice of the men; death in war was to imitate Christ.[33] Romford was quite unusual in this respect as it witnessed a nonconformist minister who directly linked Christ and the dead. The Revd Sinclair Phillips of the Congregational church made this point, and he also added the element of the lost generation:

He [Christ] was crucified at 33. That was their thought on that day when they remembered those who had gone. They were the flower of the nation – some of the best in the Church, and the home and the community.[34]

What they who were older should bear in mind was that it was the young men who had to pay the price of the faith they held. It was the young men who went to the Cross every time.[35]

A similar point was made in Ilford during the civic service in 1923 when the dead were described as 'representing Christ'.[36]

The dead soldiers were also portrayed as spectators, sitting at Christ's side, watching events on earth: during the West Ham Territorial Army service in 1923 it was stated that 'those who had passed on to the Great Beyond . . .

---

[30] *EHE*, 18 Nov. 1927.

[31] Ibid. 18 Nov. 1932. Rudyard Kipling's short story 'The gardener' implies a Christ-like presence in a British war cemetery. A bereaved mother is helped to locate a grave by a mysterious man; she is very grateful for his help and leaves 'supposing him to be the gardener'. The words echo John xx. 15 when the Risen Christ meets Mary Magdalen in the Garden of Gethsemane: 'She, supposing him to be the gardener, saith unto him, Sir, if thou have borne him hence, tell me where thou hast laid him': A. Rutherford (ed.), *Rudyard Kipling: war stories and poems*, Oxford 1990, 310–20.

[32] *ELO*, 24 Nov. 1923. William Russell first coined the phrase 'the thin red line' to describe the British army in the Crimea: R. Furneaux, *The first war correspondent: William Howard Russell of The Times*, London 1944, 54.

[33] *ET*, 14 Nov. 1925.

[34] Ibid. 12 Nov. 1927.

[35] Ibid. 16 Nov. 1929. The theme of youth against age and the nature of the war is discussed by Samuel Hynes in his book *A war imagined*, 383–407. However Sinclair Phillips does not use the image in the accusatory way that is identified in the Hynes thesis.

[36] *IR*, 16 Nov. 1923.

would be looking down upon them to see if they were doing their duty'.[37] East Ham's Church Army service of 1927 mixed this consoling message with the ethos of Muscular Christianity: the Revd W. C. Dyckworth said that the dead 'were watching over them as spectators at a race – watching and encouraging them by their example that they might run their race'.[38] Robins had used similar images at St Edward's, Romford:

> Those whom they remembered that day ran their course gloriously; they kept the torch burning, and their dying hands – for they gave their lives in the effort – passed on the torch to us as they fell that we might carry it still alight to the goal.[39]

It was Bunyan who provided the inspiration in Ilford; again the message was of working towards a Christian world as the dead had done. An Ilfordian wrote to the *Recorder*:

> Like the immortal traveller of the *Pilgrim's progress* we stand for a moment upon the hilltop looking back with a shudder and, at the same time, a prayer of thanksgiving at the Valley of the Shadow through which we have so lately passed and then, lifting our eyes towards the new horizon we dimly discern the outline of the Celestial City which is the end of our endeavour.[40]

The Church was thus offering the stock images of hope and consolation. But these were not enough. The people required more comfort, hence the great interest in spiritualism. Thus when the Ilford war memorial was unveiled wreaths were laid by the local psychical research society,[41] and Conan-Doyle, the viceroy of the spiritualist revival, addressed a jam-packed East Ham town hall during Armstice week 1927. His message was resolute and reassuring:

> those present that morning were assured that those vivid, living folk of the other sphere came back to them certain that when they were gathered together to do them honour, they would be there to receive it. They were

[37] *SE*, 14 Nov. 1923. For a discussion of Christ as the comrade of the soldiers see Wilkinson, *The Church and the war*, 161–4. Stanley Baldwin stated that he had felt the presence of the silent witnesses during a visit to the battlefields. He told the Canadian Vimy Pilgrims in 1936 that 'I know that feeling must have been with you at Vimy, that feeling that you were being watched by an unseen cloud of witnesses; and those witnesses are our dead, who are speaking to us today. Never can we feel that companionship and that communion more closely than at these solemn moments': S. Baldwin, *Service of our lives*, London 1937, 63.
[38] *EHE*, 18 Nov. 1927.
[39] *ET*, 14 Nov. 1925.
[40] *IR*, 9 Nov. 1928. Paul Fussell has argued that the *Pilgrim's progress* was the fundamental source of all Great War imagery, the main reason being that 'everybody had been raised on it': *The Great War and modern memory*, 137–44.
[41] *IR*, 18 Nov. 1922.

there by thousands, by tens of thousands; not changed into some etherealised form, but the same dear folks as ever, boisterous and happy.[42]

His visit clearly influenced local journalists, as the *Echo* declared of the Armistice service in Central Park:

> A company of grey shadows – the ghosts of those heroes whose names are inscribed upon the bronze tablets of the War Memorial – mingled with the crowd, sought out sorrowing relatives. Sons found their mothers, husbands found their wives, and fathers found their children.[43]

In the same year the East London Scouts held their Armistice rally at the People's Palace in Mile End. D. W. Henderson, the Chief Scout's commissioner, told the assembled boys that the dead scouts returned to stand among them during the two minutes' silence.[44] And a year later it was reported that 'the Dead prayed in unison with the living' in East Ham.[45]

Patriotism and Armistice Day: women, children and ex-servicemen

But there were other ways, aside from spiritual and religious concepts, of consoling the bereaved. Throughout the twenties constant reminder of the course of the war, and of its causes and aims, avoided any controversy over the conflict and soothed those who had suffered loss. Eardley-Wilmot told those at the Ilford Territorial drill hall that they had come together in order to remember 'those dear to us all who in the Great War made the supreme sacrifice; that justice, truth, honour and freedom might remain our heritage'.[46] His patriotism and commitment to the cause was shared by his fellow Ilfordian David Sutherland, the Presbyterian minister. In purple prose and swirling rhetoric he reiterated all the reasons why England went to war in 1914. He linked the war to history and thus placed it in an understandable context of space and time. The message was one of glory and hope:

> They were heroes, every one of them, the flower of our land and homes, and the land and the homes missed them sorely.
> They died for England, and for more than England. They died fighting for freedom, which, since the days of Boadicea, had been a precious heritage of our race.[47]

---

[42] *SE*, 19 Nov. 1927. See also K. Jones, *Conan-Doyle and the spirits: the spiritualist career of Sir Arthur Conan-Doyle*, Northampton 1989, 110, 124.
[43] *EHE*, 18 Nov. 1927.
[44] *ELO*, 19 Nov. 1927.
[45] *EHE*, 16 Nov. 1928.
[46] *IR*, 16 Nov. 1923.
[47] Ibid. 14 Nov. 1924.

England and the glory of dying for England was also at the heart of the Mile End British Legion's Armistice service. The chairman gave an equally stirring speech, full of rich images:

> the men of England played a part so noble, so heroic, that we remember it less as a great tragedy than as a great epic, in which men of every walk of life and of every race proved that in spirit and in body, in nerve and in muscle, they were not one whit inferior to the heroes of old. We were happy in those days in the knowledge that we were united; the Empire was united, and England was united as never before.[48]

Nationhood was further buttressed in 1928 when the service at the Ilford war memorial was taken by the Revd C. Reed. He reminded the crowd of the unique qualities of the British empire; he said it was an empire moulded by co-operation, not conquest; united in freedom the empire crushed the forces of militarism.[49] In the exotic racial mix of Poplar and Stepney shared nationhood and Armistice concepts were seen as solvents in which differences melted away. The Armistice service at Christ Church, Spitalfields, was marked by the fact that Jew, Protestant and Catholic ex-servicemen marched into church together.[50] They had fought together in the name of righteousness and the liberties Britain offered to its peoples. Conan-Doyle was unswerving in his belief that righteousness had triumphed. He told the residents of East Ham that if Britain had 'been the losers instead of the victors there would not have been a peace of such moderation as the Treaty of Versailles'.[51] Cinema added its considerable weight to the cause: the Super Cinema, East Ham, put on a special showing of the film *The battle of the Somme* on Armistice night 1927; in 1925 Sir Ian Hamilton addressed the North West Ham British Legion and spoke in favour of the newly released film *Ypres*. The effect of film and the cinema on Armistice Day can also be seen in Ilford, where the war film *Reveille* was put on during Armistice week 1924.[52] But one man, the Revd E. A. Gardner, became above all others the embodiment of all the wartime values. Starting in 1924, he established the Territorial Army service at All Saints', West Ham, as the great bastion of patriotism and conformity (see ch. 8). In 1927 he reminded the congregation of the long history of England and the type of men the nation forged: 'The men who fell in the war were only the successors of a long line of gallant men who had made England what it was'.[53] Exactly the same sentiment had been propounded by the headmaster of Bridge Road School in 1925: 'He recalled to their memories the names of the great men of England – men to whom

48 *ELO*, 19 Nov. 1927.
49 *IR*, 24 Nov. 1923.
50 *ELA*, 24 Nov. 1923.
51 *SE*, 19 Nov. 1927.
52 Ibid.
53 Ibid.

England had turned when she was in trouble, knowing full well they would do their duty nobly.'[54]

In constantly justifing the war, Gardner deflected any deep analysis or questioning of its conduct and nature. The glory of sacrifice and the need to be ready for further sacrifices was also the theme of the bishop of St Albans. He gave the sermon to the crowd in the Royal Exchange on Armistice Day 1926:

> Alluding to the better world, and the peace for which all were striving, and for which men had died, the Bishop said that it might be a dream and Utopian, but was it not better for a man to go over the top after having seen a glimpse of Utopia than to die in a funk-hole by the poison gas of pessimism and material-ism.[55]

The Glorious Dead had been martyred in the cause of a new world and the Armistice saw the living enlisted as labourers in the task of completing that work. In November 1923 the *Prudential Bulletin* talked of recovering material from the wreckage of world war, and using it in the foundations of a new world.[56]

Ordinary men were therefore transformed into heroes who fell in a noble cause. These facts were laid before children and teenagers: war, heroism and glorious sacrifice were constantly linked. Again the East London Scouts Armistice rally of 1927 provides an example. At this event, labelled as 'Calling to Higher Services', the dead were used to promote an image of inter-dependence and teamwork within a disciplined hierarchy. In his address Henderson told the boys that

> They must ask themselves what sort of figures they were cutting on the good ship scouting, whether they were serving in the crew or were only passengers or stowaways, and too, on that night they must realise the place their Move-ment took in the future of the world.[57]

He reminded the scouts of the sacrifices made by their predecessors and told them to 'raise your standards high in proud thankfulness, and look high your-selves'.[58] East Ham Technical College and Secondary School made the day a central part of its calendar. At no point was the message one of disillusion or doubt; the value of the sacrifice was ever sure, as was the confidence that the boys could match it if need be. In 1923 the whole school paraded past the memorial. The editor of the school magazine noted that 'One feels that it is in such moments that deep impressions are made and many secret high resolves are formed to be worthy of the sacrifices made by those who gave

[54] Ibid. 14 Nov. 1925.
[55] *CP*, 13 Nov. 1926.
[56] *PB*, Nov. 1923, 17.
[57] *ELO*, 19 Nov. 1927.
[58] Ibid.

their lives for us.'[59] It was the duty of the children to heed and follow their illustrious predecessors: 'The fight for righteousness and peace . . . is now for them to wage. It is a fight that will last all our lifetime and theirs . . . the only hope for the human race is for each boy and girl, to don his armour and cheerfully fill up the ranks of heroes.'[60]

The young were therefore targeted during the Armistice observances; they were the inheritors of the sacrifice and they were constantly reminded of it. The war was, in fact, constantly being refought. Alf French, born in West Ferry Road in 1917, remembered that

> As a young child I heard an awful lot about the Great War; we virtually lived in the Great War as we went along, so that places like Passchendaele and Ypres were almost as familiar to us as Stepney Green and Whitechapel. The result was that we tended as children to take tremendous interest in the Great War, and to know who served in it and who didn't and whose father was in it and what regiment he was in, and that sort of thing.[61]

George Lighterness, born in 1912 in Stepney, recalled Armistice Day in the twenties in his memoirs, written at the age of seventy-seven:

> Patriotism, in those Imperialistic days, was in the hearts and minds of most. The War had been fought for love of KING and COUNTRY, the Union Jack and Empire, each extolled as our Heritage, something that was significant to the great Deeds that had made Britain what it was.[62]

This emphasis on the young, which included such events as the special Armistice service for children held at St Edward's, Romford, in 1923 did not prevent the idea developing towards the end of the twenties of a gap between supposedly disinterested youth and respectful adults.[63] In November 1926 the rector of St Giles, Cripplegate, made special mention of the young in his comments on Armistice Day. He believed that the two minutes' silence served to concentrate the minds of young and old on their task of making the world a better place:

> Eight years ago, on November 11th, the bugles sounded the 'Cease Fire' in the Great World War. A new generation is growing up which must find it difficult to realise, as we older ones, what that momentous signal meant. Still they can say 'our fathers have told us', and all up and down the land, in remote villages, no less than in busy centres of life and of commerce: in school and in university as well as in factory and dockland: there stand the memorials which tell of a sacrifice paid.

[59] NHL, *EHTCSS Magazine*, Jan. 1924, 4.
[60] Ibid. Jan. 1925, 7.
[61] Quoted in Hostettler, *Childhood on the Isle of Dogs*, 34.
[62] THL, G. A. Lighterness, 'The life and times of an Eastender; in those days', typewritten autobiography, 1989.
[63] *ET*, 17 Nov. 1923.

It is well that we should be reminded of that sacrifice, for, as the hymn says, 'we forget so soon' . . . Armistice Day may well recall us all to serious thoughts beyond the Two Minutes.[64]

In 1929 the editor of the *Essex Times* bemoaned the 'aloofness and something of indifference among those young people who have grown into early manhood and early womanhood during the eleven years which have gone'.[65] But that does not quite tally with a letter from an ex-serviceman, complaining about his treatment during the 1928 Armistice services in Romford. He said the services were:

led by all kinds of organisations, largely composed of juveniles, many of whom know nothing of the war. This in itself has caused many a grouse and kept many ex-servicemen from attending, but when comrades . . . are refused admission to the church, while the aforesaid juveniles are admitted, I think it time that a protest is made, so that in future years service may be recognised before uniform, pomp and show.[66]

The pomp and show put on for children also worried the Revd G. A. Studdert-Kennedy of St Edmund, King and Martyr, in the City. He was a respected authority on matters to do with the war, for during the conflict he had been a chaplain and had won great respect and affection as the ciga-rette-donating 'Woodbine Willie'.[67] In 1922 he said 'that the tradition that was growing up around Armistice Day should not be one which would teach future generations to fight but should be so shaped in the direction of peace'.[68] He reiterated this message in a wireless broadcast in 1925 entitled 'What the Armistice means for the children'.[69]

The most impressive Armistice services in the East End were those of the two great Docklands Settlements, one in Canning Town and the other in Wapping. The services in these areas reveal the tight links of remembrance and community. In Canning Town the Docklands Settlement developed a communal and highly ritualistic Armistice ceremony. Each Armistice night was marked by a torchlit procession, led by the warden of the settlement.[70] Such a sense of novelty, excitement and involvement no doubt helped to keep the event alive in the minds of the children. The same atmosphere permeated the Wapping settlement. In 1927 a huge procession took place as more than 1,000 people followed the torches through the streets to Thermopylae Gate Square where a service was held under a massive, illumi-

64 GBL, St Giles, Cripplegate, parish magazine, Nov. 1926.
65 *ET*, 16 Nov. 1929.
66 Ibid. 17 Nov. 1928.
67 For biographical details see W. E. Purcell, *Woodbine Willie: the life of G. A. Studdert-Kennedy*, London 1962.
68 *CP*, 18 Nov. 1922.
69 Ibid. 14 Nov. 1925.
70 *SE*, 14 Nov. 1925.

nated cross. Wreaths were then cast into the Thames.[71] The gender element was given extra coverage in the *Stratford Express*: the journalist spoke of the grey-haired old ladies, their eyes full of tears: 'Thus it was that Dockland paid homage to its dead, and the solemn procession went on until a late hour. The most wonderful moments were those when mothers, daughters and wives of those men laid down their floral tributes at those shrines. What a great heart has Canning Town.'[72]

Women were often associated with Armistice ceremonies: as wives and mothers it was natural that they should be portrayed as the most pathetic of the bereaved. In 1923 they reclaimed the East Ham memorial as a substitute grave and revealed the curious duality of remembrance, that of its individuality and communality in equilibrium. The *Echo* spoke of vast crowds of women and 'the procession of beautiful floral emblems for husbands or lovers, sons or brothers, buried far away across the water'.[73] St Anne's, Limehouse, arranged a special Armistice meeting for the Mother's Union in 1924, when the rector urged the women 'not to think only of the sorrow, loss and suffering after the war but of the splendour of the sacrifices'.[74] The local papers certainly made much of the presence of women at Armistice services. The *East London Observer* noted the pathetic sight of a mother falling to her knees in anguish during the Silence in 1921.[75] It was the sobbing of women that Jack Farmer most clearly remembered in his memories of Armistice Day services of his youth in South Woodford: 'Women sobbing in church and at war memorials, was extremely disturbing to a young lad of eight years, and is something I will never forget! Anyone who did not stand stock still during the two minutes silence, was liable to be knocked down, so deeply did the nation mourn its dead.'[76]

Indeed tearful women and crying children were the two great clichés of the silence. In 1924 the *Stratford Express* noted that the sobs of a woman broke the silence.[77] At the conclusion of the Poplar and Stepney Rifles' service in 1929 'women in the seats reserved for the relatives of the dead were seen to be crying'.[78] In 1925 the *Ilford Recorder* noted the fumbling with handkerchiefs during the two minutes. Ilford war memorial was surrounded by a huge crowd in 1928 in which 'women formed a larger part of the throng'.[79] During the same Armistice, Canon Elliott took the service in the Royal Exchange and spoke of the struggle handed on to youth by their parents:

71 *ELO*, 19 Nov. 1927.
72 *SE*, 19 Nov. 1925.
73 *EHE*, 16 Nov. 1923.
74 THL, St Anne's, Limehouse, parish magazine, Dec. 1924.
75 *ELO*, 12 Nov. 1921.
76 J. Farmer, *Woodford as I knew it*, Theydon Bois 1986, 92.
77 *SE*, 15 Nov. 1924.
78 *ELA*, 16 Nov. 1929.
79 *IR*, 16 Nov. 1928.

The generation rising would be the men and women of tomorrow, and on them would fall the duty of working out some of the most complex problems resulting from the War. It was well that they should be told of how their inheritance had been battled for by their fathers – and, indeed, the mothers too for it was always the woman who suffered most.[80]

In some ways this is deeply ambiguous as it suggests that the world's problems sprang from the war, rather than being pre-existent to it, so that the inheritance given to them by their fathers was hardly a glorious one. But such anomalies do not appear to have bitten too deeply into the psyche of the day. In 1927 the most complex interpretation of gender and remembrance was seen when a series of tableaux were performed at the Super Cinema, East Ham. 'A particularly striking scene was that representing a mother bidding farewell to her sons – a soldier and a sailor.' That such a scene was performed shows how little values had changed since the war: this could have been a report of a recruiting campaign in 1915 for it encapsulated the spirit of the wartime poster 'Women of Britain Say Go', or the letter of the 'Little Mother'.[81] Doubtless it struck a chord with many women in the audience, but it only serves to highlight the unwittingly painful nature of remembrance in the twenties. The whole event did not look forward, only back: the dead had gone to their graves supposedly to create a new world, but in its absence, remembrance was exactly that; a constant looking back, a reaffirmation of the past, truly a bitter-sweet form of consolation.

The poppy appeal

The poppy appeal continued to be a female preserve. In Ilford it was now the personal domain of Mrs Pitt, wife of Councillor Pitt. She organised the campaign throughout the twenties with a religious zeal. The female volunteers were out on the streets at an early hour on Armistice Day 1922 and, as in 1921, the poppy supply was soon exhausted.[82] A year later the chairman of the council wrote to the *Recorder* expressing his gratitude to the lady collectors: 'I know some actually started to collect as early as 3 a.m. showing their love and devotion to those who so strenuously fought for us in the Great War.'[83] The amounts collected in Ilford climbed steadily during the twenties

---

80 *CP*, 16 Nov. 1928.

81 *EHE*, 18 Nov. 1927. For wartime posters see M. Rickards, *Posters of the First World War*, London 1968, 38. The 'Little Mother' was the author of a letter printed in the *Morning Post* in 1916. In pathetic and touching terms it spoke of the resilience of mothers and the awful but necessary sacrifice of their sons. Robert Graves made wry reference to it in his work *Goodbye to all that*, London 1990 edn, 188–9. For an autobiographical account of a wife and mother during the war and her feelings after it see E. M. E. Richardson, *Remembrance wakes*, London 1934.

82 *IR*, 18 Nov. 1922.

83 Ibid. 23 Nov. 1923

Table 1
Income from poppy sales, 1923–9

	1923	1924	1925	1926	1927	1928	1929
Bethal Green	£210	£136	£139	£186	£199	£343	£364
Poplar	£187	£123	£94	£551	£657	£829	£809
Stepney	£321	£290	£96	£390	£441	£770	£904
East Ham	£322	£387	£387	£522	£679	£795	£849
West Ham	–	£261	£261	£272	£330	–	–
West Ham (N.)	–	–	–	–	–	£936	£957
West Ham (S.)	–	–	–	–	–	£362	£479
Ilford	£556	£727	£837	£922	£1,181	£1,282	£1,414
Romford	£133	£192	£182	£191	£253	£350	£409

Source: Royal British Legion Poppy Appeal, Aylesford, Kent. Figures are rounded to the nearest pound.
Note that in 1928 West Ham was divided into two collecting districts, north (which for a time included Wanstead), and south.

as the new communities within the district, especially those at Becontree and Chadwell Heath, expanded. It added to the difficulties of collecting however; in 1928 Mrs Pitt was forced to call for more volunteers as 'owing to the rapid growth of the borough more helpers are required every year'.[84]

The poppy appeals in the other districts show varying levels of success (*see* table 1). Although the poppy had a significant grasp on the imagination of East Londoners, it is clear that certain variables affected the amount collected. Bad weather and a lack of collectors obviously had the affect of pushing sums down but most important was the continued economic depression and poverty of many areas particularly in Poplar and Stepney.

Ilford's total kept pace with its residential development. East Ham matched this with a steady climb upwards, but still did not match Ilford by 1929. West Ham's totals reveal the division of the borough between its richer, northern districts and its poorer, southern ones. However, it too did not reach the same level as Ilford. Romford appeared to show the benefit of its rapidly expanding housing estates in the late twenties. The figures for Poplar and Stepney display the importance of wearing a poppy, despite the poverty of the area: it may also reflect the influence of the organisers for the campaign was in the hands of the Revd G. H. Lancaster vicar of St Stephen's, Bow, and chaplain to the Poplar and Stepney Rifles (and his wife). The tenth anniversary of the Armistice clearly helped the appeal as all districts witnessed quite a dramatic leap forward.

[84] Ibid. 9 Nov. 1928.

Armistice Day traditions in the City

Although the aim of the day was to provide comfort and sympathy, and despite the role of women in caring for various memorials in the City, the presence of women was largely overlooked by the *City Press*. The easiest answer to this paradox, given the preponderance of the favourite weeping women cliché in all the other local newspapers, is that the City was still a male preserve, despite the changes forced by wartime manpower require-ments. The *City Press* adopted its own Armistice cliché, one closely linked to London life – the pigeon. The tradition started in 1924: 'When the first gun was sounded, followed by a maroon at the Cannon Street Fire Station, there was absolute silence but for the fluttering of the frightened pigeons over-head.'[85] Pigeons were mentioned again in 1925, 1926, 1927 and 1928. The noise of their wings breaking the silence was the *City Press*'s version of the heart-felt sobs of bereaved women.[86]

The City also managed to combine its own, historic ceremonies with the newer tradition of Armistice Day. As it happened Armistice Day came just two days after the Lord Mayor's Show, the pageant in which the newly-elected Lord Mayor formally took office in a procession through the City to the Law Courts.[87] November was therefore already a time of formal and historic observance into which Armistice Day was neatly incorporated, becoming one of the first public duties of the new Lord Mayor. This meant that when the Revd J. H. Ellison took the service in the Royal Exchange he saw no irony in mixing remembrance, commerce and Christianity: '[He] asked the congregation to pray that that day's Act of Remembrance might keep alive among us a high standard of devotion to the common weal, and that God's blessing might rest upon the municipal year just begun.'[88] Ellison kept up this theme; he included in his prayers in 1927 the wish 'that God's Blessing may rest upon the industries of the City in the coming year'.[89] As the war had been to protect the decency of British civilisation there were no qualms over prayers for the well-being of its esteemed institutions. The symbolism of the heart of a trading and commercial empire stopping totally for two minutes each year was therefore a particularly poignant salute to the dead: 'For a few moments the machinery of the business life of the Empire will be brought to a standstill and we shall think of those who made the Supreme Sacrifice and laid down their lives for their friends.'[90]

---

[85] *CP*, 15 Nov. 1924.
[86] Ibid. 14 Nov. 1925, 13 Nov. 1926, 19 Nov. 1927, 16 Nov. 1928.
[87] Weinreb and Hibbert, *London encyclopaedia*, 496–7.
[88] *CP*, 14 Nov. 1925.
[89] GML, A379/4ext, Royal Exchange Armistice Day order of service, 11 Nov. 1927.
[90] *PB*, Nov. 1927, 22.

Dissent or duty?

Evidence for unequivocal pacifism during Armistice observation is even harder to come by. In 1925 the Ilfordian loose cannon, the Revd H. Dunnico, by this time a Labour MP, had told the No More War Movement at East Ham town hall that 'there had been a marked difference in the outlook of the people since 1918. The cry of "hang the Kaiser" and "Make Germany pay" were things of the past'.[91] In 1928 the *Echo* saw a battle of correspondence over the militaristic content of Armistice Day. One reader complained that due to mistiming the Last Post had been omitted from the service in Central Park. Another replied that it 'was not an insult to those we mourn or those who mourn, but rather a healthy sign that the public is becoming averse to any kind of military show on Remembrance Day'.[92] But only in 1929 can a significant change of opinions be detected. At Stratford Congregational church the congregation were warned of the dangers of sentimental patriotism. They were told that it

> could [never] again blind them to the brutality and futility of war. To make war not only impossible, but unthinkable, that was their task. The soldierly virtues of courage and loyalty were fine virtues, but these should be developed in the service of the Prince of Peace.[93]

Dunnico addressed the war memorial service in Ilford. He told the crowd that the men of Ilford had died in order to crush militarism and establish a new international order of conciliation and peace. The *Recorder* proved to be a good barometer of the slowly changing atmosphere as for the first time the limbless and crippled were present at both the Ilford and Dagenham services. The headline for the Dagenham service read 'The Curse of Nationality' and went on to quote the vicar of Dagenham: 'in glorifying the nation they had banished from their thoughts the spirit of universal brotherhood'.[94] But some remained too deeply disfigured by grief; they simply could not face any sort of service. James Mee recalled his mother's reluctance to attend the service at British Street School:

> They used to ask the parents to come to the Memorial Service they used to hold in the school, but my mum would never go, she'd say 'I don't need that to remind me'. It must have been terrible, one boy of eighteen and one boy of nineteen . . . I wasn't even born until one of them was killed, even . . .[95]

Occasionally, the horror of another great conflict was referred to. When the Honourable Artillery Company memorial was dedicated at St Botolph,

---

[91] *EHE*, 20 Nov. 1925.
[92] Ibid. 23 Nov. 1928.
[93] *SE*, 13 Nov. 1929.
[94] *IR*, 15 Nov. 1929.
[95] Quoted in Hostettler, *Childhood on the Isle of Dogs*, 34.

Bishopsgate, the rector noted that one wall was left blank for their memorial to the next war. He then thundered: 'There will be no memorial of the next great war because there will be no church to hold it and no people of London to receive it.'[96] The vicar of St Luke's, Ilford, told his congregation that another war might result in the destruction of whole populations with 'all civilisation . . . swept away'.[97] An equally powerful message was delivered at St Dunstan-in-the-East in 1927. The Revd Arthur West told the congregation that 'such incredible stupidity, such maniacal passion shall not again enslave and torture us; shall not thus ruin the last years of those who have, in self-denial and love, slowly built the sacred home'.[98] Such emotional pacifist comments were sometimes lightened by the progress of international events and the call for a commitment to the League of Nations. In 1925 the scent of the Locarno honeymoon was very much in the air; the Revd G. W. Hudson said at St Botolph, Bishopsgate, that 'for the first time since the War, the Armistice Day services are being held in an atmosphere of real Peace'.[99] On Armistice night the mayor of East Ham addressed the League of Nations Union and stated that 'On that Day of Remembrance of their glorious dead they should pledge themselves to do all in their power to make war impossible. Personally he placed great hopes in Mr Austen Chamberlain's efforts at Locarno. (Applause).'[100] The League of Nations Union was often promoted during Armistice week and its work praised. At St Luke's, Ilford, the vicar praised the league as an instrument of international co-operation and urged his congregation to join the union.[101] Sir Arthur Steel-Maitland addressed the Ilford League of Nations Union on Armistice night 1928; he warned against militaristic toys such as soldiers and rifles and spoke of the 'need for history books that do not glorify war'.[102] The positive result that had come out of the sacrifice was seen in the affirmation of a world without war, safeguarded by the League of Nations. The Revd Sinclair Phillips of Romford Congregational church said that the war had been truly one to end war.[103] A year later Councillor J. Macpherson addressed the Romford League of Nations Union and noted that the war had not been fought to hang the Kaiser but as 'the war to end war'.[104]

But Armistice Day could also be used to highlight a far more controversial cause, the poverty and unemployment of ex-servicemen. By the mid-twenties it was clear that a new social utopia was not about to descend on Britain and

96   *CP*, 18 Nov. 1922.
97   *IR*, 14 Nov. 1924.
98   *CP*, 12 Nov. 1927.
99   Ibid. 14 Nov. 1925
100   *EHE*, 14 Nov. 1925.
101   *IR*, 14 Nov. 1924.
102   Ibid. 16 Nov. 1928.
103   *ET*, 17 Nov. 1923.
104   Ibid. 22 Nov. 1924. For a full history of the League of Nations Union see D. Birn, *The League of Nations Union, 1918–1945*, Oxford 1981.

neither was a state of full employment. Armistice Day was a potent vehicle of protest for ex-servicemen; the pride they took in their wartime record was balanced against the unfulfilled promises of the government. 'Wayfarer', writing in the *East London Advertiser*, noted the regular demonstrations against unemployment staged by the Stepney British Legion.[105]

In West Ham two ex-army chaplains articulated the disillusionment of the ex-servicemen. Canon T. G. Rogers, rural dean of West Ham, recounted his wartime experiences and then told his congregation:

> They remembered that day many were living in affluence and wealth while numbers of those who guarded the wealth of the country during the war were still living in poverty. It was those who had suffered the least who became most morally dull and keenly alive to everything that served their own pleasures. It was significant that in all parts of London there would be Armistice Dances that evening. They remembered that day the failure to seize the opportunity that was given by the men who died, of remaking the world. The world was ridden by the nightmare of the Treaty of Versailles.[106]

Just a few hundred yards down the road the Revd M. S. Evers was addressing the Territorial Army service. His sermon was remarkably similar in nature; he too spoke of his service on the Western Front and added 'But who in 1918, when the war was over, would have thought that five years later they would have the problem of unemployment on such a gigantic scale.'[107]

1926 was the year in which the Armistice tenets were fully tested. The General Strike seemed to highlight all the ideals mentioned on Armistice Day, but how they were perceived depended upon an individual's conditioning. One correspondent to the *East Ham Echo* bemoaned the lack of unity found in Britain and stated that

> It was thought by many that the last great war was to end war. It does not appear so if we look round, for if there is no foreign enemy to fight then they must needs fight among themselves. There are frequent industrial wars, class wars, industries are stopped, many thrown out of employment. . . . We are living in times when everybody seems to want something for nothing![108]

Samuel Hynes has argued that the General Strike was presented as a war both in its physical manifestation and in its rhetorical constructs.[109] That certainly seems true of the *Prudential Bulletin*'s Armistice comments:

---

[105] *ELA*, 24 Nov. 1923.
[106] *SE*, 14 Nov. 1923.
[107] Ibid.
[108] *EHE*, 12 Nov. 1926.
[109] Hynes, *A war imagined*, 353–83, 407–23. His thesis, and particularly his ideas on the General Strike as a war, seem to find proof in Evelyn Waugh's *Brideshead revisited* (London 1945), a novel written eighteen years later, during 1944, by a serving officer. Charles Ryder,

We approach the day of commemoration under the shadow of a prolonged industrial dispute which must inevitably set back the progress of the community towards better conditions. . . . We have however passed through days of darkness and gloom and have learnt not to despair. The memory of those who faced death and suffering in the Great War should be our inspiration in our present difficulties.[110]

Hynes has further stated that the Great War entered the nation's consciousness in the twenties and its images infiltrated every aspect of life.[111]

The Revd H. C. Robins of Romford certainly seemed obsessed with images of the military and conflict. In 1928 he announced that 'England was still at war. The war was still on only now it was spiritual warfare, the issue today was Christ or the secular view of life.'[112] Any elements of protest or dissent were usually met with conformist replies and a simple buttressing repetition of the tenets of 1914. In fact it was the job of the living to continue the struggle initiated by the dead. The Revd G. H. Lancaster told the Poplar and Stepney Rifles that it was within their power to change the world, but at least he recognised that there were problems:

He hoped that the Armistice of 1929 would influence their hearts to the highest ideal of national righteousness. It should arouse them to do something about the slums, unemployment and the distress in the ranks of their people. He felt that was what those who died would have them do if they spoke from the grave.[113]

There was also no room for political extremism. Havelock Davidson told his congregation that

the heart of England was sane and sound. It was not represented by the noisy and blatant voices of the Communists, or the Diehards, the Bolshevists, or the Fascists. But it was represented in the inarticulate masses of the people, those who lived ordinary, quiet and well-ordered lives.[114]

The Armistice message was thus one of teamwork and hierarchy. Everyone had a place and it was not wise to question the political make-up of England,

---

the narrator of the novel, enlists as a special constable during the strike: 'We went to a number of night clubs. In two years Mulcaster seemed to have attained his simple ambition of being liked in such places. At the last of them he and I were kindled by a great flame of patriotism. "You and I", he said, "were too young to fight in the war. Other chaps fought, millions of them dead. Not us. We'll show them. We'll show the dead chaps we can fight, too."/ "That's why I'm here", I said. "Come from overseas, rallying to old country in hour of need."/ "Like Australians."/ "Like the poor dead Australians."/ "What you in?"/ "Nothing yet. War not ready" ' (pp. 181–2).

[110] *PB*, Nov. 1926, 17.
[111] Hynes, *A war imagined*, 407–23.
[112] *ET*, 17 Nov. 1928.
[113] *ELA*, 16 Nov. 1929.
[114] *IR*, 14 Nov. 1924.

after all the sacrifices that had been made to protect that very form of existence. Addressing the Eastern District Post Office workers at Whitechapel
church, the Revd J. Mayo told them that it was their job to make England a
better nation and absolved the politicians from any further blame:

> they must see to it that this land was a land for heroes. A very fine thing to say
> and strive for, but no statesmen, politics, industrial security or housing could
> make this country fit for heroes. Heroes must make the country themselves.[115]

There were comments on the disappointing progress of the new world but no
one said that the sacrifices had been in vain. The *Prudential Bulletin* spoke of
the 'disappointingly slow progress' of international co-operation in 1928.[116]
At St Giles, Cripplegate, during the Armistice of 1926 it was noted that 'the
world is still like a sick man slowly recovering after a serious illness'.[117] But
these incidents hardly amounted to a rejection of the war or remembrance
and were always within the bounds of conventional commemoration.

They were also very firmly balanced by statements on the more conventional notions of maintaining peace. The ironic message, always reiterated,
was the belief that the best way to honour and remember the dead was a
commitment to imitate them if need arose. At the Armistice service of the
Stock Exchange battalion, Ellison spoke in glowing, chivalrous, Christian
terms:

> When in days to come you look in at our church doors, and see the Colour of
> your old Regiment laid up in God's House, you will be able to feel that it still
> stands for the stern qualities which carried you through the Great War, and
> remains to inspire generations as yet unborn.[118]

The Revd A. E. Wilkinson of the 'Cast Iron Sixth', told the men that

> it still remained the duty of young men, both as citizens and Christians, to
> train themselves so that they might be able when all else had failed, and as a
> last resort, to defend their homes against aggression and wrong. . . . He con-
> cluded by appealing to us all to recapture the spirit of service and self-sacrifice
> which was so manifest during the days of war and to apply it to present day
> problems by devoting our life to service.[119]

The same point was made by the superintendent of Smithfield Market at the
market men's service:

> Every living front-line soldier in the Last War prays for the immediate and
> lasting success of the League's endeavours. In the meantime every thinking

115 *ELO*, 19 Nov. 1927.
116 *PB*, Nov. 1928, 21.
117 GBL, St Giles, Cripplegate, parish magazine, Nov. 1926.
118 *CP*, 14 Nov. 1925.
119 *City of London Rifles Quarterly Journal*, Dec. 1928.

man knows that there is only one thing to do to stabilise the peace of Europe of the past ten years, and that is to be instantly ready and prepared for War.[120]

A year before the ex-servicemen of Mile End were told that those who were unprepared could never defend 'great possessions . . . we must be ready to defend ourselves and our place in the world when [not if] need arises if we are to do so we must be a unified nation and a healthy one'.[121]

Even League of Nations Union meetings could become a little paradoxical: the Revd Sinclair Phillips proved this when he spoke in favour of internationalism and the fraternity of nations to the Romford branch, but then said:

> no day could touch the depths of their souls like Armistice Day; the two minutes' silence was a spiritual influence. They communed with their noble dead. It brought home to them the great sacrifice made for them; remembering that 900,000 Britishers gave up all that men held dear for the land they loved and for those ideals that made the land great in the eyes of the world.[122]

Armistice Day in the twenties was therefore an event of many strands and ingredients, but was utterly constant in its devotion to the dead. Every part of the City and East London stood stock still for two minutes as the day became entrenched in both the civic and religious calendars of the district. Indeed it became so firmly entrenched that Sir Charles Wakefield suffered an attack of amnesia over his earlier views on the day:

> The Two Minutes' Silence of Armistice Day has established itself as one of those occasions upon which it is true to say that all hearts beat as one. . . . It is the only one of the many possible ways of celebrating the cessation of hostilities nine years ago that is rightly becoming a permanent part of national life. Year by year the silence itself becomes more moving, more beautiful, more pregnant with meaning. . . . It is a fitting tribute to our glorious dead, and a reaffirmation of our hopes for the future.[123]

He had come a long way since he suggested that repetition of the silence would cheapen its impact.

Perhaps the best way to judge the importance of the day is to look at the reaction when events did not meet the expectations of the public. This happened in Ilford on the tenth anniversary of the Armistice, when the 11th fell on a Sunday. The council organised an afternoon service at the war memorial but this did not stop two crowds forming at eleven o'clock, one at the town hall, the other at the war memorial. It is particularly paradoxical that the

---

120 *CP*, 15 Nov. 1928.
121 *ELO*, 19 Nov. 1927.
122 *ET*, 12 Nov. 1927.
123 *CP*, 19 Nov. 1927.

much-maligned memorial actually managed to attract a crowd quite spontaneously and then found no one there to mark the occasion. The day was
saved by a resident of Seven Kings who, without prompting, climbed onto the
memorial and improvised a short address. His gesture was greatly appreciated.
The editor of the *Recorder* praised his efforts and many letters of thanks were
sent to the newspaper. 'Wounded' wrote that:

> I am personally grateful to him for stepping into the breach once again, as he
> doubtless did in the Great War, for every inch of him had a soldierly bearing,
> Mr Deacon's actions saved many a soul from the thought that their heroes had
> been forgotten at the appointed hour recognised throughout the Empire.
>
> The handshakes he received after the ceremony, I can assure him, were from
> the heart.[124]

Others gave vent to their anger. Middle-class sensibilities were obviously
rattled and it was seen as a civic disgrace. 'Citizen' divided his anger between
the Churches, eager to put their 'magazines through one's letterbox' but
'could not spare a few minutes to be at the memorial at 11.00 a.m'. The
disgust is quite clear: 'I should imagine that this was probably the only memorial in the country and possibly in the world where no members of the clergy
were present, thus further wounding the feelings of the large numbers of
people present.'[125]

At the town hall matters were not quite so bad as the Salvation Army
band arrived and organised an impromptu service.[126]

The silence and its observance at the correct time was obviously very
important. It was also perceived as the epitome of Englishness. Even the
Scottish minister of Ilford Presbyterian church, David Sutherland, preaching
to a congregation mainly of Scots ex-patriates, stated that it was a fine thing
to die for England and quoted from 'Jerusalem' in his sermon.[127] The day held
a deep grip on the imagination of the nation as was reflected in the *Prudential
Bulletin*: 'Armistice Day, that with the years has gathered about it so much of
hallowed custom, is again approaching [emphasis added].'[128]

Armistice Day in the twenties thus quickly attained a state of familiar
maturity. East Londoners, led by their clergy and councillors, settled into a
comfortable routine of simple, self-evident truths about the war. In return
local journalists responded with a set repertoire of images and concepts: the
Englishness of the silence and its tearful interruption by women and children

---

124 *IR*, 16 Nov. 1928.
125 Ibid.
126 Ibid.
127 Ibid. 14 Nov. 1924. That the silence was regarded as a peculiarly English phenomenon
can be seen in Sir Lawrence Weaver's guide to the Scottish National War Memorial. He
wrote that 'the silence on Armistice Day is symbolic of the English temperament [and on the
Cenotaph] England has made an ethereal monument of her inarticulateness': *The Scottish
national war memorial*, London 1928, 22.
128 *PB*, Nov. 1929, 25.

often provided the backbone of Armistice Day coverage. The constant references to the past were never balanced with a full vision of the newborn world that had been bought with the blood of the dead. This made Armistice Day a proud, melancholic occasion: it was confidently stated that the dead rested in blissful Paradise but little hope for the temporal future was offered. The years after 1929 saw the day become conscious of the outside world as it began to reflect contemporary fears concerning politics, armaments and international relations.

8

The Years of Flux, 1930–1935

Armistice Day entered a period of flux between the years 1930 and 1935. A number of themes, present but not stressed in the Armistice Day observances of the twenties, became increasingly important. Thus the wider domestic problems of slump and unemployment found a greater role in East London ceremonies. Equally, out of the sudden realisation that international relations were being threatened by the totalitarian states of Europe and Japan came the general desire to support League of Nations disarmament conferences. At the same time the traditional values survived, and it was not impossible to hear completely contradictory messages during the same service. Armistice Day reached a crossroads as a new generation came to the fore and 1914 seemed to slip into distant history.[1]

The years between 1930 and 1935 turned Armistice Day into something of a cocktail in East London as pacifism and elements of protest blended with the traditional elements of the day. But it is difficult to find evidence of a concentrated assault on Armistice observation; respect for the dead was always too strong for that to happen. In 1931 Communists tried to hold a meeting at the conclusion of the ceremony in Central Park. Far from being able to capitalise on renewed economic depression they were jeered and jostled and as the crowd sang *Rule Britannia* the police shepherded them away.[2] Any attempt, real or imagined, to interfere with the sacred day was met with an innate conservatism. Much the same traits can be seen a year later at Stratford where it was rumoured that the National Unemployed Workers' Movement was planning a disturbance. The *Express* reported that

> As soon as the maroons sounded the silence the contingent . . . stood bare headed and silent but half a dozen men in the road shouted '1914, on the roll; 1932 on the dole', till they were spoken to by a police inspector. Then they too, ceased.[3]

---

[1] For the nature of British politics and society during this period see G. Williams and J. Ramsden, *Ruling Britannia: a political history of Britain, 1688–1988*, Harlow 1990, 383–404. For the European situation and international relations see M. Kitchen, *Europe between the wars: a political history*, Harlow 1988, 47–76.
[2] *SE*, 14 Nov. 1931.
[3] Ibid. 16 Nov. 1932. For the role of the NUWM in Armistice Day see W. Hannington, *Unemployed struggles, 1919–1936*, Ilkley 1973 edn, 75–8. The Labour Government elected in 1929 collapsed amid financial pressures in 1931. A National Government was then elected to steer the country through the crisis and it adopted deep cuts to the benefits system; although nominally a coalition it was in fact dominated by the Conservative Party.

This report shows that despite the rumours the NUWM largely upheld the silence and the protest came from few men; even they had no real stomach for the desecration of the dead. In other districts Armistice Day was used as a platform for protest. The Poplar and Stepney branches of the British Legion used it to highlight the level of ex-service unemployment. In 1933 the chairman of Bow, Bromley and Old Ford British Legion wrote to the editor of the *East London Advertiser* stating that over 500 ex-servicemen queued up for Legion welfare payments at St Stephen's, Bow, every fortnight.[4] A year later the South Poplar branch complained of 'idle shipping, commerce at a standstill, millions out of work'.[5]

Even conservative respectable Ilford had marches of the unemployed to the war memorial by the 1930s: in 1932 more than 200 unemployed ex-servicemen marched from the Employment Exchange to the memorial and then laid a wreath.[6] A year later the mayor of Ilford made special reference to the problem of unemployed ex-servicemen in his Armistice Day address.[7] When Captain L. H. Green of Ilford Salvation Army spoke to the League of Nations Union in 1934 he went one stage further and directly linked the war to unemployment: 'They spent some six or seven millions a day for the duration of the war, and it brought the country where it was, with two and a half millions unemployed.'[8] The mayor of East Ham, speaker at the Old Contemptibles' Association on the same Armistice night, stated that:

After the War it was said that the efforts of the men were appreciated and England 'would be made a land fit for heroes to live in'. Sometimes I ask whether

---

The National Governments survived the thirties and one-party rule did not return to British politics until 1945. See Williams and Ramsden, *Ruling Britannia*, 396–8. Noel Coward caught perfectly the mood of the time in his play *This happy breed*. The play has a particular relevance to this whole study as it was written in the spring of 1939 and set in the South London suburb of Clapham: therefore in terms of location and attitude it is very close to this subject of investigation. Coward himself wrote that 'Having been born in Teddington, having lived respectively at Sutton, Battersea Park and Clapham Common during all my formative years I can confidently assert that I know a great deal more about the hearts and minds of South Londoners than they [the critics] gave me credit for.' One of the scenes in his play is set after what appears to have been an Armistice Night regimental reunion in 1931, which the two main male characters, Frank Gibbons and Bob Mitchell attend – the National Government had been elected only a few weeks earlier. They express their concerns for old comrades and the fears of the time: 'FRANK: When I see before me all these well-remembered faces and recall, with a tug of the 'eart-strings, the hardships and perils we endured together . . . / BOB: Well, it's a strange world and no mistake. I was thinking that tonight looking at all those chaps in your regiment – wondering what they were feeling like – some of 'em looked all right, of course, but some looked under the weather./FRANK: We've been lucky./ BOB: You've said it': R. Mander and J. Mitchenson (eds), *Noel Coward: plays: four*, London 1987 edn, pp. xiii, 326, 330.

4   *ELA*, 25 Nov. 1933.
5   Ibid, 17 Nov. 1934.
6   *IR*, 17 Nov. 1932.
7   Ibid. 16 Nov. 1933.
8   Ibid. 15 Nov. 1934.

anything has been done to make it so. . . . Are we doing what we ought to do or what we promised?[9]

Nevertheless the service at the Central Park memorial was marked by respectful silence, perfectly kept 'even by those derelicts, who possibly had the bitterest cause to remember, the unemployed'.[10]

But such elements were usually countered with a conformist answer. Ironically, for all their moments of protest, the Poplar and Stepney British Legion branches also provided conservative solutions to the problem of unemployment. In 1933 the Poplar British Legion Armistice rally turned into a statement concerning the relief work of the branches within the borough. Major H. C. Joel, president of the local branches, made a speech in which he appeared to praise the National Government at the expense of the preceding Labour government:

> Whilst their organisation was a non-political one, the meaning of the word politics was good government, and the following facts were interesting. In Poplar in 1931 the unemployment figures in registered trades were 10,797; in 1932 they were 10,220; and in 1933 the figures had fallen to 8,290. (Applause). That meant that in the last twelve months 1,830 men had been set to work.[11]

The chairman then resurrected the war by stating that a large dose of the 1914–18 spirit would soon unite the nation and restore it to happiness.[12]

The Revd H. C. P. Belcher, chaplain to the Poplar and Stepney Rifles, reminded his congregation of riflemen and residents that the state of the world lay in their hands. He urged those present to work hard and not to blame God for Britain's problems: 'if we felt that the fruits of that victory were very disappointing then that was not God's fault, it was our own'.[13] His message was simple: everyone had their own role to play, if they did it to the best of their abilities the system would work; it was all rather woolly but it bore the seal of the glorious dead and that made it a concept beyond reproach.[14]

---

[9] *EHE*, 17 Nov. 1934. The Old Contemptibles' Association was specifically for original members of the BEF who had been within range of enemy artillery between 5 August and 22 November 1914: K. Simpson, *The Old Contemptibles: a photographic history of the British Expeditionary Force, August–December 1914*, London 1981, 129.

[10] Ibid.

[11] *ELA*, 18 Nov. 1933.

[12] Ibid.

[13] Ibid. 16 Nov. 1933.

[14] This was not a phenomenon unique to British ex-servicemen. Antoine Prost has shown that French ex-servicemen were liable to be equally vague about politics and their own role within society other than expressing an ill-defined sense of superiority conferred on them by their war service: 'Just as France was for them the beacon-nation the veterans formed a privileged group, the forces of sanity capable of showing the road to well-being and speaking for justice and right. This is what they expected to confirm when they spoke of their "moral

Pacifist concepts underwent the same process. The Revd Stuart Scott of Stratford Congregational church was one of the first consistently to make pacifist statements, but he never questioned the sacrifice or the day. He merely advocated an alternative form of remembrance:

it was better now that a procession of peace societies, representative of the League of Nations, should file past the Cenotaph on November 11th than that regiments of armed soldiers should still interpret the symbolic meaning of the day which is *so sacred to us all* [emphasis added]. It was impossible to think of peace whilst the nation was garbed in the panoply of war.[15]

The presence of soldiers at memorial services had come up in Romford in 1928. However, far from objecting to their presence, an ex-gunner complained that the ceremony had too little to do with the proper military observations and suggested a drumhead service.[16]

It is hard to find evidence of absolute pacifism or even a commitment to unilateral disarmament in the City. The simple explanation for this seems to be the innate conservatism of the City; radical pacifism was not a concept likely to thrive in such an atmosphere. In 1934 the bishop of Fulham took the Royal Exchange service. His message was in tune with the findings of the League of Nations Union 'Peace Ballot' conducted earlier that year. The 'Peace Ballot' sought to ascertain people's views on the correct procedure for dealing with international disputes. Instead of turning into a pacifist plebiscite as many predicted, it illuminated a desire to maintain collective security and intervene, with armed force if necessary, in international conflict provided it was done in accordance with the covenant of the League. But the wording of the ballot paper seemed to imply that disputes could be settled without resorting to force:[17]

He had seen armies growing up which were at the disposal of fanatics. He was, therefore, no advocate for such disarmament as would leave us defenceless. What he wanted was that out of remembrance should come a widespread

legislature". . . . For this reason the aims of the veterans' movement in the political arena were concealed and it was not easy to perceive them beyond stereotyped moralising rhetoric. . . . The veterans' political discourse seems empty because its function excludes explicit conclusions'; *In the wake of war: les anciens combattants and French society, 1914–1939*, Eng. edn, Oxford 1992, 98–9.

15 *SE*, 14 Nov. 1931.

16 *ET*, 17 Nov. 1928. The parades of soldiers at Armistice services was a current subject of debate. In October 1929 a Tory MP asked the Labour Home Secretary whether the Cenotaph service would follow the lines of the usual ceremony. The Home Secretary confirmed that it would, although with a reduced number of servicemen present, as 'there is an increasing public feeling that, while we continue to pay our tribute to the dead, as far as possible these ceremonies should partake of a civilian aspect more and more' and he cited the wishes of the deceased men's relatives: quoted in Hynes, *A war imagined*, 466.

17 Birn, *The League of Nations Union*, 143–55: M. Ceadel, *Pacifism in Britain, 1914–1945: the defining of a faith*, Oxford 1980, 123–46.

resolve to prevent wars of oppression by the cultivation of a feeling of greater trust and confidence among the peoples of the world.[18]

During the same Armistice, the chaplain of the Honourable Artillery Company urged them to 'think in terms of brotherhood' and 'of those ten millions who on all fronts and on either side had made the supreme sacrifice'.[19] This was an affirmation of the need to build a new world with a solid commitment to co-operation first, force second; exactly the sentiments expressed in the 'Peace Ballot'.

The new atmosphere was felt in Ilford, where in 1930 the League of Nations Union organised an Armistice Day service at the war memorial for the first time.[20] As League of Nations concepts slowly permeated the day the East London press sometimes found indicators which were not perhaps all they seemed. In 1935 the *East Ham Echo* reported that the town hall was packed for the visit of George Lansbury and people were turned away. But the headline for the Armistice service itself read: 'Apathy of the Public/Are People Forgetting?' and went on to complain that 'only a handful of people collected at the Cenotaph in Central Park'.[21] What the journalist neglected to mention was that an incredibly thick fog had rolled in from the Thames that morning covering both East and West Ham and that this certainly affected the service at West Ham.

There was an undoubtedly new force behind the calls for peace and a greater commitment to international fraternity. Miss L. D. Bentley became the first female mayor of Bethnal Green in 1933. Her diary reveals exactly these sentiments:

> Saturday, November 11th [1933]. An impressive Armistice Ceremony in front of our Public Library. A children's Armistice I should like to call it and as such I love to remember it. . . . The silence was beautifully kept, there seemed a deep hush over Bethnal Green, 'the two minutes' were reverent and profound. Thought the planting of the poppy crosses in the field of remembrance a charming, simple and touching innovation. When I laid our Borough Wreath before our Memorial Window I prayed most solemnly for the Peace of Bethnal Green, the Peace of London, the Peace of the British Empire, the Peace of the World.[22]

The residents of Ilford witnessed some particularly virulent attacks on the 1914 ethos. The Revd E. Rutherford Lane referred to the men suffering from respiratory problems and blindness due to poison gas; his speech to the League of Nations Union built up to a climax in which he stated that 'When

---

[18] *CP*, 16 Nov. 1934.
[19] *HAC Journal*, Dec. 1934, 6.
[20] *IR*, 14 Nov. 1930.
[21] *EHE*, 15 Nov. 1935.
[22] THL, L. D. Bentley, mayor of Bethnal Green, 1933–4, manuscript diary. Note also the strong sense of community in this piece, shown in the repetition of 'our'.

I hear men and women on Armistice Day, or when I hear in clubs, or read in the papers about the "glory of war" . . . then I say the glory of war be damned. (Applause).'[23] Captain L. H. Green of Ilford Salvation Army launched an even more devastating assault when he addressed the Union on Armistice night 1934:

> In 1914, full of generous impulses, he and thousands of others volunteered and went filled with the belief they were going out to help little Belgium. Today they knew more. It was lies and worse that they were taken in by. The people in charge were playing with them.[24]

When the Revd G. E. Mitchell of Goodmayes Wesleyan church took the war memorial service in 1932, he was unequivocal in his condemnation of war and stated that no young person would 'be flung into another war to murder their friends in other lands'.[25] It looked indeed as if the consensus on the glory of the sacrifice was finally falling apart; the harsh realities of the European and global situation seemed to be putting too much pressure on the rhetorical framework of the day. In 1935 the LCC councillor, Mrs Stamp, told the Goodmayes Youth Group of the League of Nations Union that the annual silence was 'almost a mockery' and asked

> when you have this big armaments race going on at the same time, can you believe that the display on Armistice Day is sincere? The men who died in the last war believed it was a war to end war. But it was not. There's one going on this minute.[26]

The shadow of the armaments race loomed large over Armistice Day during this period. It formed a key part of the Revd Robinson Whittacker's service at the Methodist Central Hall, East Ham, when he told his congregation to 'think of the ten million dead' and urged them to

> Think that, when the last shot had been fired, there were ten million cripples in the world and twenty million wounded. Can you realise now that £850 million is being spent on armaments. I do not want to speak of the horror of it all. The horror lies in the homes: in the young lives that have been cut off. How are we going to remember them? By hating War and saying 'Never again'. War unsettles everything. How can bayonets make brotherhood? How can force make fellowship? It is building a new world on the sand.[27]

The Revd W. E. Clapham of Bow Road Methodist church combined an attack on the armaments manufacturers, statesmen and bellicose Chris-

---

23 *IR*, 14 Nov. 1930. For a general survey of pacifism in this period see Ceadel, *Pacifism in Britain*, 62–82, 123–46.
24 *IR*, 15 Nov. 1934.
25 Ibid. 17 Nov. 1932.
26 Ibid. 14 Nov. 1935.
27 *EHE*, 17 Nov. 1934.

tianity. He said that the munitions factories had been busy since 1918 and 'fifteen years later, they were busier than ever and the devastating horror of war was still hanging over people's heads. Statesmen talked, but had not talked peace'.[28]

He then went on to condemn any justification of war stating that it was completely contradictory to the Sermon on the Mount. A year later Clapham repeated his theme and added that British soldiers had been killed in the Great War with guns made in England. But he refused to state that the sacrifice had been in vain; the dead served as the greatest reminder of the horror of war and would temper the ambition of unscrupulous politicians:

> Those men of theirs did not die in vain. There was now a determination never to fight again in the hearts of millions of men throughout the world. Let statesmen beat the big drums of war as they would, they would be confronted by a big army of men who believed in peace. They must strip war of its glamour, make peace glorious.[29]

Clapham added another very important theme to his Armistice sermons; the role of women. He stated his belief that worldwide peace would be obtained within months if there was an all-female peace conference.[30] Councillor A. Baker attended Clapham's service in 1934 and expanded upon this idea. He recounted that he had seen a woman holding up a little girl in order for her to see the wreaths laid at a local war memorial. The child asked her mother what was happening to which the woman replied 'that is in memory of all the daddies who have died'.[31] The pathetic symbolism of the story must have been obvious as Baker went on to say that such a scene of desolation should never be repeated. Such was the atmosphere that he could even admit to having been a conscientious objector during the conflict; it would have been impossible to have made such a statement ten years previous.[32] In 1922 'A Citizen' had written to the *City Press* complaining that some people did not show enough respect when passing the London Troops memorial. He blamed ' "Conchies" . . . "khaki-dodgers" and their whole tribe'. But a day or two

---

[28] *ELA*, 18 Nov. 1933. This was the feeling which was believed to have shaped the East Fulham by-election just a few weeks earlier. A relatively safe Conservative seat was taken by a pacifist Labour candidate. The government took it as a key indicator of popular pacifism and used it to justify a policy of low armaments expenditure. As such it later became a point of bitter political controversy: M. Ceadel, 'Interpreting East Fulham', in J. Ramsden and C. Cook (eds), *By-elections in British politics*, London 1973, 118–40.

[29] *ELA*, 18 Nov. 1933. King George V also believed that the dead served the cause of peace. On a pilgrimage to the Imperial War Graves Commission cemeteries in 1922 he had stated that 'I have many times asked myself whether there can be more potent advocates of peace upon earth through the years to come than this massed multitude of silent witnesses to the desolation of war': quoted in F. Fox, *The king's pilgrimage*, London 1922, 4.

[30] *ELA*, 18 Nov. 1933.

[31] Ibid. 17 Nov. 1934.

[32] Ibid.

earlier he had seen 'a little telegraph messenger carry his hand at the salute whilst passing. Good lad! What an example to some of his elders'.[33]

The symbolism of the widow and the bereaved mother as particularly poignant reminders of the effect of the sacrifice therefore continued to loom large. The *Recorder* noted the preponderance of 'sad-faced women – many of them war widows' at the war memorial in 1932.[34] In 1935 the *Echo* recorded the presence of a very large wreath at the memorial, paid for and laid by the mothers of Alvestone Road, Manor Park.[35] But the nature of the symbolism had slightly shifted; the widows were far more a symbol of the pity of war than they had been in the twenties; the widows were a living symbol of the desolation of war.

Bethnal Green made the greatest commitment to peace during this period in an attempt to warn the public against the glory of war. In January 1935 the borough council approved a plan put forward by Bermondsey council to abandon the word Armistice in 'the teachings of peace principles in schools'.[36] Then in June 1935 the council voted to change the name of the war memorial to 'Peace Memorial'.[37] This reveals a perception that the word Armistice was in some way tainted with militarist and aggressively nationalist concepts. There is no evidence of any great public opposition to this move.

Questions over the nature of the armed forces dominated the Armistice of 1932 in East Ham. An ex-chaplain to the Guards, T. L. B. Westerdale, wrote to the *Echo* defending the need for strong armed forces lest 'a gang of godless, unscrupulous, murdering muscovite monkeys' overrun the empire.[38] This provoked a furious reaction in the following issue. An anonymous correspondent asked why Westerdale had not joined the army in preference to the ministry; another asked how many sons he was prepared to send to war. The Revd Eric Pilton stated that 'if Peace is a Christian ideal then war is anti-Christian'; and another advocated collective security and disarmament. It all culminated in a great irony as the correspondence column also contained a letter calling for international disarmament signed by all the local Free Church ministers including Westerdale.[39]

Some even began to doubt whether the day should continue at all. In 1932 Lieutenant-Colonel Dan Burgess VC, governor of the Tower, addressed the Honourable Company of Cordwainers and told them of his distress at learning of a body committed to the abolition of Armistice Day.[40] But as an article in St Luke's, Ilford, parish magazine showed, the day just had too much significance and too much of a grip on the public imagination. Under the

33 *CP*, 8 July 1922.
34 *IR*, 17 Nov. 1932.
35 *EHE*, 15 Nov. 1935.
36 THL, metropolitan borough of Bethnal Green, council minutes, 17 Jan. 1935.
37 Ibid. 25 June 1935.
38 *EHE*, 14 Nov. 1932.
39 Ibid. 21 Nov. 1932.
40 *CP*, 18 Nov. 1932.

title 'The festival of peace – a keynote for Armistice Day' the piece stated that:

> The critics of Armistice celebrations must be somewhat deficient in their knowledge of mass psychology, when they clamour for their discontinuance or curtailment. With eager interest worshippers continue to fill our Churches as the sad anniversary recurs. What a conflict of emotions! What ghostly memories! Faces staring up before our very eyes, as we, at these services of thanksgiving and remembrance, sing the Warriors Hymn: O Valiant Hearts. . . . If any change in name be ever contemplated, why not call Armisticetide – 'All Heroes Day'?[41]

The Church could also, of course, claim the ancient significance of November and remembrance, as was reiterated by the parish magazine of St Clement's, Great Ilford, in November 1934:

> November is inevitably a month of remembrance for all church people; for not only have we the commemorations of All Saints and All Souls, but Armistice Day also brings to us the remembrance of the noble stand made by our Country for high principle and of the great sacrifice given by so many of our 'dearest and best'.[42]

Respect for the day thus remained strong and there was no tailing off of public interest. In 1930 the *City Press* noted that 'There seemed to be no dimunition

---

[41] St Luke's, Ilford, parish magazine, Nov. 1932. The permanence of Armistice Day had also been discussed in the Commons in 1929. During the same exchange, on the number of soldiers designated to parade at the Cenotaph, Major Brunel Cohen MP of the British Legion had asked 'Does the right hon. gentleman imply that when there are no relatives of ex-servicemen left the Armistice service will be dropped?' The Secretary of State for War, Tom Shaw, ironically a wartime pacifist, replied 'I cannot answer hypothetical questions, but I hope that when there are no relatives of ex-servicemen left we shall have forgotten what war is.' For a discussion of this debate see Gregory, *Silence of memory*, 121–3. The Army perceived the 'spit and polished' troops drawn up at the Cenotaph as a good advert for recruiting: K. Jeffrey, 'The post-war army', in Beckett and Simpson, *Nation in arms*, 218.

[42] St Clement's, Great Ilford, parish magazine, Nov. 1934. The quote 'dearest and the best' comes from the Cecil Spring-Rice poem 'I vow to thee, my country'. Stephen Gwynn, the poet's biographer, wrote on the poem that 'In 1911 and 1912, Spring-Rice's imagination was ceaselessly at work on the thought of a war in which England must fight for her very life; and he wrote of her helmeted and sword-wielding. But in 1918, after he had seen three years of war, he struck out all the panoply and noise of battle to glorify the single aspect of patriotism that seemed worth celebrating – the passion of self-sacrifice. What he kept, in 1918 as in 1911, was the vision of man's other country, a vision of gentleness and peace. . . . These lines are the extreme quintessential expression of Sir Cecil Spring-Rice's spirit; but they have received a wider acceptance. They have been spoken broadcast on the day in November when England remembers her dead; yet it would mean more to their writer that they were chosen to be inscribed as the last words of the Golden Book of Eton, at the end of the long list of those whom the school that he loved sent forth during the Great War to make the "final sacrifice" ': S. Gwynn (ed.), *The letters and friendships of Sir Cecil Spring-Rice: a record*, ii, London 1929, 432–3. In 1921 Gustav Holst set the words to music and thus made it a powerful hymn: M. Short, *Gustav Holst: the man and his music*, Oxford 1990, 197.

in the number present; certainly there was no sign of a slackening in the public observance.'[43] Five years later it was just as well observed:

> Despite the fact that seventeen years have passed since the Armistice, the Day of Remembrance continues to make a strong appeal to citizens. . . . The Two Minutes seemed an eternity and it was so complete as to become an oppression. Never has there been so complete a hush – a hush made more intense by the soft lapping of the pigeons overhead.[44]

1935 was also the year when fog ruined the service at West Ham. At the last moment the service was forced inside the memorial hospital, which meant that many were being left outside unable to see or hear. The *Stratford Express* received a host of indignant complaints; the improvised service clearly ruined the day for many, and even the bishop of Barking thought it had been a shoddy affair.[45] This shows that if an element of doubt had entered the day by the early thirties, it was certainly not reflected in the numbers present at the services. The *Essex Times* reports of the Romford services show no dimunition in interest from the people: 'One of the largest crowds ever seen at the annual Armistice Day parade was attracted to the Market Place in the afternoon';[46] 'The congregation this year at the town's service was greater than ever, and the passing of the years seems not to have lessened a whit the interest that is taken';[47] 'The two minutes' silence was heralded by maroons at the fire station, and the stillness was unbroken for a space, while watching thousands lining the road and the surrounding windows waited bareheaded.'[48]

In fact, interest was so great that in 1935 the official service was moved from St Edward's to the Plaza Cinema in order to accommodate the greater numbers. There were some complaints that a secular building was being used for a holy act but it was noted that the important thing was 'the spirit which permeates' the act.[49] In the event all 1,500 seats in the cinema were easily filled and the crowd spilled out onto the streets. Thus two essential social habits of the age were combined, cinema-going and Armistice Day observance.[50]

---

43 *CP*, 14 Nov. 1930.
44 Ibid. 15 Nov. 1935.
45 *SE*, 16 Nov. 1935.
46 *ET*, 15 Nov. 1930.
47 Ibid. 14 Nov. 1931.
48 Ibid. 18 Nov. 1933.
49 Ibid. 8 Nov. 1935.
50 Ibid. 15 Nov. 1935. The impact of modern technology was revealed at Bow Road Methodist church in 1934 when the Cenotaph service was broadcast live to the congregation. The wireless served to make the nation a true community as all could feel part of the events at the national memorial at the precise moment they happened: *ELA*, 17 Nov. 1934. In 1928 an Ilford woman wrote an irate letter to the *Recorder*; she complained that interference had ruined her reception of the broadcast and was convinced it was the work of local prank-

The fact that Armistice Day fell on a Sunday in 1934 was seen as a reason for its increased signifcance. The *Ilford Recorder* stated that:

> The scene was more impressive this year than for many years. Sunday gave an opportunity for many who have been unable to attend because they have been at work to be present and the attachments [*sic*] of the British Legion men and Territorials were larger than usual.[51]

Exactly the same sentiment was felt at All Hallows', Bromley-by-Bow:

> The fact that November 11th falls on a Sunday gives opportunity this year for a fuller observance of this national commemoration than is sometimes possible. . . . It is hoped that many ex-servicemen and others who desire to recall before God the valour and sacrifice of those who had died that we might live will be present at the Men's Corporate Communion at 10 o'clock.[52]

A good yardstick was provided in the City. The *City Press* predicted a diminished turn-out, and they believed that they were proved right. The crowd only numbered about 4,000 at the London Troops' memorial, half the usual figure according to their correspondent and St Paul's Cathedral was only filled instead of spilling out over the steps and into the churchyard. It still seems pretty impressive.[53]

Alongside the traditional interest in the day, went the traditional subjects of the day. Despite the shift in emphasis it was still possible to refer to the solid, patriotic values that had so marked the day in the twenties without a hint of irony. The message was also clear: the war was still seen as a necessary and righteous struggle, no suspicion of futility being allowed to filter. When the dean of St Paul's addressed the crowds in the Royal Exchange in 1935 he told them not to 'forget to be grateful for the deliverance'.[54] He obviously did not doubt that Britain had indeed been delivered from a demonic fate thanks to the sacrifices made in the war. It was an achievement to be proud of as the *Prudential Bulletin* stated: 'nothing can diminish the pride that fills our hearts as we remember their valour, their fortitude and their devotion to the cause in which they have taken up arms'.[55]

Elsewhere wartime values continued to flourish. Good old-fashioned suspicion of the Germans remained a part of the memory of the war. A letter

---

sters. The letter was printed under the headline 'Wireless Fiends'!: *IR*, 16 Nov. 1928. For a general discussion of the role of radio in Armistice Day see Gregory, *Silence of memory*, 133–42. See also J. M. Mackenzie ' "In touch with the infinite": the BBC and the empire, 1923–53', in J. M. Mackenzie (ed.), *Imperialism and popular culture*, Manchester 1986, 165–92.

51 *IR*, 15 Nov. 1934.

52 GLRO, P88/ALL2/13/4/26/27, All Hallows', Bromley-by-Bow, parish magazine, Nov. 1934.

53 *CP*, 16 Nov. 1934.

54 Ibid. 15 Nov. 1935.

55 *PB*, Nov. 1930, 16.

on the Zeppelin raids was printed in the *East Ham Echo* during the Armistice-tide of 1933. It concluded on a note of caution, tinged with sarcasm: 'over in Germany a nation tries to camouflage the fact that it is still unrepentant. In our own England we have those who still trust the Hun. Seems funny somehow'.[56] The wife of a shell-shocked ex-serviceman wrote a piece on the poetry of Rupert Brooke for the *Echo*. She included a comparison between Hitler's ambitions and those of imperial Germany, but her main preoccupation was with the resilience of women throughout the war and their desire to see the sacrifices properly remembered:

> It was a time of devotion to duty and great courage. In the last year of the war many of the older girls gladly and proudly saw the lads they loved or friends that they might have loved, go to France – and all did not return. These are remembrances that shall never be taken from us in spite of the talk of so-called Pacifists. . . . The men who died – the men who were wounded – the men who were shell-shocked, the people who gave their future health to their country in 1914–1918 did so to keep England and her honour unviolated, and it is 'up to us' and future generations to carry on their ideals – the ideals of men like Rupert Brooke.[57]

It seems as if it was too painful to admit that the sacrifices had been made in vain. A large slice of anti-German feeling was also perceptible at the East London Scouts Armistice rally in Stepney. The boys were reminded of the peculiar nature of German militarist *kultur*: 'Nearly 21 years ago they were threatened with the loss of their liberty; threatened by enslavement by a power which for generations had been taught to worship a great military force.'[58]

The patriotic themes were buttressed by the same militant Christianity that had justified the war and defined Armistice Day throughout the twenties. The Revd E. A. Gardner of West Ham displayed the most perfectly preserved tenets. He compared Armistice Day to Good Friday; the implication that the dead had imitated Christ was common but the connection with Good Friday was another of Winnington-Ingram's wartime dictums.[59] Whether it was 1915, 1925 or 1935 certain facts remained solid and self-evident to Gardner and many others.

The war was still presented as a sacred cause in which the dead followed the path of Christ. The vicar of Romford, the Revd H. C. Robins stated that 'if they looked at them [the dead] under the light of the Cross, they had done the same as Christ did, they bore the sins of the world'. During the same

---

[56] *EHE*, 17 Nov. 1933.
[57] Ibid. 10 Nov. 1933.
[58] *ELA*, 16 Nov. 1935.
[59] *SE*, 14 Nov. 1931. Winnington-Ingram stated during Holy Week 1919 that 'I have said through the war, and I say it again here today, that those boys of ours died for the same cause and in the same way as Jesus Christ died on Good Friday.' See his collected sermons in *Victory and after*, London 1919, 214.

Armistice the Revd H. B. Young of St Andrew's, Romford, compared the German occupation of Belgium with the Roman oppression of Palestine,[60] but when the Revd Sinclair Phillips of Romford Congregational church made a similar point his attitude implied that the ideals were coming into doubt:

> Those boys who passed out of their homes and churches did not go forth because of their love of warfare. They went through the compelling power of high ideals. Their country's honour was at stake; its name was written on a scrap of paper. They were going to make the great war the last war and they were prepared to pay whatever price was asked from them. It was their ideal that was in danger of being forgotten now.[61]

In 1926 he made an identical point, linking sacrifice with idealism, and had said that 'Redemption always meant a Cross, and the boys were willing to pay that price'.[62] Armistice Day traditions appeared impervious.

Consolation too remained part of the day and it was still possible to refer to a Christ-like sacrifice without incongruity tainting the statement. The Revd B. Cockett led the joint Salvation Army–British Legion service at the Ilford Citadel in 1932. He told the assembly that he did not see the tragedy in the deaths:

> We dare not . . . sorrow for those who gave their lives – we sorrow for ourselves only. If Christ had lived a long life, He might have been a great carpenter, but He died at 33, and became the Saviour of the world. We commemorate the memory of the fallen by wearing a scarlet poppy with a black cross hidden in its heart, the emblem of the greatest thing in life, salvation through sacrifice. The death of the men we knew, made plain the meaning of the sacrifice of Christ.[63]

In 1930 a new term was introduced to East London – Armisticetide. Heavy with iconographical and canonical overtones, it shows how the Armistice had come to be a Christian occasion. The secular embodied in the Cenotaph was lost as Christianity and Anglicanism in particular took the day into its calendar. Armisticetide also gave the occasion an air of great antiquity and Englishness, despite the growing sense of internationalist pacifism. It was first used in *Dockland Outlook*, the journal of the Docklands Settlements, in 1930; in 1932 it was quoted in the parish magazines of St Clement's, Great Ilford, and All Saints', Goodmayes, and the *East London Advertiser* used it in November 1934.[64]

---

[60] *ET*, 14 Nov. 1931.
[61] Ibid. 15 Nov. 1930.
[62] Ibid. 13 Nov. 1926.
[63] *IR*, 17 Nov. 1932.
[64] St Clement's, Great Ilford, parish magazine, Nov. 1932; All Saints', Goodmayes, parish magazine, Nov. 1932; *ELA*, 17 Nov. 1934. It is slightly odd that it took so long for the term to become common parlance in East London as Adrian Gregory has identified its use as early as 1925: *Silence of memory*, 76.

That Armistice Day remained firmly in the possession of the bereaved, was revealed in 1931 when the vicar of St Andrew's, Bethnal Green, conceptualised it entirely in terms of bereavement: 'Armistice Day has many tender memories for the passing generation; many of our mothers and fathers look back to the children who gave their lives at the call of their country's need.'[65]

Ex-servicemen still tended to perform their own rituals away from the scrutiny of the general public. At the Poplar and Stepney Rifles service Lieutenant-Colonel Watts took the opportunity to promote the Territorial Army to his audience of riflemen and ex-riflemen. He used the traditional carrot of good food and a good life, while doubting the ability of pacifist idealists:

> Our peace leaders were inclined to go too fast, and should they be wrong what a horrible position would arise. Theirs was a very grave responsibility. He appealed to young men to join the Territorials which would make them fit and healthy, ready to respond to war if it came whilst if it did not so much the better.[66]

The Old Comrades present, who had seen the horrors of war, seemed to have had no qualms about this very obvious call to arms in case of another. The memory of the war was truly a complicated one for these men. In 1936 Brigadier-General J. T. Wigan addressed the Old Comrades' Association of the 4th (Ilford) battalion, Essex Regiment. He told the old sweats to encourage their sons and relatives to join the Territorial Army and experience all the benefits of service life. Soldiering had obviously not become a redundant or contemptible profession even among those who had fought in what was believed to be the war to end war.[67]

In November 1934 the men of the Whitechapel, Jewish (Maccabean) branch of the British Legion were addressed by Dr O'Donovan, Conservative MP for Mile End and vice-president of the Mile End and Limehouse British Legion. He emphasised the gap between servicemen and society, highlighting the deep sense of solidarity that war service imparted, a sense of being apart which was intensified among the Maccabeans by virtue of their religion: 'The soldier carried on his back the destiny of the civilian. If civilians would lose their senses and go to war, soldiers were their agent and soldiers who knew war were the best apostles of peace.'[68]

Ex-servicemen never lost pride in their achievements or their feelings towards their lost comrades. The 1st City of London battalion, Royal Fusiliers, and its Old Comrades' Association marked their debut in action by celebrating Aubers Ridge Day each May; it was their own remembrance day. A spirit of commemoration was combined with a proud sense of their special connection with the City:

65 THL, St Andrew's, Bethnal Green, parish magazine, Nov. 1931.
66 *ELA*, 18 Nov. 1933.
67 *IR*, 12 Nov. 1936.
68 *ELO*, 4 Nov. 1934.

In the distance can be heard the hum of the traffic of the City, while a hundred or two hundred yards away up Cheapside and Queen Victoria Street can be seen masses of red omnibuses already brought to a standstill by the density of the crowd. At 10.59 the buglers sound the last post and, as the last note dies away, the Colours are lowered, and for two minutes absolute silence reigns in the 'Hub of the World', broken only by the fluttering of some pigeon.[69]

The London Rifle Brigade's journal responded to the 1933 Armistice in equally complex terms. Its message tackled the questions of the lack of progress towards the new world and the fact that the war was very definitely slipping into the past; but the memory of the dead remained inviolate, as did the glorious war record of the imperial armies:

For a great and increasing number of our people it [the war] is now nothing more than history, and history, unfortunately, except to those that made it is not always a thrilling subject. And there are other influences at work which tend to force the war into oblivion. No thinking man can look forward to another conflict with anything other but horror, nor can anyone seriously imagine that the result of another European conflagration will be anything but the collapse of such things as are good in our civilisation. But it would be a grim tragedy if such thoughts blinded us to the deeds of 1914–1918. And it is well if we pause on occasion to consider the immensity of the Empire's sacrifice. It is not the fault of the Dead if that sacrifice has so far failed to produce the millennium.[70]

Two themes were clearly being given extra weight during this period: the passing of time and the new generation. There were ambivalent messages however: the exhortation to imitate the dead was still present, but so was the cautionary lesson that only by remembering the dead could the horror of war

---

[69] *The Tudor Rose: Magazine of the 1st City of London Battalion, Royal Fusiliers*, May 1933, 9. The choice of alternative dates as days of remembrance was a common theme in Britain; the alternative was usually the anniversary of the début in action of a local regiment or battalion. Bury, intimately connected with the Lancashire Fusiliers, who were barracked in the town, provides a good example. On 25 April 1915 the Fusiliers took part in the Gallipoli Landings and achieved the heroic feat of 'Six V.C.s before breakfast'. After the war Gallipoli Day was reverently marked in the town (and indeed still is). Gallipoli Day is also celebrated in Australia under the title ANZAC Day in memory of the Australian and New Zealand troops who also took part in the assault. An excellent study of the importance of the Lancashire Fusiliers and Gallipoli to the town of Bury can be found in G. Moorhouse, *Hell's foundations: a town, its myths and Gallipoli*, London 1992, 124–41, 179–237. For ANZAC Day see A. Thomson, *ANZAC memories: living with the legend*, Oxford 1994, 3–4, 129–31, 133–42, 201–2. Other dates were sometimes floated as alternative remembrance days: the *Ilford War Memorial Gazette* announced in May 1921 that 30 May was to be 'Inter-Allied Memorial Day'. It noted that it was already observed in America and stated that 'it will be consecrated in memory of the Great Silent Army'. However the public response was minimal; the date had no emotional appeal and simply could not compete with the significance of 11 November or dates of peculiar, local importance: RHL, *Ilford War Memorial Gazette*, no. 4 (May 1921), 3.

[70] *LRB Record*, Nov. 1933, 9.

be averted. In 1935 the dean of St Paul's said that the young must never be allowed to forget the war,[71] while the *Prudential Bulletin* seemed to suggest that some sort of mystical gnosis held young and old together on Armistice Day:

> Many changes have taken place since the 11th November, 1918. A new generation which has no knowledge of the War, a generation to whom it is but one of Childhood's undefinable memories. To all of us – to those who have never known – comes the two minutes' silence, our tribute to the dead. We are united in a common bond of pride and sympathy, and strengthed thereby in our determination to go forward with undaunted spirit.[72]

Not everyone agreed with this, as was clearly seen in Romford in 1934 when the *Essex Times* printed the banner headlines: 'Debunkers of Armistice Day/ Does the Great Sacrifice Mean Nothing Now?/War is Nature's Suicide – Not a Purge.'[73] The sermon of the Revd P. S. Abrahams, of St Edward's, was at the heart of the matter. He had asked how many boys or girls aged around sixteen believed that the Armistice had any value at all. He also said that many believed that the victory had been hollow and that cynics sought to undermine the whole day. At the same time he maintained that there was an undeniable truth at the bottom of it all which was that 'deeds of courage and self-sacrifice could never be destroyed'.[74] A year earlier the mayor of Ilford had made exactly the same point when he told the crowds outside the town hall that 'the younger element did not understand the meaning of Armistice, and did not enter into the spirit of it'.[75] The theory that the young were ignorant to the meaning of the day seemed to find justification in 1930 when the *Ilford Recorder* ran a banner headline stating 'Disgusting Incidents during Tuesday's Silence'.[76] The story concerned the fact that the grammar school girls continued their games lesson in Valentines Park during the silence. Numerous letters of complaint were printed in the *Recorder*. Strangely no one seemed to blame the teachers; rather it was the girls who were portrayed as disrespectful iconoclasts.[77]

The young, who had not known the trials of war or even the deceased, could not grasp the significance of the occasion with quite the same intensity of those who had experienced it. The vicar of St Andrew's, Bethnal Green, realised this and wrote that 'The rising generation (we are told) knows little of the war days. The fresh young lives which were sacrificed for their country

---

71 *CP*, 15 Nov. 1935.
72 *PB*, Nov. 1932, 13.
73 *ET*, 17 Nov. 1934.
74 Ibid.
75 *IR*, 16 Nov. 1933.
76 Ibid. 14 Nov. 1930.
77 Ibid.

are to them not even a memory: those who lived and loved and laughed with us and died at the call of duty are but *names*.'[78]

The experience gap was fully appreciated by the Revd E. M. Porter Goff of Ilford who told the League of Nations Union that it would be a disaster if Armistice Day was discontinued. He believed it was vital in teaching lessons about the horror of war to the young; his conclusion was hardly optimistic as he stated that 'I don't think it is likely that there will be another Great War for the next 25 years.'[79] In other words the Armistice message would die with the present generation.[80] Mr Atkins of the Union then concluded the Armistice night rally by stating that the Union was an important agent of fraternity as it transcended age barriers. This uniformity guaranteed an apostolic succession of the League's principles as 'there was another generation coming along to whom "1914–1918" would be something like 1066'.[81] During the same Armistice the vicar of Romford told the crowd that the young had to be brought up in the ways of peace as their fathers had died to save them from the horrors of war.[82]

Armistice concepts could also be used to instill far more traditional values in the young. The boys of East Ham Grammar School (previously the Secondary School) were constantly reminded via the medium of Armistice Day of their duty to the school and to maintain its honour:

As the boys go about the hall of their building they see the ever-lit torches shining on the names of the gallant company who, in the dark years of 1914–1918, gave their lives in the faith that those who came after would see that they had not died in vain. That faith is for the boys and girls of today to fulfil. To them comes the task of building a new world. The Grammar Schools are in existence mainly to train generations of devoted men and women, who will give the ability of trained minds and the enthusiasm of loyal hearts to the solution of the problems of the changing world.[83]

[78] THL, St Andrew's, Bethnal Green, parish magazine, Nov. 1930. The vicar went on to draw a most vivid comparison between the act of communion on Armistice Day and communion with the glorious dead: 'Yet there are for many of us cherished memories of noble men and women, and the years have not blotted them out from our minds. So we will gather before the Altar and keep the Silence – remembering them and praying for their souls' rest: and we will join them in offering their sacrifice with the sacrifice of God's only Son – joining together with Saints and Angels in the greatest and most beautiful Act of Worship which binds together Heaven and earth. Many lessons of the war are still unlearned, but this we will remember.'

[79] *IR*, 14 Nov. 1930.

[80] Geoff Dyer has examined the peculiar memory of the Great War and he identified this very theme: 'Every generation since the armistice has believed that it will be the last for whom the Great War has any meaning': *The missing of the Somme*, 18.

[81] *IR*, 14 Nov. 1930.

[82] *ET*, 15 Nov. 1930.

[83] NHL, *East Ham Grammar Schools Magazine*, Nov. 1932, 3.

A year later the boys were reminded of their role in the continuing fight for peace. It was a struggle:

> [that] began in the mud, and filth of Flanders and France, on the scorching plains of Gallipoli and in the East, and in the air with their hidden, desperate foes. 'A war to end war' was a phrase indicating a reality to those men. Yet 'the war to end war' means also a long struggle in times that are called days of peace.[84]

Clearly the dead had not achieved a new world devoid of strife and struggle. Concepts of duty to the country were therefore still very much alive. A year later the Old Comrades of Romford Intermediate School donated a flag as a memorial to the dead of the school. The headmistress saw it as a symbol of obligation and honour; she spoke of the boys who had 'served their country so nobly' and added that 'a memorial had been raised which should remind the children always to be ready to do their best for the school'.[85] A year earlier the Romford councillor, S. Boston, noted his desire to see children brought up in the ways of peace but then added that they should also be ready 'to defend their country against an aggressor if one should arise, and he was one who held that they must be prepared'.[86]

East London children were not allowed to escape this ethos of devotion to duty and unquestioning loyalty to a hierarchical system which found a most potent stage in Armistice Day. Over 3,000 East London Scouts gathered in Stepney in 1933. Mr Ince, warden of Roland House Church Mission Centre addressed them, in the spirit of Kipling's 'If':

> They had to be straight and honest though mixing with people who were twisters, unselfish and loyal where men were mostly selfish; helpful and cheerful in a world given mainly to the worship of blue devils; and clean in word, thought and deed.[87]

He added that the living had to make 'themselves ready and worthy to take the place of those who had given their all for England . . . and each Scout replied "I will" '.[88]

Wartime values were transformed and transposed to fit the demands of the time; in this way Armistice Day ensured its traditional, backward-looking atmosphere. The young could never quite escape the clutches of the past and the war loomed over their lives. This was most vividly shown in the magazine of the Docklands Settlement journal. The page devoted to Docklands youth in the November 1930 issue is worth quoting in full as it perfectly captures the didactic spirit of the day:

84 Ibid. Nov. 1933, 7.
85 *ET*, 14 Nov. 1931.
86 Ibid. 15 Nov. 1930.
87 *ELA*, 18 Nov. 1933. See *Rudyard Kipling's verse*, 576.
88 Ibid.

If ye break faith with us who die
We shall not sleep though poppies grow
In Flanders' Fields.

Everywhere you go for the next few weeks you will see those words emblazoned on hoardings, in shop windows, on private cars, in offices, in factories, in newspapers and on the Settlement.

Ye means YOU, whoever YOU may be and whatever you may be. US means all those who lie in graves across sea or at home, and those countless thousands who have died to everything but pain and disappointment, and who still throng the many hospitals in this country. What is the faith that we may break? Perhaps the original writer of the words was thinking of the actual enemy in the field, and the possibility of England giving up the struggle to win the war. Time alters a good many things and lends a new meaning to many phases. And so the lines which eat into our minds during Armistice-tide have for you and for me a new and very real significance. They challenge us to keep faith with the lofty ideal of 'Active Service' – active for God, King and Country. They demand from us something more than a mere penny or a magnanimous gesture of giving more to the Haig Fund than we can really afford. They challenge us to re-dedication of self to service for the greatest King, and if we answer that challenge wholeheartedly and faithfully, such things as looking after the maimed, the sick in mind, the blind and the heart-broken, ideal homes for heroes, and perfection of local government, will be mere routine duties in the wider and international stride towards perfection. Selfishness will scuttle away into the background; 'Give till it hurts' will not be the motto of the eleventh of November, but of each day from January 1st to December 31st. In those heart-searching moments of Silence into which we shall all be plunged at 11 am on Tuesday the 11th, as the faces of those we cared for, or the figures that have been burned into our minds by books and films pass in review before us, let us, in the name of Him Who died that all might live, passionately repeat with body, soul and spirit: WE WILL NOT BREAK FAITH.[89]

The *East London Advertiser* witnessed the proof of this approach at the Poplar British Legion service in 1933: 'There was not only a large number

[89] THL, *Dockland Outlook: The Journal of the Docklands Settlements*, Nov. 1930, 5. Samuel Hynes has shown that from 1926, and more particularly from 1929 when *All quiet on the Western Front* was published in Britain, there was a rush of war literature and films which started to present a new version of the war. He states that this was the time when 'the war becomes a myth'. Such works as Edmund Blunden's *Undertones of war*, Siegfried Sassoon's *Memoirs of a fox-hunting man* and *Memoirs of an infantry officer*, Robert Graves's *Goodbye to all that* and Manning's *Her privates we* were published during this period. In addition, the stage play *Journey's end* was produced on the London stage and subsequently made into a film as was *All quiet on the Western Front*. The editor of the *Dockland Outlook* seems to be referring to exactly this phenomenon when he wrote of the images 'burned into our minds by books and films': Hynes, *A war imagined*, 423–64.

of ex-servicemen and old people, but a great many young folks and children who had been taught what Poppy Day meant.'[90]

Armistice Day therefore entered a confused period in the years between 1930 and 1935. In comparison, the twenties seem all the more consistent. The old themes survived but were joined by some elements of disillusion and a mistrust of politicians as unemployment and international events intruded on the day. But the strength of conservative elements and the sheer habit of attending the services meant that true radicalism on a dangerous scale was never likely. This period also shows how the wider situation influenced the local. The debates over the war memorials had been shaped by the characters of the boroughs and districts; this is much less true of the themes surrounding Armistice Day and remembrance. This was a period when greater attention was being paid to the wider problems of the world, when a sense of history began to permeate the memory of the Great War, and when the effects of national and international trends on the locality were obvious. The industrial and working-class districts more severely affected by the slump were the ones that saw the protests of the NUWM and the Communist Party. The middle-class areas of East Ham and Ilford seemed to be more accessible to the middlebrow philosophising of the local League of Nations Unions and pacifist movements, which often found homes under the umbrella of the various churches. Thus particular local circumstances shaped the exact manner in which larger events and issues were felt and manifested.

At the same time the iconography and respect for the dead was as high as it had ever been; the same sense of achievement and deliverance remained inherent in the observance of Armistice Day. The old and the new came together, but it was not necessarily a head-on collision. Rather the dead were simply viewed from different angles and different conclusions were drawn from the lessons of war. Any attempt fundamentally to alter the nature of the day was often misconstrued as an attempt to scrap it.

[90] *ELA*, 18 Nov. 1933.

9

Into Battle, 1936–1939

The last years before the outbreak of the Second World War saw Armistice Day revert to type in East London. West Ham did see the culmination of an extreme, Christian pacifist campaign but that was almost completely rejected. Instead people seemed to find comfort and even hope in the solid views that had prevailed in the twenties. This time round the concepts were firmly anchored in the reality of the world situation.

The parishioners of Plaistow witnessed an absolutist pacifist campaign orchestrated by the Revd D. C. Tibbenham. He told his congregation that Christ had been captured and crucified without a struggle and therefore war was a sin. In a distinctly pessimistic mood he stated that 'as far as I can see another war is inevitable unless the miraculous happens'. He concluded that invasion was preferable to fighting, naively implying that it would not be such a bad thing:

> Passing under foreign control [was preferable] to the horrors of war of count-less millions, with its leading young men [led] into sin and murder, with its indiscriminate killing by shell and bomb and bullet, with its rousing of an orgy of hate and fear and lying. Of course, we did pass under foreign control in 1066.[1]

A week later the *Express* printed a letter from an ex-serviceman: he was insulted by Tibbenham's suggestion that he was less of a Christian by virtue of his war service. His letter argued that defending the country was a duty although he believed that there ought to be room 'for the genuine conscientious objector'.[2] A year later Tibbenham was again advocating total pacifism. He exhorted 'the people to realise the utter futility of war'.[3] At exactly the same moment the Revd G. H. Simpson of Romford Trinity Methodist church 'said that many of his own congregation – the war generation – were slowly coming to the conclusion that the immense sacrifice of young manhood of twenty years ago was almost in vain'.[4] In Ilford the pacifist cause blended into appeasement. A correspondent to the *Recorder* wrote to complain about:

> those people who say that we should 'stand up to Hitler'. Unfortunately it would not be a case of 'standing up to Hitler', it would be a case of throwing

1 *SE*, 14 Nov. 1936.
2 Ibid. 21 Nov. 1936.
3 Ibid. 13 Nov. 1937.
4 *RR*, 12 Nov. 1937.

millions of innocent people into a senseless mortal combat with one another, and what sane man would advocate this?[5]

The high-water mark of pacifist feeling in Stepney came in 1936 when the Stepney Council for Peace and Democracy sold white poppies in aid of the International Peace Campaign. It caused remarkably little fuss if the correspondence and news columns of the local press are anything to go by, and so does reveal a certain change of atmosphere.[6] At the same time the local League of Nations Unions found their tenets under pressure. The Revd Rutherford Lane addressed the Ilford Men's Meeting and stated that 'the League has not failed'.[7] The bishop of Chelmsford, speaking to the Romford League of Nations Union, revealed an ironic mix of clear thinking and a new emphasis on the grand, abstract Armistice themes. He said that it was ridiculous to talk of peace when there were conflicts raging over the entire globe but that was no reason to dismiss the League or the values of duty inherent in Armistice Day.[8]

Any enlightened views of world co-operation still came up against the formidable barrier of good old-fashioned patriotic rhetoric. The Revd E. A. Gardner of West Ham was the embodiment of these values: by the mid-thirties his Armistice services had become an institution in the borough of West Ham. In 1936 he preached on the ancient bonds between monarch and people in England and, in the process, he did a convincing impression of Kitchener twenty-two years on from the original:

'Your King and Country need you' was the call, and they answered it. That thought had run through the minds of Englishmen until it had become an instinct, and it was a very good and sound way in which to walk. The alliance of King and people had had a leavening effect on English politics.[9]

5   IR, 3 Nov. 1938.
6   ELA, 7 Nov. 1936. For a general discussion of the white poppy campaign see Gregory, Silence of memory, 153–7.
7   IR, 17 Nov. 1938.
8   RR, 13 Nov. 1936.
9   SE, 14 Nov. 1936. Ironically King Edward VIII had just attended his final public duty as monarch at the Cenotaph. In early December his affair with Mrs Simpson became public knowledge. See G. Talbot, The Country Life book of the royal family, London 1980, 92. The influence of Kitchener rumbled on long after his death; he became a symbol of everything the British empire stood for. His memory was evoked in 1924 by the Revd David Sutherland of Ilford Presbyterian church who used Kitchener to remind any forgetful youth of his debt to the dead: 'They did not remember a poster "Your country needs you" that caused men to throw down their tools, to leave their offices for the last time and to give up the recently opened business which was beginning to yield a profit, without a thought about the sacrifice they were making': IR, 14 Nov. 1924. In 1927 the chairman of the Mile End British Legion referred to Kitchener as the inspiration of all Englishmen: 'Men of the British Navy and Army, you would not I feel sure, wish me to speak of the dead without some reference to the greatest of them all – Lord Kitchener. His death at sea was an inspiration to Englishmen no less than his life, which he spent in the service of his country': ELO, 19 Nov. 1927. For a dis-

He believed such a philosophy was the greatest guard against extremism, and blamed the 'intelligensia' for sowing the seeds of discontent against the English way of life. By 1937 he was even more vehement; it was in the language of 1914 that he inferred that Britain's cause was God's and therefore that Britannia acted as the temporal guardian of the world:

> There was a tremendous call for patriotism; not cheap patriotism – that was dead he hoped – but willingness to serve and give themselves for England knowing that all the time they were doing that they were giving themselves for the good of the human race all over the world; and a finer thought still, that they were giving themselves to the Son of God, who gave Himself for them.[10]

The *Express* reported that Stratford church was packed for this sermon whereas the League of Nations Union meeting at the town hall was sparsely attended. Clearly Gardner was giving a lot of people what they wanted.

It was still of course possible to believe that Britain had acted as the champion of the weak and defenceless. The Revd C. W. Thomas of St Thomas's, West Ham, told his congregation that the British had acted as sportsmen throughout the conflict and were absolved from any blame:

> Never before, so far as I know has an armistice totally ended any war, but has only been a temporary cessation of hostilities. The magnanimity with which our men let the other side off after their leader had run away (inconsistent with an armistice) shows us England's innocence in things connected with war.[11]

In order to maintain the role of champion it was necessary to remember the example of the dead and follow their example of duty. Lieutenant-Colonel T. D. Chappell addressed the Scouts, Guides and Old Comrades of the Poplar and Stepney Rifles at St Stephen's, Bow, on Armistice Day 1937. He told his hearers to 'remember their comrades who made the great sacrifice and to dedicate themselves anew to serve the country for which they died'.[12]

It was still a day on which to justify the war and every sacrifice made. The dean of Manchester drew on Muscular Christian imagery when he took the Royal Exchange service, implying that the dead had achieved paradise because of their righteous sacrifice. This in turn placed an onus on the living: 'Those who had passed over had run the race well. The race of life was a relay

---

cussion of the iconography surrounding Kitchener see Sillars, *Art and survival*, 10, 21, 39, 57. There was also some unintentional irony in the reference to Kitchener's death at sea. Kitchener appears to have remained on the sinking HMS *Hampshire* to the very last. Refusing to panic or abandon ship without instruction, he seems to have let the ship sink around him: P. Warner, *Kitchener: the man behind the legend*, London 1985, 198–201.

[10] *ELO*, 13 Nov. 1937.

[11] Ibid. 6 Nov. 1937.

[12] *ELA*, 20 Nov. 1937.

one, and we all had our part in handing on the torch to those who came after us.'[13] The Revd A. St G. Colthurst, chaplain of the Honourable Artillery Company, told the men that their comrades 'died because they loved England and wanted to give Freedom and Justice' to the world.[14] Wartime values were still very much alive, and such concepts were proclaimed without irony: in 1937 the HAC veterans were told 'with them in remembrance, . . . our resolve should be – service for God and country'.[15]

Christian concepts were therefore still entwined with patriotic injunctions. The language of sacrifice was still used both as an instrument of consolation and of instruction. At Balaam Street Congregational church, West Ham, the Revd W. W. Cotton, chaplain to the local branch of the British Legion, framed his Armistice message in exactly these terms. He said that 'if they really desire peace they might have to follow Him through Gethsemane's garden and over Calvary's cruel hill'.[16]

There is little evidence to suggest that the public rejected Armistice Day or any of its tenets. The size and reverence of the Armistice crowds and congregations remained an important point of the press coverage. The *City Press* recorded great crowds in 1936: 'not a square inch of vacant ground was left, the crowds presenting to the eye a compact mass, broken occasionally by the figure of a mounted policeman'.[17] As the international situation worsened it seemed to rejuvenate the day and all it stood for still further, and perhaps provided the reassurance that the British had beaten the Germans once and they could therefore do it again. In 1938, the year of Munich, it was noted that the crowds thronged 'every available inch of space around the memorial'.[18] Armistice Day was a great agent of national cohesion, when people were brought together and presented with a largely reassuring message of duty and obedience. It was comforting and reassuring in its sheer solidity, and must have seemed like an age-old ceremony by the late thirties. '[I]n common with every city, town and hamlet throughout the Empire, Romford reverently observed the two minutes' silence on Friday for those who fell in the war.'[19] This was a common theme throughout East London. In 1936 the

[13] *CP*, 13 Nov. 1936.
[14] *HAC Journal*, Dec. 1936, 12.
[15] Ibid. Dec. 1937, 9.
[16] *SE*, 13 Nov. 1937.
[17] *CP*, 16 Nov. 1937.
[18] Ibid. 18 Nov. 1938.
[19] *RR*, 18 Nov. 1938. For a wider discussion of these 'ancient customs' see E. Hobsbawm and T. Ranger (eds), *The invention of tradition*, Cambridge 1983, 1–14. See also David Cannadine, 'The context, performance and meaning of ritual: the British monarchy and the "invention of tradition", c. 1820–1977', ibid. 101–65. The venerable nature of Armistice Day was so great that F. J. Drake-Carnell felt no qualms in adding it to his book of *Old English customs and traditions* (London 1938): 'Nearly twenty years after the end of the Great War we take it as an established custom that November 11th should see the King and the representatives of the Services, the veterans and the Government, gathered together with the people of England in Whitehall, and at other memorials all over the country, to pay tribute to those

bishop of Chelmsford told the Romford League of Nations Union that 'the general interest in the observance of Armistice Day was greater than before and there was not the slightest sign of interest in it petering out'.[20] Continued interest in the day seems to prove that the young were well aware of the sacrifices made and wanted to show their respect, or at least had no option other than to attend and receive the Armistice message. The Revd W. H. Belcher told the Poplar and Stepney Rifles that Armistice Day was a truly unique event: 'That it had not lost its fervour, its force and solemnity in 19 years was one of the most remarkable things of the present time. It was a social phenomenon and could only be productive of good.'[21] It was also an event which drew the most recalcitrant Christian to church: 'the Two Minutes' Silence are sacred moments of affectionate prayer even for those who are perhaps unaccustomed to praying with us in Church'.[22]

As well as being an element of national cohesion, the two minutes' silence served to promote the bonds of local community. The worsening of the international situation seemed to increase the desire to feel part of a wider whole; it provided strength and resolve, the simple comfort of safety in numbers. The Revd 'Tubby' Clayton certainly caught this atmosphere in 1937; he revelled in the spirit of London and beat Noël Coward to its definition by some four years. He said that frightened men were boasting and making a lot of noise:

> but London had never yet needed to boast. London Pride was just one little, humble flower, unostentatious, needing no exhibition. . . . The memory of those Londoners who died was still dear. Every street in the City had some memory of them – some tribute to pay. They possessed four great qualities – fortitude, the power to endure; fairmindedness, the root of humour, which alone rendered the intolerable endurable; brotherhood, which was no forced fellowship; and the faith, the power to hope. London, the old nurse, understood.[23]

---

who fell, and the same winter evening sees thousands of small wooden crosses on the Field of Remembrance outside Westminster Abbey, to be burnt later and the ashes scattered on the battlefields of France and Belgium. Surely the deriders of tradition would not see such things decay, or the memory of of their fathers, brothers and cousins pass away' (p. 110).

20 *ET*, 13 Nov. 1936.

21 *ELA*, 20 Nov. 1937.

22 THL, St Andrew's, Bethnal Green, parish magazine, Nov. 1936.

23 *CP*, 12 Nov. 1937. 'Tubby' Clayton ran the Christian *Toc H* movement from the City church of All Hallows-by-the-Tower. The movement was inspired by the comradeship he found whilst serving in the Great War. During the conflict he ran a Christian hostel at Talbot House, Poperinghe, near Ypres; in army signals the house was called 'Toc H' thus providing the name for his group. Its rituals were firmly based on the spirit of remembrance and wartime comradeship. Ceremonies were opened (and still are) by the lighting of the Lamp of Maintenance and the reciting of Binyon's lines from 'The fallen': T. Lever, *Clayton of Toc H*, London 1971, 122–4. Noël Coward wrote his famous song 'London pride' in 1941. It was inspired by the resilience of London during the blitz. His song reflected many of the themes Clayton spoke of (although there is no evidence that Coward was aware of Clayton's words). He wrote: 'I sat on a platform seat and watched the Londoners scurrying about in the

The Revd J. A. Mayo of Whitechapel church said 'that they were remembering the men who died to save England and to save Whitechapel'.[24] Concrete concepts of home, the physical place of residence, were therefore balanced with the largest unit of the imagined community, the nation.[25]

In many ways the interest, emotion and pride invested in the day can best be deduced from the poppy revenues. It is a lot harder (see table 2) to find patterns in the figures for the thirties than it was for the twenties. If the 1931 figures are compared with the population census figures of the same year an average contribution per head can be calculated. In all cases the sum works out at less than 1d. per head. This should not be taken as an indicator of lack of interest; the local newspapers always recorded the amounts raised by the poppy appeal with some pride. The most likely explanation for the average contribution is that poppies were sold only on the evening before Armistice Day and on Armistice morning itself which greatly reduced their relative availability. It should also be noted that much of the commuting workforce would probably have bought poppies at places of work (in this case the City) and so may not have contributed within their area of residence. The economic slump appears to have influenced the totals but not in a uniform manner: some areas felt the pinch later than the others. Local problems certainly affected the totals; the *Essex Times* and the *East Ham Echo* blamed heavy rain for the decreased totals in 1934.[26] The *Stratford Express* noted that West Ham North was sixty collectors short in 1932 and in 1930 the *East Ham Echo* recorded that no collections were made in East Ham schools.[27] Ilford, which was the most successful of the districts in the twenties, entered a more complex period. Poppy revenues were clearly affected by the depression, but in 1933 a recovery occurred, set back by the appalling weather of 1934 and another mediocre year in 1935. Thereafter the figures generally recover, hitting a peak during the increased tension over the Munich crisis. The twentieth anniversary of the Armistice, like the tenth, combined with the publicity generated by Munich caused a surge in poppy revenue in all districts. In many ways the figures for 1939 are artificially low due to the

---

thin sunshine. They all seemed to me to be gay and determined and wholly admirable and for a moment or two I was overwhelmed by a wave of sentimental pride. . . . I am proud of the words of this song; they express what I felt at the time and what I still feel.' The song contained sentiments very close to Clayton's words: Cockney feet/Mark the beat of history./Every street/Pins a memory down . . . /There's a little City flower every spring unfailing/Growing in the crevices by some London railing,/Though it has a Latin name, in town and countryside/We in England call it London Pride: S. Morley, *A talent to amuse: a biography of Noël Coward*, London 1985 edn, 222; Noël Coward, *The lyrics*, London 1983 edn, 268–9.

[24] *ELA*, 20 Nov. 1937.

[25] B. Anderson, *Imagined communities: reflections on the origin and spread of nationalism*, London 1994 edn, 6–7.

[26] *ET*, 17 Nov. 1934; *EHE*, 16 Nov. 1934.

[27] *SE*, 16 Nov. 1932; *EHE*, 21 Nov. 1930.

Table 2
Poppy revenues, 1930–9

	1930	1931	1932	1933	1934	1935	1936
Bethnal Green	£477	£550	£547	£541	£400	£378	£454
Poplar	£775	£677	£608	£788	£627	£637	£685
Stepney	£681	£795	£631	£712	£648	£727	£923
East Ham	£820	£763	£746	£776	£583	£679	£823
West Ham (N.)	£1,095	£1,138	£1,046	£1,002	£516	£1,392	£616
West Ham (S.)	£632	£595	£597	£681	–	£697	£730
Ilford	£1,547	£1,525	£1,505	£1,543	£1,223	£1,392	£1,575
Romford	£530	£566	£490	£511	£454	£495	£597

	1937	1938	1939
Bethnal Green	£384	£415	£425
Poplar	£617	£643	£554
Stepney	£745	£1,049	£798
East Ham	£807	£882	£690
West Ham (N.)	£514	£712	£661
West Ham (S.)	£701	£767	£770
Ilford	£1,536	£1,611	£1,157
Romford	£494	£560	£547

Source: Royal British Legion Poppy Appeal, Aylesford, Kent

disruption caused by the early months of the war, but it is obvious that the wearing of a poppy was still a vital Armistice habit and the figures show no sign of a real or prolonged collapse.[28]

The old gender clichés also still held true. Armistice 1936 saw the *East Ham Echo* once again stress the female memory of the war:

War widows drying a tear, thought once more of the day their husbands left for the battlefield – remembered the farewell kiss, the 'Cheerio' from home.
After eighteen years, their memory was not veiled by the midsts of years. . . . Time, the greatest healer, had not carried away their grief.[29]

But then came the ambiguity:

Schoolchildren too, were there. To them the war was something which had robbed them of their fathers, and something of which their mothers had a perpetual dread, something which gave an opportunity to men to show their mettle – yes and, perhaps, *something glorious* [emphasis added].[30]

[28] By the 1930s poppies were priced at 6d., 1s., and 2s.: Gregory, *Silence of memory*, 108.
[29] *EHE*, 13 Nov. 1936.
[30] The memories of war peculiar to women were captured by Coward in *This happy breed*. The first scene of the play, set in the summer of 1919, defined the 'perpetual dread': 'FRANK: Me perishing on a field of slaughter? What a chance!/ ETHEL: There was a

The presence of children was also noted at the Romford service: the editor of the *Essex Times* obviously believed it was of great importance:

> There was one very significant thing at the service at the war memorial on Armistice Day – it was the presence of the children who lined the railings. They had no memory of the war and knew nothing about it except what they had read in history books or had been taught in school or at home. But it was those children who they had to consider for the future.[31]

As the shadow of international problems loomed larger in the late thirties ex-servicemen seemed to grow in stature. Suddenly their own special Armistice Day gatherings took on a greater significance; the nation seemed to need their peculiar qualities once more. Ex-servicemen still indulged in their special brand of camaraderie; twenty years after the war their collective desire to remember and relive their experience of war was as strong as ever. West Ham Old Contemptibles' Association had one of their largest ever meetings with over 130 present. The chairman of the East Area explained, in a speech full of pride and emotion, why ex-servicemen were a breed apart:

> they learned something of what was called comradeship, the kind of comradeship that was responsible for the existence of every ex-servicemen's organisation they had today. They were the remnants of an old army that fought together twenty-four years ago, and they believed that those men they knew then were still the finest they could ever meet.[32]

The ex-servicemen of the City, whose remembrance services had always emphasised comradeship and belonging displayed a similar spirit. It shows perhaps a paradoxical memory of war that Aubers Ridge Day continued to be an important remembrance day to them: not to remember the day peace returned but the day when their own particular war began. The editor of *The*

---

chance every minute of every day for four years and don't you forget it. I used to feel sick every time the postman came, every time the bell rang./FRANK: Well, there's no sense in going on about it now, it's all over and done with./ ETHEL: We're lucky; it isn't so over and done with for some people. Look at poor old Mrs Worsley, two sons gone and her husband, nothing left to live for, and Mrs Cross with that boy she was so proud of done in for life, can't even feed himself properly. We're lucky all right, we ought to be grateful . . . ': Mander and Mitchenson, *Noël Coward: plays: four*, 257–8. (This also illustrates the need for memorials to comfort and console the bereaved.)

[31] Ibid.

[32] *SE*, 18 Nov. 1938. Again Coward underlined the special sense of comradeship and 'apartness' that marked ex-servicemen. The basis of the firm friendship between Frank Gibbons and Bob Mitchell in *This happy breed* is shown to be their shared wartime experiences: 'PHYLLIS: Mr Gibbons and Mr Mitchell were in the war together, weren't they?/ ETHEL: Yes, and to hear them talk you'd think they were the only ones that was': Mander and Mitchenson, *Noel Coward: plays: four*, 291, 325–6. E. J. Leed has shown that the experience of the Western Front made ex-servicemen a special group within British society, with their own way of looking at the world: *No man's land: combat and identity in World War One*, Cambridge 1979, 193–213.

Tudor Rose, journal of the 1st City of London battalion, Royal Fusiliers, mused on this and came up with both a spiritual and a severely utilitarian explanation:

> There is something quite strange to my mind, I nearly said unaccountable, that this parade is very popular, not only among those who took part in the affair at Aubers Ridge in 1915, but of many others who joined the battalion at later dates.
>
> The attendance, either at the Church Service or at the Royal Exchange Memorial following, usually amounts to a couple of hundred. The strange thing is that, when a convivial evening with dinner, etc (plenty of etc), is staged in the November following, our members fall to around fifty. Is it that in our old (?) age we are drawn more to spiritual than material things, or is it the more prosaic reason of finance?[33]

The answer is probably a little of each.

The extraordinary spirit that filled ex-servicemen was also clearly visible at Romford United Services Club Armistice Dinner in 1936. Mr M. Brazier of Romford Football Club was the guest speaker. He noted that he hoped the young men present would never have to 'kick a football over the trenches: but if that time were to come he was sure that the young men would be there just the same as their fathers had been'.[34] It was an amazing throw-back to 1916, when on 1 July the East Surrey Regiment had gone into battle kicking footballs towards the German lines and been slaughtered. But there was no intentional incongruity in Brazier's speech – the themes were seen to be equally applicable twenty years on.[35]

The Whitechapel engineering firm of Buck and Hickman had its own ex-service society, which provides a fascinating insight into the nature of community and the memory of the war. These men had worked, fought and then remembered together. Every November the society held a reunion dinner, the bosses were always present and jokes were often made about relations between them and the men; it was a good safety valve for the firm as the governors allowed themselves to be lightly mocked. In 1936 the *East London Advertiser* remarked upon 'the usual convivial atmosphere common to that of old comrades'. The selective memory of the ex-servicemen was fully revealed by the treasurer of the society, A. T. Horne, who stated that: 'Though they did, to some extent, forget the unpleasant things of war, the spirit of comradeship which came from the Great War persisted and resulted in the formation of the Society.'[36]

Naturally the living ex-servicemen always saluted the dead on these occasions. The HAC chaplain 'said that it cannot be for nothing that, in spite of

---

[33] *Tudor Rose*, Summer 1936, 13.
[34] *RR*, 20 Nov. 1936.
[35] For the assault of the East Surrey's see Middlebrook, *First day on the Somme*, 124, 254.
[36] *ELA*, 21 Nov. 1936, 1 Dec. 1934, 20 Nov. 1937.

all attempts to the contrary, the instinct is overwhelming that we must go on remembering our Dead'.[37] Pride flowed through their tributes. The chairman of the Romford United Services Club stated that

> Those of us who took part in those grim years, and, whom Providence has spared to look back upon, recall deeds of single and united heroism, and the fortitude displayed by those who responded to the call of King and Country. We who are assembled here this evening express our heartfelt gratitude, and pay silent homage to the memory of those who were firm in disaster, courageous in danger and generous in victory – they lie asleep.[38]

This statement was made in 1938 and perhaps represents the reaction to the Munich agreement, signed earlier in the autumn. One ex-serviceman certainly took the opportunity to combine the sentiments of Armistice Day with an assault on government foreign policy. Will Cullen, an ex-rifleman in the Poplar and Stepney Rifles and a self-confessed Communist, managed to sound like a good old fashioned John Bull. In a letter to the *East London Advertiser* he slated the policy of appeasement and said it made Armistice Day observance a sham:

> Yet the Government represented at the Cenotaph has betrayed the dead and the living by their foreign policy, which is responsible for landing the country into the mess in which it finds itself today. They are also responsible for the abandonment of the League of Nations and the throwing overboard of collective security, the only bulwark against Fascist aggression.[39]

He advocated an immediate show of collective will with France and Russia to prevent war. Cullen warned that if collective security were not implemented a far more awful war would ensue.[40]

1938 and Munich clearly increased interest in remembrance and Armistice Day. The *Echo* noted this and referred to 'the deeper significance that

---

[37] *HAC Journal*, Dec. 1936, 11.

[38] *RR*, 18 Nov. 1938.

[39] *ELA*, 19 Nov. 1938.

[40] His stance resembles that of Frank Gibbons in *This happy breed*. Frank argues with his sister over the Munich agreement. She perceives it as blessed relief but Frank sees it as a cowering surrender to brute force: 'FRANK: . . . I've seen something today that I wouldn't 'ave believed could happen in this country. I've seen thousands of people, English people, mark you! carrying on like maniacs, shouting and cheering with relief, for no other reason but that they'd been thoroughly frightened, and it made me sick and that's a fact! I only hope to God that we shall have guts enough to learn one lesson from this and that we shall never find ourselves in a position again when we have to appease anybody!; SYLVIA: . . . I don't care how much we appease as long as we don't have a war. War is wicked and evil and vile – They that live by the sword shall die by the sword – It's more blessed to give than to receive. FRANK: I don't think it's more blessed to give in and receive a nice kick on the bottom for doing it': Mander and Mitchenson, *Noel Coward plays: four*, 359–60. It must be remembered that this play was written in the spring of 1939, after the occupation of Prague, when the mood of the nation had significantly altered.

has become attached to Armistice Day since the crisis. There was a larger crowd than for some years at the Remembrance service'.[41] Overall the atmosphere of 1938 seems to have been one of quiet preparation for war. At the East Ham Central Methodist Hall, the Revd W. H. Armstrong subtly paved the way: 'If freedom of thought was going what was life worth? It was essential for us in this freedom loving country to do our level best to see that we do not lose the liberty of free speech.'[42] In Ilford more than 3,000 people attended the service at the war memorial and the League of Nations Union had its largest attendance for some time.[43] At the Docklands Settlement the warden warned the crowd that Britain ought to be prepared for war.[44]

Armistice commemorations did not go smoothly in Bethnal Green where they were overshadowed by a clash between the Labour council, the British Legion and the British Union of Fascists. The origins of the controversy are unclear but it seems to have started in a dispute between the council and the British Legion. On Sunday 9 October the British Legion laid a wreath at the memorial in the library in order to mark the day of international reconciliation promoted by the Federation Interalliée des Anciens Combattants (the International Federation of Ex-Servicemen). The council attempted to impose a fee for opening the library but after receiving some criticism waived the payment. At this point the BUF entered the scene and used the incident to support their claims that the Labour councillors were warmongers and anti-ex-servicemen and that the council had banned a poppy collection. They further claimed that they had British Legion support and demanded their own separate service at the borough memorial on Armistice Day. The council responded by refusing to allow the BUF to hold a separate service. This prompted the reply that the Jews were allowed to hold their own service at the Cenotaph without any opposition from the Labour Party.[45] Armistice Day was obviously such an emotive issue that the council took the decision to print and distribute a special pamphlet entitled *The Labour borough of Bethnal Green: the truth about Armistice Day: reply to the fascists*. Rather paradoxically, the Labour councillors sounded like men laden with the spirit of 1914 as they implied that fascism was another German menace:

In almost every home in Bethnal Green some life was sacrificed – what for? – to defend Britain against the German invader. . . . Fascism during the war was unknown, this new kind of horror has only sprung up since the war ended. Did any of the men of Bethnal Green sacrifice their lives for Fascism, emphatically NO.[46]

---

41 *EHE*, 18 Nov. 1938.
42 Ibid.
43 *IR*, 17 Nov. 1938.
44 *SE*, 18 Nov. 1938.
45 THL, *The letter which Labour warmongers did not publish!*; *Labour warmongers continue to insult Bethnal Green ex-service men*, BUF pamphlets, Oct., Nov. 1938.
46 THL, *The Labour borough of Bethnal Green: the truth about Armistice Day: reply to the*

Determined not to be outdone in the use of wartime imagery the BUF hit back with the words of John McCrae, stating that the 'British Union has greatest respect for all ex-service men. We do not discriminate, we shall never *break faith*' [emphasis added]'.[47] The council ended the matter by reaffirming the commonly held truth that the dead were sacroscant and could not be claimed for any political activity:

> We are certain that the majority of men and women in Bethnal Green will resent this latest stunt of the Fascists and will agree with the Labour Borough Council that politics should be kept out of the Armistice Service and that No political organisation should be allowed to hold separate ceremonies which would only be used, not to pay homage to the dead, but for the purposes of political propaganda.[48]

The most remarkable piece of the period 1936–9 came from the Reverend A. Beale, chaplain of the HAC, at their Armistice service in 1938. His sermon mixed the language of 1914 with an implication for the future. He started by making clear his dread of talking of remembrance when he was affected 'by the gloomy character of the world situation'.[49]

His sermon centred on the text 'Who shall roll away the stone from the door of the sepulchre?' Christ and the sacrifice of the dead were firmly linked and he drew in the particular pain of the widows and orphans. But comfort lay in the assurance of the Resurrection. Such an approach shows the seemingly timeless values of Armistice Day; the sermon could have been given at any time over the preceding twenty years:

> And the powers of darkness insinuated, 'Was their sacrifice then in vain?' Were the broken hearts of women, the orphan children, the blood and tears of those years to be just waste? Had Christ been crucified afresh to no purpose? The answer came swiftly when those questions were seen in the light coming from the Cross. For after the desolation of Calvary came the triumph of the Resurrection and the glory of the Risen Christ.[50]

He provided further reassurance and pride by confirming the well-known fact that Britain's cause was God's:

> He stressed that they died for justice and for truth, for democracy, of which Christianity is the Charter, for freedom to live in peace and security. They may not have been articulate, they may not have been practising Christians, but they had imbibed with their mothers' milk those principles which we in Brit-

---

fascists, pamphlet, 9 Nov. 1938. Ironically, in the same pamphlet the British Legion re-stated its non-party political role.

[47] THL, *Labour warmongers*, Nov. 1938.
[48] THL, *The Labour borough of Bethnal Green*, 9 Nov. 1930.
[49] *HAC Journal*, Dec. 1938, 6.
[50] Ibid.

ain, through centuries of effort based on the teaching of the Church, have succeeded in bringing to a measure of fruition. For our history is the story of the triumph of Christ over the weaknesses of sinful men.[51]

Masculinity flowed through the message: British men had followed a Muscular Christ: 'Not . . . the pale humanitarianism of anaemic Christ, but . . . the red-blooded sacrifice of a strong and virile Son of God who triumphed over sin and death, and rolled away the stone from the door of His Sepulchre.'[52]

The sermon ended with the exhortation to re-dedicate themselves to Christ and really begin the work of God on earth, thus keeping faith with the dead. It therefore contained the unexpressed implication that keeping faith with the dead might ultimately mean following them in equally righteous sacrifice.[53] Beale used all the great iconographic devices and displayed the utter timelessness of the remembrance message, not to mention its imperviousness to any attempt to undermine it. In some ways this sermon found its perfect, if slightly irreverent, balance a week later when the *City Press* commented on a new board game called *Invasion*, in which players had to defend Britain from assault and send an expeditionary force to the continent. People were thinking in terms of war.[54]

One year later the City found itself at war but tradition was not ignored and the dead were once again thanked for their sacrifice in a service at St Paul's Cathedral.[55] The British Legion still sold poppies in both East and West Ham and laid a wreath at the Central Park cenotaph. Of greater interest was the decision of the *Echo* to print an 'on this day' column. Each edition contained a summary of events from the corresponding date in the Great War. Such a phenomenon shows how the memory of that conflict had not been rejected by 1939 and how this newspaper at least perceived the new war as a continuation of the old one.[56] For the *East London Observer*, England was still carrying the light of liberty, as it had in 1914:

for the remembrance of our million dead, the million who willingly gave their lives so that England might live on, and lead the peoples of the earth to happiness and peace. Who dies if England lives? Not they who remember with pride and gratitude today. In our hearts and minds we salute them still in that Two

---

[51] Ibid.
[52] Ibid. Dec. 1938, 4.
[53] Ibid.
[54] *CP*, 25 Nov. 1938.
[55] Ibid. 10 Nov. 1939. The holding of a service or any sort of public gathering was, strictly speaking, forbidden due to the fear of bombing: T. Aldgate and J. Richards, *Britain can take it: the British cinema in the Second World War*, Oxford 1986, 1.
[56] *EHE*, 17 Nov. 1939.

Minutes' Silence which we believe every East Londoner will privately observe as they have publicly during the past twenty years.[57]

In Romford too the day was reaffirmed. The Revd J. Haigh, chaplain to the mayor, took the service at the war memorial and asked whether the sacrifice had been in vain. He answered his own question:

> we could say with certainty that the good things the men died for would never be lost in the sight of God or man as an example of devotion and sacrifice; and, secondly, that the real judgement of history would be given in the future when things were seen in their right perspective, and that would depend in no small measure upon ourselves.[58]

One of the columnists of the *Romford Recorder* wrote of a friend who thought the Armistice services a mockery in time of war. He had replied that 'it can be argued with every justification that the fact that war has again overcome us is no reason why the memory of 1914–1918 should be cast aside. There is much to learn from remembering'.[59] Only in Ilford was there any great variance. The *Ilford Recorder* slightly tarnished the great crusade of 1914–18 by stating that this time 'the principle at stake is so much clearer, the issues involved so much easier to understand, the course and the goal so much more plainly set before us'.[60] Ottaway said in his Armistice sermon that 'In many ways it is easier for us because we see the issues clearly. It was not so in 1914 but there is not one of us who does not realise at this time that we are facing evil things.'[61] No one had ever doubted the clear duty of righting the wrong done to Belgium in 1914 and yet suddenly here was a doubt. Throughout the twenties and thirties Ottaway had been one of the great defenders of the principles of the Great War, so his sudden defection is mystifying. Perhaps the class and religious complexion of Ilford had a bearing. As a solidly middle-class, over-whelmingly Protestant, community it may well have been that the influence of the League of Nations Union and the last remnants of the thinking of the Peace Pledge Union still lingered. Both of these organisations seemed to flourish most strongly where there was a tight connection between the religious and social function of the various churches and where middle-class intellectual tenets held sway. This might help to explain why there suddenly developed a feeling that this conflict had a much clearer morality and was justified by the provisions of the League of Nations. With regard to this

---

57 *ELO*, 11 Nov. 1939. 'Who die if England live' is a quote from Kipling's patriotic poem of 1914 'For all we have and are': *Rudyard Kipling's verse: definitive edition*, 329–30.
58 *RR*, 17 Nov. 1939.
59 Ibid.
60 *IR*, 9 Nov. 1939.
61 Ibid. 16 Nov. 1939. He also appears to be quoting Neville Chamberlain's speech (reported in the *Daily Mirror*, 4 Sept. 1939) announcing the start of hostilities with Germany: 'It is the evil things that we shall be fighting against – brute force, bad faith, injustice, oppression and persecution – and against them I am certain that right will prevail.'

sudden apostacy over the justification of the Great War, however, Ilford was out of step.

As Britain entered another war the country continued to observed Armistice Day, just as it had for the previous twenty years.[62]

---

[62] For details of the observation of Armistice Day during the Second World War see Gregory, *Silence of memory*, 212–24.

10

The East End Jewish Ex-Service Movement

This chapter will show how one particular community of the East End was affected by the Great War. The Jewish community of East London was probably its most distinctive racial minority, distinguished by its own language and customs. Mainly consisting of Russian and eastern European Jews, the community faced much suspicion and distrust up to the Great War. Indeed, during the conflict itself antisemitic sentiments were often close to the surface. However, it was also a time when many Jews rallied to their adopted country. Service in the armed forces brought death and grieving home to Jewish families. For the families of the bereaved a question was posed: should they commemorate their loved ones in a style similar to that of the Gentile communities, or find a distinctly Jewish form of war remembrance?[1]

The size of the East End Jewish community in 1914 is a matter of some debate. The Toynbee Hall survey of 1900 estimated the Jewish population of East London to be some 100,000. Julia Bush believes that this figure is a little too high but states that it had reached that point by 1914.[2] The great majority of these Jews had come to Britain in order to escape Tsarist persecution. They mostly remained where they entered London and so the metropolitan borough of Stepney took on the appearance of a *stetl*. Reliance on Yiddish and the distinctive culture of the immigrants soon made them the objects of resentment in the poverty-stricken East End. The separatist nature of the community led to the accusation that it was a seditious and unpatriotic force dwelling at the heart of the empire. Such fears seemed to have a basis in reality when the involvement of Jewish radicals in the famous 1911 Siege of Sydney Street became known.[3]

The state reacted to growing fears over immigration with the Aliens Act of 1905 which limited the number of foreign Jews who could seek asylum in Britain.[4] In order to further alleviate the situation the established Anglo-

---

[1] Tony Kushner has explored the effect of the Great War and its aftermath on the Jewish community and its relationship to the rest of the East End in his essay, 'Jew and non-Jew in the East End of London: towards an anthropology in everyday relations', in G. Alderman and C. Holmes, *Outsiders and outcasts: essays in honour of William J. Fishman*, London 1993, 12–32.

[2] J. Bush, 'East London Jews and the First World War', *London Journal*, no. 2 (Winter 1980), 147–61.

[3] For the nature of the East End Jewish community at this time see W. J. Fishman, *East End Jewish radicals, 1875–1914*, London 1975.

[4] See Kushner, 'Jew and non-Jew', 12–32.

Jewish community attempted to quell antisemitism by encouraging assimilation and integration. Walter Besant noted this development in his 1900 work, *East London*: 'I am informed, however, that the leaders of the people in London are persistent in their exhortations to the new-comers to make themselves English as fast as possible; to send their children to the Board-schools, and to make them English.'[5]

So-called West End Jewry supported a variety of Anglicising elements such as the Jewish Lads' Brigade, formed in 1895 and based in Aldgate and the Brady Street Club for Working Boys formed in 1896. The purpose of both bodies was to ensure that Jewish boys should become conformist and invisible members of society. The twelfth annual report of the Brady Street Club professed its policy thus: 'the main aim of the Club . . . is to turn its members into self-respecting English Jews'.[6]

The Jewish Lads' Brigade, formed by Colonel Albert Goldsmid as a Jewish version of the Church Lads' and Boys' brigades, had very similar aims. Upper-class Anglo-Jewish officers drilled the boys and filled them with ideas of a Muscular Judaism modelled on the existing public school codes. According to one of its early leaflets, the brigade would ensure that the 'narrow chested, round-shouldered, slouching son of the Ghetto [would be] converted with extraordinary rapidity into an erect and self-respecting man, a living negation of the physical stigma which has disfigured our race'.[7]

In 1914 these institutions led many young Jews to the Colours. But for many Russian Jews, conditioned by the brutal treatment they had received as conscripts in the armies of the Tsar, service was something to be avoided at all costs. The sight of many young Jewish men on the streets – not in uniform – resurrected the claim that Jews were not 'doing their bit'. Serious antisemitic disturbances followed as Jews became the target for abuse.[8] The government attempted to alleviate the situation by creating Jewish battalions within the Royal Regiment of Fusiliers to serve in Palestine. But these were hardly popular:[9] The *British Jewry book of honour* was forced to admit that

> They did not like life in the Army, never said that they did, but they lived up to every duty given them, behaved splendidly under fire and there was never among them any breach of military discipline. When demobilised they dispersed to their countless workshops and speak with pride of their campaign in Palestine.[10]

---

[5]   Beasant, *East London*, 165.
[6]   THL, Brady Street Club for Working Jewish Boys, *Twelfth annual report, 1907–08*. In addition, all members were encouraged to join the Jewish Lads' Brigade.
[7]   Quoted in Springhall, *Youth, empire and society*, 42. See also S. Kadish, '*A good Jew and a good Englishman'*: the Jewish Lads' and Girls' Brigade, 1895–1995, London 1995.
[8]   See Bush, *Behind the lines*, 165–92.
[9]   S. Kadish, *Bolsheviks and British Jews: the Anglo-Jewish community, Britain and the Russian Revolution*, London 1992, 223–7. See also the general history, V. Zhabotinsky, *The story of the Jewish Legion*, New York 1945.
[10] M. Adler (ed.), *British Jewry book of honour*, London 1922, 65.

This left the East End Jewish community in an ambivalent position at the Armistice. Many felt bitter about the treatment they had received while others felt that they had nobly fulfilled their obligations to King and Country. That there was much emotional commitment to the cause is reflected in the sentiments captured in Jewish war memorials in East London. Paradoxically certain sections of the Jewish community felt that the war had led young Jews too far in the opposite direction. Arthur Barnett, a rabbi to the forces, wrote to the *Jewish Chronicle* bemoaning the fact that 'Men who before had lived a fairly Jewish life, will now, after these years of de-Judaising tendencies and influences, find it difficult to recover their faded Jewish consciousness. Army life had produced a Jewish anaesthesia.'[11] Such 'de-Judaising' was, however, only partial. Those that had served the empire, particularly the willing volunteers of the East End, instead felt that Judaism had made a positive contribution to its defence and therefore stimulated a new confidence in their identity.

The various Jewish ex-service groups in the East End were responsible for using the memory of the war, their memory of their dead comrades and their own war service in a variety of forms to serve many different purposes. Remembrance was very much a two-way process, for the living honoured the dead but then used their memory and their own experiences to serve political and social ambitions for the whole Jewish community. Unfortunately hardly any records survive relating to these organisations and the story has had to be reconstructed simply using their journals and the Jewish press.[12]

One of the earliest Jewish ex-service groups to form in the East End was the Judean War Memorial Lodge of the Grand Order of the Sons of Jacob. The Grand Order was in fact a Jewish Friendly Society with its main offices in Brick Lane and Middlesex Street, at the heart of the Jewish East End. The *Jewish year book, 1919*, states that the War Memorial Lodge met in the Bromley and Bow Hall.[13] The existence of such a body shows the grip of the experience of war; these men felt the need to set themselves apart in peacetime in order to act and remember together. It is particularly incongruous in the light of the fact that they had been perceived as trench-dodgers, men who would want to put the experience of war very firmly behind them. They also appear to have been the first Jewish group to take part in the Whitehall Armistice parade.[14] This vanguard of organised Jewish ex-servicemen in East London was, therefore, composed of men who would hardly have been regarded as the most willing combatants, whilst also being perceived as those

[11] JC, 28 Feb. 1919.
[12] This was confirmed in an interview with Harry Farbey, general secretary of the Association of Jewish Ex-Servicemen and Women and chairman of the Monash branch of the British Legion, in August 1993.
[13] JG, 9 July 1926.
[14] Ibid.

most likely to want to forget their war service. This reveals the deep complexity of the memory of the war.

The most important of the Jewish East End ex-service groups, however, the Jewish Ex-Servicemen's Legion, appears to have come about as the result of the *Jewish Graphic*'s support for the plan to re-launch the military Chanukah service at the Bayswater synagogue. In 1926 it threw its weight behind H. Jerrold Annenberg, an ex-officer in the Queen's Westminster Rifles, who was attempting to organise the service.[15] Annenberg was joined by a retired colonel of the Gordon Highlanders, J. H. Levey, and from this the Jewish Ex-Servicemen's National Remembrance Committee was formed.[16] In 1927 an extra element was added for a wreath was laid at the Cenotaph before the Chanukah service. That it was a successful event and that the heart of the support for it came from the East End can be seen in the fact the Lieutenant-Colonel H. Dodge suggested 'that next year the service might be held in an East End Synagogue'.[17] After the service the Judeans' Old Comrades' Association (closely connected to the War Memorial Lodge) met the other participants and it was decided to form an ex-servicemen's organisation. The JESL was the result. The big breakthrough for the JESL came in 1929 when it organised an Armistice parade at the Great Synagogue, Aldgate, and a wreath-laying at the Cenotaph. The *Jewish Guardian* referred to it as a 'unique' event and the *Jewish Chronicle* noted the fact that it 'was the first Armistice Service organised by the Jewish Ex-Servicemen's Legion'.[18] The event did not not happen without a certain amount of controversy. Rabbi Lipson conducted the service at the Great Synagogue and bemoaned the fact 'that there was no Armistice so far as the Jew was concerned; for unjust and evil accusations were the Jewish lot and reward for bravery'.[19] But the *Jewish Guardian* preferred to frame the event in terms of positive images of Jewry and stated that it was a reminder that 'when sacrifice was needed Jews did their duty'.[20] The Jewish Ex-Servicemen's Legion had got off to a good start and its activities were quickly taken up by readers of the Jewish press.

Interest in a specifically Jewish ex-service organisation is indicated by letters in the *Jewish Chronicle* asking for more information. One old soldier wrote that he 'would be greatly interested in coming together for a Jewish ideal from an Ex-Servicemen's point of view'. He added that 'we can already join the British Legion for club advantages, and for upholding comradeship caused by the war'.[21] This is fascinating for it reveals the double sense of a special community defined by religion and war service. Mr Sarna, honorary

---

[15] Ibid. 30 Apr., 21 May, 18 June 1926.
[16] JESM, no. 1 (Nov. 1934), 3.
[17] JG, 23 Dec. 1927.
[18] JGuard, 15 Nov. 1929; JC, 15 Nov. 1929. See also *Jewish year book* 1939, London 1939, 93.
[19] JC, 15 Nov. 1929.
[20] JGuard, 15 Nov. 1929.
[21] JC, 15 Dec. 1929.

secretary of the JESL (and resident of Hackney), replied to this enquiry and stated the aims of the Legion. They are worth repeating in full for they show just how wide the aims were and how far war service had given these men a feeling of natural leadership, which won them the right to campaign for such causes:

1. To open a Club to advance comradeship.
2. To establish close contact with Jewish Ex-Servicemen in other countries, and to promote friendship and understanding between Jewish and non-Jewish Ex-Servicemen.
3. To promote the upbuilding of Palestine as the Jewish National Home especially by assisting Jewish Ex-Servicemen to settle on the land there.
4. To encourage knowledge of Jewish Culture, History and Literature, and to participate in all forms of sport.[22]

By November 1934 the Jewish Ex-Servicemen's Legion was well enough established for it to open its headquarters premises and clubhouse in Great Prescott Street, Aldgate. At the same time, it launched its own journal, the *Jewish Ex-Serviceman*. Its increased significance can be seen in the fact that the formerly subdued East London press finally started to take notice. The *East London Advertiser* covered the opening of the headquarters and reported Barnett Janner's speech. (Janner was the Jewish Liberal MP for Whitechapel and something of a local icon; whether this was because he was a Jew, a Liberal, or a Liberal and a Jew is unclear.) He reminded his audience of Britain's proud record of racial tolerance which had faced its acid test in the Great War:

England would not forget, however, what other countries had forgotten, that Jew and non-Jew had battled as brothers. Twelve thousand boys of the Jews' Free School [Whitechapel] served in the war. [He continued that he] . . . was proud indeed to join with the men of the Legion.[23]

Levey, as president, then toasted Sarna's work as secretary and revealed how far the Legion perceived itself to be something far more than just an ex-servicemen's club: 'The Legion was doing a service to the community in the East End without blowing trumpets.'[24] The *East London Observer* also waded-in with its thoughts on the Legion's new journal. The *Observer* stated, via its special Jewish affairs page, the 'Ghetto Gossip' column, that 'as a first number it gives much promise of useful success'.[25] The opening of their headquarters and the launch of the journal gave a huge boost to the Legion's

---

22 Ibid. 2 Jan. 1930.
23 *ELA*, 1 Dec. 1934. Janner's claim that 12,000 boys of the Jews Free School served is either a slip of his tongue or the journalist's pen for Michael Adler puts the figure at 1,200 in the *British Jewry book of honour*, 3, 32.
24 *JC*, 30 Nov. 1934.
25 *ELO*, 10 Nov. 1934.

membership which trebled in the three months from the opening of the club. By the summer of 1935 the Legion was at its peak; it had over 600 members, was active in the struggle against antisemitism, had a high profile in the Jewish press and represented British Jewish ex-servicemen at the World Conference of Jewish Ex-Servicemen in Paris.[26]

The Legion certainly did not worry about upsetting the Jewish establishment during this period; indeed its first campaign was against the Jewish War Memorial Committee and Scheme.[27] At the consecration of the headquarters Rabbi J. Rabinowitz expressed his disbelief that so little had been done for Jewish ex-servicemen:

> not a single penny of that large sum collected as a Jewish War Memorial, has been devoted to the needs of ex-servicemen. Alone of all creeds and denominations, alone of all Jewries, we have not given a thought to those who came back. . . . It is unfair that it should have been left to a handful of individuals to erect a permanent meeting place for Jewish Ex-Servicemen.[28]

This buttressed an earlier piece on the subject, by Levey, in the *Jewish Chronicle*, in which he stated that

> the money will be devoted to establishing, in connection with Jewish education and worship, an organisation to carry on Jewish tradition. Must we have a Great War to obtain large sums of money before we carry on our old traditions of religion? Surely the subscribers were never told this at the time, and when the sacrifices of the dead and the survivors were green in their memory. Did not the subscribers have in their mind a practical memorial in the heart of the Empire? – a memorial hall with the names of the dead inscribed therein and which would be available for the living survivors to meet in and re-establish that great spirit of comradeship which only those who served can understand. Are we to be the only race to ignore this debt of gratitude we owe to the living and the dead?[29]

In June 1935 Levey once again raised the question of a Jewish war memorial. He believed that the plaques in the synagogues were not enough; he wanted something big, public and visible:

> Every city, town, village and hamlet throughout the length and breadth of the country has its own local Memorial, but there is nothing in the centre of the East End of London or the Jewish centres of Manchester or Leeds, which can

---

[26] *JESM*, no. 4 (Feb. 1935), 12–13; *JC*, 21 June 1935.
[27] The Jewish War Memorial scheme was established in 1919; the original aim was to collect over £1 million from Jews across the empire in order to fund a Jewish college and seminary at either Oxford or Cambridge. The fund-raising continued for many years and during that time controversy grew as the plans were altered and inaction seemed to paralyse the committee: *JC*, 31 Oct. 1919, 13 Nov. 1925.
[28] *JESM*, no. 2 (Dec. 1934), 5.
[29] *JC*, 20 Nov. 1931.

compare in any way even with that of a local Memorial in a small village. [Levey then accused the Jewish War Memorial Committee of having failed in] their obligations to the dead and the living.[30]

Levey had grand plans for all Jewish ex-servicemen and his vision was closely connected with the idea of a communal war memorial. He wanted to unite all Jewish ex-servicemen into one association. He believed that this would have an extremely beneficial effect for 'By these means we shall provide visible evidence of Jewish loyalty which the eye can see.'[31] The idea was floated at a conference of Jewish ex-service groups in London, which included delegates from Leeds, Manchester and Newcastle on 30 June 1935. All Levey's proposals were carried, reflecting the importance attached to the decisions of the London-based Legion:

> 1. The formation of a united body of Jewish Ex-Servicemen to be known as the Jewish Ex-Servicemen's Association of the British Empire. (a) Organisations of Jewish Ex-Servicemen throughout the Empire to be invited to join this Association. (b) That the Association should foster a feeling of good fellowship of all Ex-Servicemen irrespective of creed. (c) The Association to work in the closest co-operation with the British Legion. (d) That the Headquarters of the Association should be in London.
> 2. (a) To erect in London a visible War Memorial in the form of a dignified Association Headquarters building in memory of those who fell in the War. (b) To inscribe on the walls of the entrance, the name of every British Jew who lost his life. (c) The building to be named after General Sir John Monash, Commander of the Australian Forces.[32]

The aim was not to force men to drop membership of other ex-service organisations, rather it was to complement them. Levey stated that: 'the majority of ex-servicemen belong to Old Comrades Associations and such-like organisations. There is nothing inconsistent in a Jew belonging to both the British Legion and a Jewish Ex-Servicemen's organisation simultaneously'.[33] He received support from the Leeds Jewish Clive Beherens branch of the British Legion when it voted to affiliate to the new empire-wide body, which was to take up offices in Lower Regent's Street, thus leaving the JESL behind in the East End.[34] The concept ran into the assimilation argument for many Jews were not interested in a single Jewish body separate from the British Legion. The problem was two-fold: first there were a plethora of small, independent Jewish ex-service organisations such as the Jewish Ex-Servicemen's Associa-

---

[30] *JESM*, nos 8–9 (June–July 1935), 17.
[31] *JC*, 21 June 1935.
[32] Ibid. 5 July 1935. Sir John Monash was an Australian Jew who had won great respect by his daring and intelligent command of the Australian Imperial Force on the Western Front: P. A. Pedersen, *Monash as military commander*, Melbourne 1985.
[33] *JESM*, nos 10–11 (Aug.–Sept. 1935), 9–10.
[34] *JC*, 30 Aug. 1925; *JESM*, nos 17–18 (Mar.–Apr. 1936), 15.

tion with its branches in such places as Southend-on-Sea, Newcastle, Swansea and Sheffield, which were being asked to affiliate to a body created by the president of a London-centric organisation.[35] Secondly, there were also Jewish branches of the British Legion in, for example, cities such as Newcastle, Manchester, Glasgow and Leeds.[36] The British Legion Charter did not actually allow for sectarian branches but these, in reality, were *de facto* Jewish ones.[37] Moreover, in Whitechapel itself, running alongside the JESL, was the Maccabean branch of the British Legion. This was the group that was most obviously affected by the actions of Levey and the Jewish Ex-Servicemen's Legion. From its relatively quiet beginning in 1933 the Maccabeans overtook the Legion to become the most important Jewish ex-service group in the East End and, by 1938, the whole country. The Maccabeans were formed after a meeting at the Grand Palais, Commercial Road, Whitechapel in October 1933. It began with a two minutes' silence in memory of dead comrades. Then Colonel F. D. Smith, the wartime commander of the 40th Judean battalion was elected president. In his speech, reported by the *East London Observer*, he revealed the desire of Anglo-Jewry to prove the loyalty of the entire Jewish community: 'Jews who had the happiness to live in Old England should have for their motto "Our Country first, right or wrong", and he was sure that was the motto of all present. (Cheers).'[38] The first full meeting was held a month later when membership already stood at 500. Dr W. O'Donovan, Conservative MP for Mile End and vice-president of the Mile End and Limehouse branch of the British Legion, addressed the men. Highlighting the deep sense of solidarity war service imparted, a sense of being apart which was intensified among the Maccabeans by virtue of their religion, he stated that 'The soldier carried on his back the destiny of the civilian. If civilians would go losing their senses and go to war, soldiers were their agent and soldiers who knew war were the best apostles of peace.'[39]

When, therefore, Levey began his drive to unite all Jewish ex-servicemen under the extended aegis of the Jewish Ex-Servicemen's Legion, he revealed the confidence of the East Enders but was also entering the minefield of the Jewish community's sense of belonging in a host nation.

In February 1935, at the Legion's annual general meeting, it was proposed that they apply for affiliation to the British Legion. Some, however, believed that only by remaining separate would the true interests of Jewry be served;

---

35 *Jewish year book, 1939*, 93.

36 Ibid.

37 Graham Wootton, in his *Official history of the British Legion*, largely ignores the question of the Legion charter and its relationship with Jewish members; they are only mentioned once, on p. 197.

38 *ELO*, 4 Nov. 1933.

39 Ibid. It is interesting to note that the *ELO* covered all Maccabean stories within the main body of the newspaper whereas Jewish Legion of Ex-Servicemen matters were confined to the 'Ghetto Gossip' column. This implies the total Jewishness of the Legion compared with the more mainstream activities of the British Legion Maccabeans.

others believed that belonging to a Jewish group and affiliated British Legion membership would provide the best of both worlds, and that any sort of self-imposed ghetto was a dangerous concept. The issue of affiliation produced considerable debate. Alexander Ben Joseph, for example, a member of the Jewish Ex-Servicemen's Legion, wrote that although he believed that totally independent Jewish ex-service groups would not carry enough weight, if they were swallowed up by the British Legion it would be equally disastrous. He said that the Jewish branches of the British Legion were 'for Jewish purposes . . . non-existent', and that the best option was affiliation to the Legion.[40] Sarna, general secretary of the JESL, unsurprisingly backed Levey's call for affiliation, but he then pointed out the very real need to remain autonomous:

> A 'Jewish' branch of the British Legion isolated in the East End or Stoke-on-Poge is ineffective from a Jewish point of view. The Armistice Parade unites us for one occasion; why not all year round? Can a British Legion branch undertake Jewish propaganda? Has any branch or individual in the British Legion been efficient in this respect? The British Legion Delegation is now in Germany where Jews are being persecuted – are any Jewish members there to raise the Jewish question? Would not a united body affiliated to the British Legion be more useful?[41]

The *East London Observer*'s 'Ghetto Gossip' columnist gave cautious support to the idea stating that:

> On the whole we think that this solution of the problem would be a wise one, because the special needs and interests of the Jewish ex-soldiers can be best served by preservation of their identity. It is possible for the best organisation in the world to be too big for good and useful management.[42]

Some Jews seemed bemused by the whole thing and saw such a division of energies as a potentially dangerous phenomenon. Rabbi Barnett wrote to the *Jewish Chronicle* expressing his concern that there were now two Jewish ex-service organisations in the East End:

> Each has a headquarters in the East End. Geographically they are very close to one another. But if rumour is to be trusted, unhealthy rivalry and enmity place them leagues apart. I hold no brief for either party. Both are doing useful work. But this exhibition of internal dissension is a sorry commentary on the avowed object of both sides, of presenting to the outside world the facts of Jewish loyalty and solidarity. The community has the right to know why this 'Chevra-dom' should be perpetuated and reinforced, at its expense, in brick

40 *JESM*, no. 6 (Apr. 1935), 8.
41 *JC*, 19 July 1935.
42 *ELO*, 10 Aug. 1935.

and stone. And the Community would do well to withhold its support until it receives a valid answer.[43]

He then went on to raise the great fear of established Jewry, that of the self-imposed ghetto: 'Is it desirable that Jews should separate themselves from their non-Jewish comrades in arms by remaining outside the British Legion – a national movement which is free from all distinctions of creed?'[44] It was exactly this theme that Major Benn Brunel Cohen, Conservative MP and honorary treasurer of the British Legion, took up in his letter to the *JESM*. He asked 'why is there this desire to segregate ourselves?' and went on to add that 'if you want some special concession given to you merely because you are Jews, then I am afraid that I cannot see eye to eye with you'.[45] In the same issue, the 'Scrutator', a regular columnist in the *Jewish Chronicle*, stated in reply that:

> Major Cohen seems to have forgotten that many Ex-Servicemen are not interested in joining any ex-service movement. The proposed Empire Association [which was also seeking affiliation to the British Legion], however, wishes to unite Jewish Ex-Servicemen *not only* because they served in HM Forces, but for the principle [*sic*] reason that they are concerned in Jewish affairs.[46]

Dual motivation and allegiance was therefore stressed once again. But it did not cut much ice with Rabbi Michael Adler, chief rabbi to the armed forces and the British Legion, who was firmly in favour of one organisation only – the British Legion. He addressed all Jewish ex-servicemen via the pages of the *Jewish Chronicle* and stated that:

> There are no Roman Catholic or Nonconformist organisations of ex-soldiers – and there exists no valid object or purpose why we Jews should isolate ourselves in this good work. . . .
> At all functions of the Legion, including the Annual Conference, the members of the Jewish branches take their place side by side with all others thus keeping alive the spirit of unity and good fellowship that marked all sections of the British Army during the Great War itself. Those who remain apart, like the non-British Legion organisations, deliberately exclude themselves from co-operation with their ex-comrades of other faiths and plough their own lonely furrow.

And then he lobbed in the real grenade: 'I am officially authorised to state

---

43 *JC*, 12 July 1935.
44 Ibid.
45 *JESM*, nos 12–13 (Oct.–Nov. 1935), 7. Major Benn Brunel Cohen was the son of the owner of a large chain of department stores in Manchester, Liverpool and Birmingham. He was crippled in the Great War while serving on the Western Front with the King's Liverpool Regiment. See his autobiography, *Count your blessings*, London 1956.
46 Ibid. 7.

that . . . "affiliation" is impossible under the Royal Charter of the Legion. The sooner this is realised by Jewish ex-Servicemen the better for all concerned.'[47]

It seems strange that negotiations that had been instigated in February 1935 had dragged on until July only for this impasse to be reached; surely such a fundamental problem would have negated any discussions from the start? Perhaps negotiations collapsed in the summer of 1935 because the British Legion went on a tour of Germany, a fact that brought forth a mixture of sarcasm and exasperation from many Jewish ex-servicemen. The August-September issue of the *JESM* was dominated by the event. It kicked off with congratulations to the Glasgow Jewish branch of the British Legion, which had persuaded the Scottish branches not to send any delegates to Germany. The British Legion version seems to differ from this account, for Graham Wootton, it's official historian, states that 'Jewish Legionaries made . . . little stir'.[48] The JESL took its own line stating that any move towards international co-operation was welcomed, but they would not 'shake hands with a Government who treats its own Ex-Servicemen, who are Jews, and their brethren with such intolerance and persecution'. Two months earlier the JESL had attended the World Convention of Jewish Ex-Servicemen in Paris and they now attributed their success at the meeting to the fact that they were not 'fettered by Charters of such bodies as the British Legion. Hence the need for the Association of Jewish Ex-Servicemen of the Empire. Unity is strength'.[49] The most passionate piece came from Rabbi Rabinowitz in the *Jewish Chronicle*. In support of the independence of the JESL he stated that:

> Has the British Legion ever protested against the exclusion of German Jews from the sister organisation in Germany? Or has it, the week after the living bretheren of the 12,000 German Jews who gave their life to their Fatherland were compared to fleas – a comparison which presumably includes the Treasurer of the British Legion, Major Brunel Cohen – sent a delegation to Germany which witnessed the disgraceful anti-Jewish riots in Berlin?[50]

Deadlock had been reached on the question of affiliation by the autumn of 1935 and it was exactly at this point that the star of the JESL started to wane. The reasons for this are unclear, but it seems that the negotiations with the British Legion, the desire to create an empire association, were a bit too lofty and a bit too irrelevant to the average East End Jewish ex-servicemen. There were problems to be faced on the doorstep, namely the fight against blackshirt aggression, and many turned their faces to that. Nevertheless

---

[47] JC, 26 July 1935. When attempts were made to see the minutes of the meetings between the JESL and the British Legion it was claimed that no such negotiations took place, and thus that were no records.

[48] JESM, nos 10–11 (Aug.–Sept. 1935), 9–10; Wootton, *Official history of the British Legion*, 197.

[49] Ibid.

[50] JC, 26 July 1935.

negotiations were reopened with the British Legion and eventually a compromise was reached: in July 1936 the Monash Branch of the British Legion was established which essentially gave JESL members dual status, but shifted the focus from the East End to Woburn House, Bloomsbury, the administrative centre of British Jewry and the seat of the Board of Deputies.[51] The influence of the British Legion and Anglo-Jewry was obvious and can be seen in 1938, when Sir Robert Waley-Cohen addressed the men during Armistice week. He promoted a conformist, unquestioning line on governmental policy, typical of much of influential, assimilated Anglo-Jewry: 'They had not realised the depth of feeling of their people for peace and appeasement in the world. If there was to be peace and appeasement then it would mean departure from the terrible hatreds and persecutions which had marred certain countries.'[52]

But the old independent spirit of the JESL did not quite die, for in the spring of 1939, Sarna changed its name and founded the Association of Jewish Ex-Servicemen, AJEX, the group which has become the central, independent Jewish ex-service organisation.[53]

Jewish ex-servicemen and the fight against fascism

It is in the fight against fascism that the example of the war dead, the authority invested by active service and the comradeship of the trenches was most obviously used by the Jewish community for specific, contemporary purposes.

First, the experience of war was certainly felt to give the ex-servicemen a sense of leadership and importance. The JESL and its members quite obviously perceived themselves to be in the advance guard of Jewish defence. Mr I. Amswyth stated in the *JESM* that:

> There is one thing which confounds Mosleyites and anti-semites, and that is the sight of Jewish Ex-Servicemen maintaining their identity and proclaiming their services to their Mother Country, of which we can be proud. . . . There are matters in Jewry which only Jewish Ex-Servicemen can tackle freely and unhampered.[54]

Levey thought that the defence of Jewry was an important part of the empire association: 'The Association has come to stay – and will remain until the Jew is no longer singled out for attack, and is treated with respect – as are his fellow citizens. The loyalty of Jewish citizens has been impugned.'[55] Mr H. Harris of Bethnal Green backed this up and claimed that:

51 Ibid. 17 July 1936.
52 *ELA*, 12 Nov. 1938.
53 JC, 31 Mar. 1939. See also *Jewish year book, 1996*, London 1996.
54 *JESM*, no. 14 (Dec. 1935), 13.
55 Ibid. nos 17–18 (Mar.–Apr. 1936), 18.

The Jewish Ex-Servicemen's Legion should be regarded as a group of men on active service. We are not banded together simply for the purpose of commemorating old glories and celebrating old triumphs. On the contrary, a chief aim should be to look forward rather than backward. Our purpose, as I see it, is to weld together an organisation of Jewish defence of those who are banded together by common experience.[56]

The clearest example of East End Jewish ex-servicemen using their position to confront fascism can be seen in the Ex-Servicemen's Movement Against Fascism. Though nominally a national, non-political and non-sectarian movement, its base was Fashion Street E1, and of its 1,000 members 700 were Jews.[57]

How was the memory of the war used in this fight? The message the ex-servicemen wanted to put over was that they had been loyal and courageous servants of King and Country and were therefore entitled to live their distinctive lifestyle – a subtly different approach to that of the proponents of assimilation. The wider British public had to be taught that Jews had fought and died, and in the absence of a central war memorial the Armistice parades were the best way to do this. The JESM made the following point on the 1934 Armistice:

> Over 3,500 Jewish Ex-Servicemen, representing 50,000 Jews who had fought for the British Empire, proved that Anglo-Jewry had done its duty as citizens. . . . The importance of these annual Parades cannot be exaggerated. In view of the constant attacks on Jewry, the opportunity of proving to the British Public that we Jews have stood side by side with our fellow citizens in time of stress, cannot – and must not – be ignored by a single Jewish Ex-Serviceman.[58]

When William Hurtz issued his instructions for the 1938 parade he emphasised this very aspect:

> The Service on Horse Guards is of the utmost value to the good name and prestige of Anglo-Jewry. Ex-Servicemen should not only regard attendance as an act of homage to their fallen comrades but also regard themselves as living witnesses to the readiness with which British Jews discharged responsibilities as loyal and proud citizens of this country.[59]

Even Gentiles recognised the need to maintain a high profile; in 1934 one of the guests of honour was Major-General Sir Frederick Maurice, who addressed the men and noted that 'In these days when your faith is subject to so much persecution, it is necessary to remind your fellow-countrymen that

---

[56] Ibid.
[57] JC, 31 July 1936.
[58] JESM, no. 2 (Dec. 1934), 4. The Jewish Armistice parades were held on the Sunday before the actual Armistice anniversary in order to give the event a higher profile: ibid. no. 1 (Nov. 1934).
[59] JC, 4 Nov. 1938.

you are true citizens of the Empire. I believe that the spirit of service and comradeship is going to see us through the difficulties of peace.'[60]

That the parades served their purpose can be seen in 1938, albeit in a highly charged year, when more than 7,000 Jewish ex-servicemen marched past the Cenotaph and it was estimated that over 100,000 people crowded into Whitehall to witness the scene.[61] In 1935 technology came to the aid of the organisers when the BBC broadcast the service for the first time, not only to Britain but relaying it on to the empire and the USA as well.[62]

But there were other ways in which to ram home the patriotic message whilst maintaining the pressure against fascism, most obviously via direct protest. In July 1933 more than 50,000 people marched to Hyde Park to protest at German antisemitism. The rally was organised by the United Jewish Protest Committee and included a contingent of 6,000-plus Jewish ex-servicemen. The presence of the ex-servicemen was perceived as a great morale booster precisely because of the weight they carried. The *Jewish Chronicle* stated that:

> Six thousand Jewish ex-servicemen are on parade, wearing their war decorations, and many of them showing clearly the wounds they received in the Great War when fighting in the British Army – men with one arm, faces scarred and bearing testimony to the treatment of plastic surgery. The ex-soldiers' banner declares '1914 we defended Freedom against the Huns; 1933 we must defend Jews against Hitler's atrocities'.[63]

A few years later, when the threat was much closer to home, a rally was held in Victoria Park, Bow, and of the 10,000 people present over 3,000 were ex-servicemen. Once again, the imagery revolved around the patriotism of the ex-servicemen and its ability to confound fascist jeers:

> Many Union Jacks fluttered in the air and the ex-Servicemen were heavily be-medalled for services to their country in the Great War. These are the men whom the Fascists stigmatise as unpatriotic and un-British! [Much was also made of the fact that these men also sang the old wartime songs including 'Tipperary'][64]

And, once again, the authority of ex-servicemen was emphasised in a message from the earl of Listowel: 'In mobilising the ex-Servicemen in the fight against Fascism in this country you are doing a very great service indeed for

60 Ibid. 9 Nov. 1934.
61 Ibid. 11 Nov. 1938.
62 Ibid. 15 Nov. 1935.
63 Ibid. 21 July 1933. Jews were well aware of the paradox that they had fought German Jews in the Great War. Indeed in 1935 a German Jewish Iron Cross winner joined the Armistice Parade, and AJEX, on its formation, worked hard for refugee German-Jewish ex-servicemen and their families: ibid, 15 Nov. 1935, 31 Mar. 1939.
64 Ibid. 4 Sept. 1936.

all those who believe in democratic institutions and parliamentary government.'[65]

The militancy of the ex-servicemen and the survival of their wartime spirit
can be seen in the whole-hearted support given by the JESL to the call for a
boycott of German goods. A member wrote to the *JESM* agreeing with the
proposal:

> who better to assist the boycott than the organised bodies of the Jewish
> Ex-Servicemen, a body of men who having proved that they are 100 per cent
> British, should proudly tell the world that they are also 100 per cent Jewish.
> There are many who may be of Jewry but are certainly not in Jewry.[66]

The JESL urged a united front and called upon the Board of Deputies to set
an example. Sarna wrote to the *Jewish Chronicle*, he too seemed to imply that
established Jewry regarded the threat of fascism as something that was not as
important to them as it was to other sections of British Jewry:

> This is a question which is the business of *all* Anglo-Jewry, and as such should
> be undertaken by a representative body, such as the Board of Deputies, who
> should be in a position to speak and act for Jewry . . . . Defence against Fascism
> in England, which is using Jewry as the scapegoat, must be undertaken by a
> representative body having the confidence of the whole Community. The
> Jewish Ex-Servicemen's Legion and, I feel sure, every other organised group
> and individual in Jewry will be prepared to rally around the Board of Deputies.
> . . . We shall welcome a lead from our communal headquarters to co-ordinate
> all efforts to meet a common danger.[67]

This was a theme that was soon taken up by other members of the JESL, Mr J.
Glick wrote to the *JESM* and asked: 'What are we doing to stem the tide of
Anti-Semitic attacks on our people? Let us rise to the occasion in one united
effort. The tragic part is the pandering of so many of our fellow Jews to the
assimilation cult which makes united efforts so abortive.'[68] Further, it was felt
that East End Jewry was being left to shoulder the full load in the anti-fascist
campaign. Mark Mitchell, a JESL member, wrote to the *Jewish Chronicle*
stating his grievances against 'comfortable' Jewry:

> Being an Ex-Serviceman I joined in the demonstration which took place on
> Sunday at Hyde Park. I marched from Stepney Green with a contingent of
> Ex-Servicemen which headed the procession, which was followed by a few
> thousand Jews, 99 per cent residing in the East End. What has become of our
> Jewish brothers living in Hampstead, Golders Green etc. Are they content to

65 Ibid.
66 JESM, nos 17–18. (Mar.–Apr. 1936), 22.
67 JC, 10 July 1936.
68 JESM, no. 5 (Mar. 1935), 8.

stay at home and leave it every time for the East End to lead the way? I suppose North and North-West London will want to join in when it is too late.[69]

This is not to imply that East End Jewry, or East End Jewish ex-servicemen, had a monolithic unity. It is likely that many ex-servicemen might have felt that any strong affiliation to anti-fascist or political causes would have been better expressed through overtly political organisations, with a wider agenda. This is something that was not possible solely by being a member of the British Legion or the JESL, for both groups stressed their apolitical nature. The evidence shows that the Jewish ex-servicemen were far from clear as to their true nature. They had only one absolute solvent – war service – because, for Jewish ex-servicemen, differences in class and wealth often cut through religious bonds.

Occasionally, this feeling seemed close to taking on an overt, combined class-religion message. The most damning assault on established Jewry came via the Ex-Servicemen's Movement Against Fascism, in the form of a pamphlet entitled *Mosley in motley*. The author was A. C. Miles, former director of industrial propaganda for the BUF, who had recanted his beliefs. Written in 1937, after the passing of the Public Order Act, the pamphlet warned nevertheless that 'the absence of the uniform from our streets serves to conceal the existence of its [BUF] members but in no way guarantees that they have ceased to exist'.[70]

Miles then launched into his attack. He obviously believed in a class conspiracy that transcended religious divides, and he proceeded to indict some of the leading-lights of the Anglo-Jewish establishment. Donald Van Den Bergh was picked out. It was stated that as a director of Unilever he had a vested interest in keeping high the prices of certain commodities. Miles further claimed that Mosley was receiving funding from Unilever, which meant it was exempt from fascist propaganda about the subjugation of the working class. Van Den Bergh rode out these criticisms: as president of the Maccabean branch of the British Legion, there is no evidence that his leadership was called into question over these matters. Lord Melchett was also attacked for allegedly stating that fascism was 'the embodiment of his ideas on industrial policy'. Similarly short shrift was given to the Rothschilds, for they were 'singularly reluctant to identify [themselves] with any opposition to Sir Oswald Mosley'.[71]

The final page exhorted ex-servicemen to remember their comradeship and rally to the defence of democracy. Memory of the war was obviously a potent weapon and was to set an example to Britain's youth:

[69] JC, 1 Nov. 1935.
[70] A. C. Miles, *Mosley in motley*, London 1937. The Public Order Act was passed in 1935. It banned the wearing of uniforms and made it harder to get permission for public demonstrations which could possibly lead to violence: R. Benewick, *Political violence and public order*, London 1969, 235–62.
[71] Miles, *Mosley in motley*.

Who better fitted than the survivors of the 'Great War of Civilisation' to be leaders in that defence? Who better fitted than those who received their experience on the blood-soaked fields of Flanders, on all the battlefields of the Great War, to rally the forces of Democracy, to lead the Youth of Britain, to the gaining of that world fit for mankind to dwell in, that can never be, for centuries at least, if Fascism prevails.

For the sake of those fighting for freedom now, we cannot fail.[72]

Then on the very last line, it rammed home the message by using McCrae's lines from 'In Flanders Fields', fully revealing how that poem had been engrained into the British consciousness and its prolific employment to justify almost any action by ex-servicemen: 'If ye break faith with we who died we shall not sleep, though poppies grow in Flanders Fields.'[73]

Paradoxically, it was just at this time that government policy and the mood of the country generally, began to change as the shadow of war started to loom. What had once been an 'unfashionable' radicalism was becoming mainstream. It often did not simplify matters, instead it made them rather ironic. The Monash branch of the British Legion were lectured on the virtues of appeasement during the 1938 Armistice week. On the same evening the men were encouraged to join the emergency and civilian defence services and to urge the younger members of the Jewish community to join the armed forces.[74] Exactly the same message had pervaded the Jewish Armistice parade a week earlier. Lord Reading addressed the men and managed to combine reasoned appeasement with the prospect of active service:

> every Jew who at the present time did not take his place in the national service was not only betraying himself but being an enemy to the Jewish community . . . if there was to be general appeasement among the nations some effort might be made to mitigate the horrors and dangers of the Jewish position the world over. Any real appeasement must be founded on the principles of justice, tolerance, and freedom.[75]

The Maccabeans vehemently supported initiatives to encourage Jewish recruitment. Mr Hurwitz, a committee member, addressed the men in forceful tones at a meeting in January 1937: 'I am positively disgusted . . . when I see many young Jewish 'Cissies' walking about the countryside who ought to be wearing a uniform and submitting to some discipline.'[76] When the new Maccabean headquarters was opened in Commercial Road in 1939, the Jewish Councillor Frankel took the opportunity to urge all Jews to help

---

[72] Ibid.
[73] Ibid. The actual line is 'If ye break faith with us who die . . .': Gardner, *Up the line to death*, 49.
[74] *ELA*, 12 Nov. 1938.
[75] *JC*, 11 Nov. 1938.
[76] *ELO*, 9 Jan. 1937.

prepare 'this country and the democracies of the world against attack'.[77] AJEX, from its inception, was committed to encouraging Jews to join up and affiliated itself to the National Services Committee in order to do so.[78] The motivation seems to have been a mixture of wanting to oppose fascism actively and to avoid perpetuating the antisemitic rumours of the Great War. These activities therefore reveal that Jewish ex-servicemen, both inside and outside the British Legion, were at one with the will of the government by 1939.

In conclusion it can be said that the nature of Jewish remembrance was shaped to make a comment about the entire Jewish community and shows that the experience of war buttressed a sense of identity rather than weakening it. East End Jews were at the heart of British Jewry and Stepney was the motor of Jewish ex-service activity. Divisions with established Anglo-Jewry can easily be seen, but it was not totally clear-cut, for a man like Levey had a long service career behind him, with the rank of lieutenant-colonel. It is easy to overstate the radicalism of the ex-servicemen. Levey himself noted that no group could ever attract all ex-servicemen; he stated that even 'the British Legion represents only about one-sixth of the total of the Ex-Servicemen in Britain'.[79] In 1939 the Maccabeans, the most powerful Jewish ex-service group in the country, had a formal membership of only 632.[80] But the numbers are, to a certain extent, irrelevant, for the image counted for a lot more. The Jewish press and, a little belatedly, the East London press, came to see Jewish ex-servicemen as the conscience and vanguard of their community, living proof of the honour won on the battlefield. The old soldiers also prove how far images of struggle and war dominated the twenties and thirties. These men never lost their air of combat and were a lot less sanguine about prospects for peace. Ultimately, Jewish ex-servicemen were extremely loyal members of the state. Their forceful and often outspoken actions were based upon a sense of distinctiveness, of loyalty to their dead and an authority gained by experience of war – an experience that, in the final analysis, not only permeated their community but the whole of British society in the inter-war period.

[77] Ibid. 14 Jan. 1939.
[78] JC, 31 Mar., 21 Apr. 1939.
[79] JESM, nos 10–11 (Aug.–Sept. 1935), 9–10.
[80] JC, 13 Jan. 1939.

Epilogue

Given the importance of war memorials in the lives of East Londoners after the Great War what then happened after the Second World War? In 1944 a War Memorials Advisory Council was formed under the chairmanship of Lord Chatfield. Mass Observation then organised a survey which indicated that most people objected to stone or sculptural memorials and preferred parks and gardens, 'which would be useful or give pleasure to those who outlive the war'.[1] How did East London respond to its war dead in 1945? Romford added the dates 1939–1945 to its Great War memorial and erected a recreation hall which included plaques inscribed with the names of both the civilian and military dead. Finally, the borough had its practical memorial.[2] Ilford also added the dates 1939–1945 to its memorial, compiled a book of remembrance, again for civilian and military dead, and unveiled a bronze tablet recording the work of the civil defence services.[3] In accordance with the findings of Mass Observation and after having studied the literature of the War Memorials Advisory Council, East Ham decided to opt for a Garden of Remembrance in Central Park and a Book of Remembrance.[4]

Poplar, Stepney and Bethnal Green, like West Ham, do not appear to have planned much, at least not in the ten years immediately after the war. However, West Ham Council did discuss a grand volume detailing its war record and Bethnal Green and Poplar erected memorials to the council employees who were killed.[5] Finally, in the City, the court of common council voted to add a new inscription to the London Troops' memorial.[6]

Arnold Whittick, the art historian, writing in 1946, noted the lack of desire for 'true' memorials and the enthusiasm for gardens and parks but deplored the attraction of utilitarian memorials.[7] The evidence from East London seems to suggest a slightly more complicated reaction to the Second World War than the simple theory that memorials were rejected and replaced with a desire to erect something useful. Only Romford actually built a truly utilitarian memorial and this was no different from what had been suggested in the town at the end of the Great War. Other districts had indeed built

---

1   See Longworth, *Unending vigil*, 183.
2   HHL, Romford borough council, minutes, 19 Dec. 1950, 29 Jan. 1952.
3   RHL, dedication of the Ilford book of remembrance, order of service, 27 Apr. 1949.
4   NHL, county borough of East Ham, council minutes, 27 Nov. 1944, 26 June, 8 Aug. 1945, 5 June, 30 Sept., 3 Oct. 1946.
5   NHL, county borough of West Ham, council minutes, 3 Dec. 1946; THL, metropolitan borough of Bethnal Green council, memorandum, 1 Nov. 1948; *EEN*, 16 Nov. 1951.
6   CoLRO, minutes of the court of common council, 22 Oct. 1953.
7   A. Whittick, *War memorials*, London 1946, 1–2.

practical memorials after that conflict. East Ham's memorial, though arguably utilitarian, was in fact aesthetic – a flower garden, a thing of beauty. And it must be noted that the Great War memorials were not rejected; instead new inscriptions were added to them. This seems quite natural for these memorials were already the centre of so much emotion and, in sheer practical terms represented a large cash input – they were already fitting memorials for the new dead too and the newly bereaved gathered at them to remember. In some ways this may have helped to bring about the concept of the twenties and thirties as the long weekend, a mere gap in a prolonged Anglo-German conflict.

In general, however, far fewer memorials were erected after the Second World War.[8] A few ideas can be put forward in order to explain this. The Second World War saw civilians become casualties on a large scale, though military casualties still easily outnumbered them. This served to distort the image of the war and the nature of the war memorial. A 'pure' war memorial, such as those erected after the South African War and the Great War, commemorated men buried far away from home and was erected by people largely ignorant of the true nature of war. In 1945 this was no longer the case, for the division between combatant and non-combatant had been blurred: who was to commemorate who and how? It can also be said that the Great War was fought for the most ethereal of ideals; the liberation of Belgium was indeed a physical necessity but it was justified in a most spiritual way. The domestic issue of homes fit for heroes was belatedly added to British war aims but did not dominate the ethic of the war. At the war's end only an aesthetic, spiritual response was truly fitting. In contrast, the Second World War had its lofty ideals very firmly entwined with extremely utilitarian ones. Beveridge's plans and the 'People's Peace' to match the efforts of the 'People's War' were not only war aims but a war memorial as well; the new Britain was to be put in place in memory and gratitude for the struggle of all, soldier and civilian.[9] There was no formal end to the war. The cessation of hostilities in Europe was not the end of the conflict and even when Japan was beaten there was no grand treaty. Wartime drifted into austere peacetime and then into Cold War.

8   See Borg, *War memorials*, pp. ix–x. At an imperial level, however, the Imperial War Graves Commission got on with the job of setting out a whole new set of cemeteries and building new memorials: Longworth, *Unending vigil*, 161–213.

9   See the work of Paul Addison and Angus Calder for a discussion of these ideas: P. Addison, *The road to 1945*, London 1982 edn, 211–28; A. Calder, *The people's war: Britain, 1939–1945*, London 1992 edn, 524–86. A number of post-war British films touch upon the debate about war memorials and the new Britain and they show that memorials were still a subject of interest. *Silent Dust* (1948), revolves around a landowner's plans to erect a war memorial to his son and the villagers desire to have a communal war memorial. *Vote for Huggett* (1948) concerns the plans of crooked local builders to exploit the desire for a community centre as a war memorial. I am grateful to Stephen Guy for supplying this information. See his PhD thesis, 'Back to business: British cinema and society, 1946–1951', London (in progress).

There were no clear breaks as in 1918. Then the signing of the Armistice, the ending of all hostilities, began the rush to memorialise; this was then followed in 1919–21 by a set of peace treaties. Peter Hennessy states that VE Day was an anti-climax, quoting Kingsley Martin: 'V-Day . . . will not be at all like Armistice Day, 1918. For one thing, very few people then had been expecting the war to end: one just couldn't believe it.'[10]

The communities of East London marked their losses and expressed their pride in their dead of the Great War via their war memorials. These monuments, although unprecedented in scale, were not innovatory, for they continued a tradition of monumental and funerary architecture. The memorials enshrined a series of set values, reflecting grief and mourning, but also intense pride and indeed glory. The degree to which this array of emotions was reflected was conditional on the type of community that the memorial served. To the smallest units of community, the streets, parishes and congregations where cash was necessarily more restricted and where the gaps in society were far more keenly felt, grieving and funerary symbols were more important. In schools, workplaces, colleges and clubs, more often dominated by masculine virtues and a sense of teamwork, corporate pride and honour took central stage. And of course regimental, battalion and military memorials enshrined much the same set of values. At the municipal level the memorials served to enhance civic identity and pride and often included a utilitarian element in order to impress the worth of the sacrifice and the civic commitment to the dead on generations yet to come.

The war memorial once unveiled and dedicated then became the altar around which the annual rites of the war dead were enacted. Armistice Day held the imaginations of the people of the City and East London throughout the twenties and thirties. The day enshrined the symbols of the memorials and the beliefs of 1914. The four phases of Armistice Day can be seen as nearly a full circle. The years 1919–21 were times of improvisation and development. Then from 1922 to 1929 it became a solid, reassuring ceremony with everyone involved, ignoring any ambiguities involved and almost completely oblivious to change. 1930–5 saw some new attitudes towards commemoration, but they vied with the old elements and never toppled them. From 1936 the day began to revert to its former consistency. By ritual and repetition, the glorious dead of East London retained their revered status as martyrs for the cause of humanity. The day was one for the bereaved, and in particular the female bereaved. Ex-servicemen, who were both consciously and unconsciously a breed apart, often celebrated the day in their own peculiar way and had memories of the war far more complex, and in many ways far more contradictory, than any other group.

Big Words did not die on the Western Front or any other theatre of the Great War. The people of East London did not reject the values which sent

10 P. Hennessy, *Never again: Britain, 1945–1951*, London 1992, 56.

many of them to war in 1914. That the Second World War produced some variants on memorialising should not be taken as a conscious decision to put the Great War into the shadows. November continued to be the month of the dead; in 1945 11 November fell on a Sunday and was observed as a day of Remembrance. In 1946 Clement Attlee announced that the nearest Sunday to the eleventh would be kept as Remembrance Day in memory of the dead of both world wars.[11] However Remembrance Sunday had been part of an Armistice week of commemoration long before 1939: once again there was continuity alongside a necessary adaptation.

The war memorials of East London and the Armistice Day ceremonies conducted around them, provided private sentiments of remembrance and grieving with a fitting public expression and then fixed the dead in a mantle of pride and glory. It all served to remind the living of the fact that they were part of a community of the bereaved throughout the period 1919–39.

[11] For a full discussion of these events see Gregory, *Silence of memory*, 215–22.

Bibliography

Unpublished primary sources

Aylesford, Kent, Royal British Legion poppy appeal
Poppy appeal statistics, 1923–39

Chelmsford, Essex Records Office
A6865 Holy Trinity, Canning Town, vestry and PCC books
D/NC4/18 Romford Congregational church, church meetings books
D/NM/20 Ilford High Road Wesleyan Methodist church, trustees minute books
D/NM20/492 Goodmayes High Road Wesleyan Methodist Mens' Meeting, committee minute books
DP/590/29 St John the Evangelist, North Woolwich, vestry and PCC books

Ilford, Redbridge Local History Library
Dedication of the Ilford book of remembrance, order of service, 27 Apr. 1949
Ilford Urban District Council minutes, 1918–26, 1945–49
Ilford War Memorial Gazette, nos 1–6 (1920–27)

London, City of London Records Office
Court of common council minutes, 1918–20, 1944–53
File 605A–6C 1920/9A
File Misc MSS 18.34

London, Greater London Records Office
Acc 1850/147/1 Bow Road Wesleyan Methodist church, trustees' minute books
N/C/21/4 Burdett Road Congregational church, deacons' minute books
P72/JSG/11/1; P72/JSG/118/1 St James the Great, Bethnal Green, vestry books, scrap and cuttings book
P72/JUD/49 St Jude, Bethnal Green, PCC books
P72/MTW/190 St Matthew's, Bethnal Green, PCC books
P72/MTW/244/1–11–265/1–12 St Matthew's, Bethnal Green, parish magazine, 1916–37
P72/PET/32–33 St Peter, Bethnal Green, faculty papers
P88/ALL2/13/14/26/27 All Hallows, Bromley-by-Bow, parish magazine, 1916–36
P88/All2/70/1 All Hallows, Bromley-by-Bow, PCC book
P88/MRY2/66–67 St Mary, Bromley St Leonards, vestry and PCC books
P93/CTC1/202 Christ Church, Spitalfields, vestry and PCC books
P93/DUN/383 St Dunstan, Stepney, vestry books
P93/MRY3/32 St Mary, Cable Street, vestry books
P93/PAU2/20 St Paul, Dock Street, vestry and churchwardens' books

London, Guildhall Manuscripts Library

A379/4ext Royal Exchange Armistice Day order of service, 11 Nov. 1927

L64.6 MS 14,600 London Stock Exchange Company, general purposes committee books, vols 105–8

L64.6 MS 21,291 London and Lancashire Insurance Company, annual general meetings minute books

L64.6 MS 21,291 London and Lancashire Insurance Company, printed annual reports

L64.6 MS 21,296 London and Lancashire Insurance Company, general purposes committee books

L75.1 MS 21,313 London and Lancashire Insurance Company, account of unveiling of company war memorial, war memorial book, 31 Mar. 1922

L75.23 MS 17,716 Inns of Court Yeomanry and Officer Training Corps, papers relating to Armistice celebrations, 1928, 1934

L75.23 MS 17,716 Inns of Court Yeomanry and Officer Training Corps, scrapbook 1914–28

L75.24 MS 6438A City of London Volunteer Regiment (5th battalion), Old Comrades' Association scrapbook, 1919–47

L92 MS 2590 St Lawrence, Jewry, vestry books

L92 MS 3193/1–11 St Sepulchre, Holborn, churchwardens' memorandum book

L92 MS 3990 St Bartholomew-the-Great, vestry books

L92 MS 4251 A&B St Andrew, Holborn, vestry and PCC books

L92 MS 4436 St Mildred, Bread Street, vestry books

L92 MS 4526 St Botolph-without-Bishopsgate, vestry books

L92 MS 6048 St Giles, Cripplegate, vestry books

L92 MS 6554 St Bride's, Fleet Street, vestry books

L92 MS 8014 St Andrew-by-the-Wardrobe, vestry books

L92 MS 11,261 St Edmund, King and Martyr, PCC book

L92 MS 14,375 St Bartholomew-the-Great, scrap and cuttings book

L92 MS 18,319/21/46 St Andrew-by-the-Wardrobe, faculty papers

L92 MS 18,319/42b St Botolph-without-Bishopsgate, faculty papers

L92 MS 18,319/43 St Vedast-alias-Foster, faculty papers

L92 MS 18,319/44 St Edmund, King and Martyr, faculty papers

L92 MS 18,319/44/48/58 All Hallows-by-the-Tower, faculty papers

L92 MS 18,319/47 St Dunstan-in-the-East, faculty papers

L92 MS 18,319/47 St Olave's, Hart Street, faculty papers

L92 MS 18,319/52 St Bartholomew-the-Great faculty papers

L92 MS 18,319/52 St Michael's, Cornhill, faculty papers

L92 MS 18,319/92 St Mildred, Bread Street, faculty papers

L92 MS 18,319/95 St Sepulchre, Holborn, faculty papers

L92 MS 18,319/136 St Bride's, Fleet Street, faculty papers

L92 MS 21,738 St Michael's, Cornhill, vestry books

L92 MS 779,801 St Vedast-alias-Foster, vestry books

L92 MS 858,1706/7 St Olave's, Hart Street, vestry books

London, Guildhall Printed Books Library

Pam 264 Order of service, war memorial unveiling, City of London Royal Field Artillery, St Lawrence, Jewry

Pam 2541 Order of service, war memorial unveiling, Corporation of the City of London, St Lawrence, Jewry
Pam 17411 Order of service, war memorial unveiling, St Botolph, Bishopsgate
Pam 17412 Order of service, war memorial unveiling, Honourable Artillery Company, St Botolph, Bishopsgate
St Giles, Cripplegate, parish magazine, 1919–26
SL64/6 Stock Exchange war memorial book, Apr. 1923

London, Imperial War Museum
Archives of the National Inventory of War Memorials

London, Isle of Dogs Local History Trust
Archive of aural history transcripts

London, Jewish Lads' and Girls' Brigade headquarters, South Woodford
Jewish Lads' Brigade, council meeting minute books, 1919–21

London, Prudential Assurance
Prudential Bulletin, 1920–38
Roll of honour, 1920

London, Queen Mary and Westfield College.
East London College Magazine, 1923

London, Royal Fusiliers Museum, Tower of London
M18 War memorial papers
M23 Instructions for unveiling of war memorial

London, St Bartholomew's Hospital
Book of Remembrance: *Pro Patria 1914–1918*
League news: Journal of St Barts Nurses League, Sept. 1926
War memorial unveiling, order of service

London, Tower Hamlets, Gas Museum
The Co-Partners: journal of the Gas Light and Coke Company, 1914, 1920–26

London, Tower Hamlets Local History Library
All Hallows', East India Dock, parish magazine, 1916–22, 1927–36
Bentley, L. D., mayor of Bethnal Green, 1933–34, manuscript diary
Bethnal Green war memorial, general committee minute books
Bethnal Green war memorial, sub-committees minute books
Brady Street Club for Working Jewish Boys, annual reports, 1896–1908
Dockland Outlook: The Journal of the Docklands Settlements, Nov. 1930
Labour borough of Bethnal Green: the truth about Armistice Day: reply to the fascists, pamphlet, 9 Nov. 1938
Labour warmongers continue to insult Bethnal Green ex-service men, BUF pamphlet, Nov. 1938
Letter which Labour warmongers did not publish!, BUF pamphlet, Oct. 1938

Lighterness, G. A., 'The life and times of an Eastender; in those days', typescript autobiography 1989

Metropolitan borough of Bethnal Green, council minutes, 1918–22, 1935–36, 1945–55

Metropolitan borough of Poplar, council minutes, 1918–24, 1944–55

Metropolitan borough of Stepney, council minutes, 1918–22, 1945–55

Our Mag. (the magazine of the Poplar Rangers), Apr. 1924

Oxford House magazine, Nov. 1931

Poplar, central ward, public war memorial, fund-raising circular, 17 Apr. 1920

St Andrew's, Bethnal Green, parish magazine, 1916–21, 1930–36

St Anne's, Limehouse, parish magazine, 1918–29; order of service for the unveiling and dedication of war memorial

St George's Jewish settlement, annual reports, 1919–31

St Michael and All Angels', Bromley-by-Bow, parish magazine, 1917–24

Stepney Jewish Lads' Club, 1901–1926: a short history, London [1926]

Upper North Street School memorial, fund-raising circular

Wolveridge, J., *'Aint it grand; or this was Stepney*, London 1989

Romford, Havering Local History Library
Official guide to Romford, 1908, Romford 1903
Romford borough council, minutes, 1944–53
Romford Urban District council, minutes, 1916–25

Stratford, Newham Local History Library
'Brief synopsis of the history of Woodgrange Baptist Church', manuscript [1940]
Councillor Dyer's cutting book, 1914–15
County borough of East Ham, council minutes, 1916–25, 1944–50
County borough of East Ham, education committee minutes, 1916–24
County borough of West Ham, council minutes, 1916–25, 1944–50
County borough of West Ham, tramways department, reports of the general manager, 1922
East Ham Hospital, annual reports, 1918–30
East Ham parish magazine, 1920–27
East Ham Presbyterian church, council minute books
East Ham Technical College and Secondary School (later *East Ham Grammar Schools) Magazine*, 1919–34
East Ham Trinity Presbyterian church of England, *Jubilee handbook, 1900–1951*, London 1951
Forest Gate Congregational church, annual manual 1921–22, church council minute books, Sunday schools committee minute books
Great Eastern Railway Magazine, 1919–24
John Cornwell papers, 1916–70
Plaistow Congregational church, church council minute books
Queen Mary's Hospital for the East End, annual reports, 1917–27
Queen Mary's Hospital for the East End, general committee books, 1918–24
St Matthew's, Manor Park, Mens' Meeting magazine, *The Steeple*, 1922–23
Stratford church parish magazine, 1923–24
Stratford Trinity Presbyterian church magazine, 1919–24
Way Down East: The Magazine of the Mansfield House University Settlement

West Ham Central Secondary School Magazine, 1920–36
West Ham Hospital, general committee minute books

Material *in situ*
All Saints', Goodmayes, parish magazine, 1916–35
City of London School for Boys, *City of London School Magazine*, 1919–26
Ilford County High School, *ICHS Chronicles*, 1918–46
St Andrew's, Romford, vestry books
St Bartholomew-the-Less, vestry books
St Clement's, Great Ilford, parish magazine, 1916–39, vestry books, PCC books
St Luke's, Ilford, parish magazine, 1925–39
St Sepulchre, Holborn, vestry and PCC books
SL64/6 Stock Exchange memorial book, Apr. 1923

Journals and newspapers

Bethnal Green News
Bulletin: Journal of the National Federation of Discharged and Demobilised Sailors and Soldiers
Buzzer: Journal of the National Union of Disabled Ex-Servicemen
City of London Rifles Quarterly Journal
City Press
Daily Chronicle
Daily Mirror
Daily News
Daily Telegraph
East End News
East Ham Echo
East London Advertiser
East London Observer
Eastern Post
English Churchman
Essex Times
Evening News
Evening Standard
Hackney and Kingsland Gazette
Honourable Artillery Company Journal
Ilford Recorder
Jewish Chronicle
Jewish Ex-Serviceman: Journal of the Jewish Ex-Servicemen's Legion
Jewish Graphic
Jewish Guardian
Jewish World
London Gazette
LRB Record
Memories: Journal of the 19th Battalion, St Pancras Rifles
Northampton Independent
Old Contemptible: Journal of the Old Contemptibles' Association

Romford Record
Romford Times
Royal Fusiliers Chronicle
Stratford Express
Tablet
The Times
Tudor Rose: Magazine of the 1st City of London Battalion, Royal Fusiliers
Westminster Gazette
Ypres Times: Journal of the Ypres League

Primary printed sources

Adcock, A. St John, *The ANZAC pilgrim's progress*, London 1918
———— *For remembrance*, London 1918
Adler, M. (ed.), *The British Jewry book of honour*, London 1922
Armitage, F. P., *Leicester, 1914–1918: the wartime story of a midland town*, Leicester 1933
Asquith, M., *The autobiography of Margot Asquith*, London 1920
Baker, H., *Architecture and personalities*, London 1944
Baldwin, S., *On England*, Glasgow 1926
———— *Service of our lives*, London 1937
Bavin, W. D., *Swindon's war record*, Swindon 1922
Beavan, A. H., *Imperial London*, London 1901
Beckles-Willson, H., *Ypres: the holy ground of British arms*, London 1920
de Bergerac, B., *The Oxford victory pageant, 1919*, Oxford 1919
Besant, W., *All sorts and conditions of men*, London 1882
———— *East London*, London 1903
Blackman, A. J., *The Corporation of the City of London: its ceremonies and importance*, London 1924
Blackman, R. J., *London for ever the sovereign city*, London 1932
Bliss, A., *As I remember*, London 1970
Blomfield, R., *Memoirs of an architect*, London 1932
Boisseau, H. E., *The Prudential staff and the Great War*, London 1938
Brazier, R. H. and E. Sandford, *Birmingham and the Great War, 1914–1919*, Birmingham 1921
Brice B. *The battle book of Ypres*, London 1927
———— *Ypres: outpost of the Channel ports*, London 1929
———— and W. Pulteney, *The immortal salient: an historical record and complete guide for pilgrims to Ypres*, London 1925
Brief record of Cheveley men in the war, Cambridge 1920
British Legion, *The British Legion album*, London 1924
———— *The British Legion children's annual*, London 1931–7
———— *Ten memorable days*, London 1938
Brittain, V., *Poems of the war and after*, London 1934
Brooke, R., *The complete poetical works of Rupert Brooke*, London 1918
Buchan, J., *These for remembrance*, London 1987 edn
———— and H. Newbolt, *Days to remember*, London 1923
Burnett, R. G., *Chudleigh: a triumph of sacrifice*, London 1932

Butler, A. S. G., *The architecture of Sir Edwin Lutyens*, London 1950

Callwell, C. E., *Field Marshal Sir Henry Wilson*, London 1927

Canadian Battlefields Memorial Commission, *Canadian battlefields memorials*, Ottowa 1929

Carrington, C., *Soldier from the wars returning*, London 1965

Cartmell, H., *For remembrance: an account of the part played by Preston in the war*, Preston 1919

Charteris, J., *Field Marshal Earl Haig*, London 1929

Christie, O. F., *A history of Clifton College, 1860–1934*, Bristol 1934

Church of England liturgies: special forms of prayer for Armistice Day, London 1925, 1926, 1928, 1929, 1930

City of London guide, London 1939

Codrington, G., *The rules of the road*, London 1934

Cohen, J. Benn Brunel, *Count your blessings*, London 1956

Cooper, C. S., *Outdoor monuments of London*, London 1928

Cooper, D., *Haig*, London 1935–36

Coward N., *The lyrics*, London 1983 edn

Digby Planck, C., *History of the 7th (City of London) battalion, the London Regiment*, London 1947

Ditchfield, P. H., *The City of London*, London 1921

Drake-Carnell, F. J., *Old English customs and traditions*, London 1938

Edmonds, J. E., *Military operations France and Belgium, 1915*, ii, London 1928

Errington, F. H. L., *The Inns of Court Officer Training Corps in the Great War*, London 1922

Farmer, J., *Woodford as I knew it*, Theydon Bois 1986

Fellowes, R. A., *Sir Reginald Blomfield: an Edwardian architect*, London 1985

Fleming, A., *How to see the battlefields*, London 1919

Fox, F., *The king's pilgrimage*, London 1922

Gardner, B. (ed.), *Up the line to death: the war poets, 1914–1918*, London 1986 edn

Gildea, J., *For remembrance and in honour of those who lost their lives in the South African war*, London 1911

Glasspool, A. J., *The Corporation of the City of London: its ceremonies and importance*, London 1924

Gleichen, E., *London's outdoor statuary*, London 1928

Godfrey, E. G., *The Cast-Iron Sixth: a history of the 6th battalion, London Regiment (The City of London Rifles)*, London 1938

Goold Walker, G. (ed.), *The Honourable Artillery Company in the Great War, 1914–1919*, London 1930

Gosling, H., *Up and down stream*, London 1927

Gowing, E. N., *John Edwin Watts-Ditchfield*, London 1926

Graham, S., *The challenge of the dead*, London 1921

Graves, R., *Goodbye to all that*, London 1929

—— and A. Hodges, *The long weekend: a social history of Great Britain, 1918–1939*, London 1940

Green Cross Society, *Roads of remembrance as war memorials*, London 1920

Gwynn. S. (ed.), *The letters and friendships of Sir Cecil Spring-Rice: a record*, ii, London 1929

Haig, Dorothy, *A Scottish tour*, Edinburgh 1935

—— *Douglas Haig: the man I knew*, London 1936

Hamilton, A. S., *The City of London Yeomanry (Roughriders)*, London 1936

Hamilton, I., *The friends of England*, London 1923

—— *Listening for the drums*, London 1944

Hannington, W., *Unemployed struggles, 1919–36*, Ilkley 1973 edn

Harrington, C. H., *Plumer of Messines*, London 1935

Hart-Davis, R. (ed.), *Siegfried Sassoon diaries, 1915–1918*, London 1983

Harter, J. and L. J. D. Garvin, *The story of an epic pilgrimage*, London 1928

Hatton, C. F., *The yarn of a yeoman*, London 1930

Hay, I., *Their name liveth*, London 1931

Hill, A. W., *Our soldiers graves*, London 1920

History of the London Rifle Brigade, 1859–1919, London 1921

Holloway, S., *Wiv a little bit o' luck*, London 1967

Holloway, W. H., *Northamptonshire and the Great War*, Northampton 1921

Hostettler, E. (ed.), *Memories of childhood on the Isle of Dogs, 1870–1970*, London 1990

Howarth E. and M. Wilson, *West Ham: a study in social and industrial problems*, London 1907

Hurst, S. C., *The silent cities*, London 1929

Hussey, C., *The work of Sir Robert Lorimer*, London 1931

—— *The life of Sir Edwin Lutyens*, London 1950

Hutchinson, G. S., *Pilgrimage*, London 1935

Ilford charter day, October 21st 1926, souvenir book, Ilford 1926

Imperial War Graves Commission, *Annual reports* [1920–39], London 1920–39

In memoriam: Gallipoli, Auckland 1918

Inskip, J. T., *A man's job: the autobiography of James Inskip, second bishop of Barking*, London 1948

Jarratt, J. E., *Municipal recollections: Southport, 1900–1930*, London 1932

Jerrold, W. (ed.), *The complete poetical works of Thomas Hood*, Oxford 1911

Jewish War Memorial, *The overseas dominion's visit*, London 1923

Jewish year book [1939], London 1939

Jones, S. R., *England in France*, London 1919

Kelly's directory of Essex [1911], London 1911

Kelly's directory of Ilford [1916–22], London 1916–22

Kenyon, F., *War graves: how the cemeteries abroad will be designed*, London 1918

Kernot, C., *British public school war memorials*, London 1927

Kipling R. *The graves of the fallen*, London 1919

—— *Rudyard Kipling's verse: definitive edition*, London 1966 edn

Lever, T., *Clayton of Toc H*, London 1971

Lloyd B., *Poems written during the Great War*, London 1918

—— *Paths of glory*, London 1919

London statistics, 1921–1923, xxxviii, London 1924

Longbottom, F. W., *Chester in the Great War*, Chester 1920

Lumsden, C., *My Poplar Eastenders*, Stepney 1991

Mander, R. and J. Mitchenson (eds), *Noel Coward: plays: four*, London 1987 edn

Masefield, J., *St George and the dragon: the war and the future*, London 1919

Mason, M. H. H., *The Whitgift grammar school book of remembrance*, London 1920

Masterman, C. F. G., *England after war*, London 1922

Maude, A. H. (ed.), *The 47th (London) Division, 1914–1919*, London 1922

Mayo, K., *Soldiers what next?*, London 1934

Michelin, *Guides for visits to the battlefields*, Paris–London 1917–25

Michin, J. H. C. (ed.), *The Legion book*, London 1929

Miles, A. C., *Mosley in motley*, London 1937

Moore Keatley, H. and W. C. Sayers Berwick, *Croydon and the Great War*, Croydon 1920

Morriss, H. F., *Bermondsey's 'bit' in the greatest war*, London 1923

Mosley, O. E., *My life*, London 1970

Mottram, R. H., *The Spanish farm trilogy*, London 1927

———— *Ten years ago*, London 1928

———— *Through the Menin Gate*, London 1932

———— *Journey to the western front*, London 1936

Moult, T., *Cenotaph: a book of remembrance in poetry and prose for November the eleventh*, London 1923

Mudie-Smith, R. (ed.), *The religious life of London*, London 1904

Mullins, C. F., *Shocked and disillusioned*, London 1919

Murray, W. W., *The epic of Vimy*, Ottawa 1936

New survey of London life and labour, III: *Survey of social conditions: the eastern area*, London 1932

Newcastle-under-Lyme, *The book of remembrance*, Newcastle-under-Lyme 1922

Newman, B. and I. O. Evans (eds), *Anthology of Armageddon*, London 1935

Official guide to the Great Eastern Railway, 1892, London 1892

Official guide to Ilford, including Seven Kings and Goodmayes, Ilford 1921

Official guide to the metropolitan borough of Poplar, London 1927

Official guide to Romford, 1908, Romford 1908

Osborn, E. B., *The muse in arms*, London 1917

———— *The new Elizabethans*, London 1919

Oxenham, J., *High altars: the battlefields of France and Flanders as I saw them*, London 1918

Paget, E. K., *Henry Luke Paget*, London 1939

Pankhurst, S., *The home front*, London 1987 edn

Pemberton, T. J., *Gallipoli today*, London 1926

Pensioners of the Great War, London 1922

Pepper, H., *Seven-days soup: growing-up in London's Chinatown*, London [1981]

Purcell, W. E., *Woodbine Willie: the life of G. A. Studdert-Kennedy*, London 1962

Rawlinson, A., *The defence of London, 1915–1918*, London 1923

Rice, S., *Neuve Chapelle: India's memorial in France*, London 1928

Richardson, E. M. E., *Remembrance wakes*, London 1934

Robertson, W., *Middlesbrough's effort in the Great War*, Middlesbrough 1921

Rowse, A. L., *A Cornish childhood*, London 1942

Rowson, J. W., *Bridport and the Great War*, Bridport 1923

Royal Fusiliers in an outline of history, 1685–1938, Aldershot 1938

Rutherford A. (ed.), *Rudyard Kipling: war stories and poems*, Oxford 1990

St Barnabas Hostels, *Ypres–Somme*, London 1924

———— *Gallipoli and Salonika*, London 1927

———— *The Menin Gate pilgrimage*, London 1927

Scott, W. H., *Leeds in the Great War*, Leeds 1923

Shaw Sparrow, W. (ed.), *The Gospels in art*, London 1904

Sherren, W., *The rights of the ex-service man and woman*, London 1921

Southern Railway Company, *Belgium, Ostend and the coastal resorts*, London 1924–34

Star and Garter home for disabled sailors and soldiers, London 1930

Stone, G. F. and C. Wells, *Bristol and the Great War*, Bristol 1920

Swinton, E., *Twenty years after: the battlefields of 1914–1918 then and now*, London 1934–6

Tabor, M. E., *The City churches*, London 1924

Taylor, H. A., *Goodbye to the battlefields*, London 1928

Their nameth liveth, London 1954

Thomas, B., *Ben's Limehouse: recollections by Ben Thomas*, London 1987

Thorne, W., *My life's battles*, London 1989 edn

Toc H., *The pilgrims' guide to the Ypres salient*, London 1920

—— *The gallant adventure: the Toc H annual*, London 1928

—— *Over there: a little guide to pilgrims to Ypres, the salient and Talbot House, Poperinghe*, London 1935

—— *A birthday book*, London 1936

Townroe, B. S., *A pilgrim in Picardy*, London 1927

Trotter, J. T., *Valour and vision*, London 1920

Walbrook, H. M., *Hove and the Great War*, Hove 1920

War Office: Department of General Staff, *Battle of Le Cateau: 24 August, 1914, tour of the battlefields; Battle of the Aisne: 13–15 September 1914, tour of the battlefields*, London 1934

Ward, Lock and Company, *Handbook to Belgium and the battlefields*, London 1924

Ware, F., *The immortal heritage*, Cambridge 1937

Waugh, E., *Brideshead revisited*, London 1945

Weaver, L., *The Scottish national war memorial*, London 1928

Webb, M. de P., *Britain victorious! a plea for sacrifice*, London 1920

Wetherell, J. E., *The Great War in verse and prose*, Ontario 1919

WGT, *For those who mourn*, n.p. 1917

Whittick, A., *War memorials*, London 1946

Winnington-Ingram, A. F., *The potter and the clay*, London 1917

—— *Victory and after*, London 1919

—— *Fifty years work in London (1889–1939)*, London 1940

Wolveridge, J., *Aint it grand; or this was Stepney*, London 1981

Woodward, E. L., *Short journey*, London 1942

Secondary sources

Addison, P., *The road to 1945*, London 1982 edn

Aldgate, T. and J. Richards, *Britain can take it: the British cinema in the Second World War*, Oxford 1986

Anderson, B., *Imagined communities: reflections on the origin and spread of nationalism*, London 1994 edn

Aries, P., *Western attitudes toward death from the Middle Ages to the present*, London 1974

Beckett, I. F. W. and K. Simpson (eds), *A nation in arms: a social history of the British army in the First World War*, Manchester 1985

Benewick, R., *Political violence and public order*, London 1969

BIBLIOGRAPHY

Betjeman, J., *The City of London churches*, London 1974

Birn, D., *The League of Nations Union, 1918–1945*, Oxford 1981

Blythe, R., *The age of illusion: England in the twenties and thirties, 1919–1940*, London 1963

Boorman, D., *At the going down of the sun: British First World War memorials*, York 1988

Borg, A., *War memorials: from antiquity to the present*, London 1991

Bracco, R. M., *Merchants of hope: British middlebrow writers and the First World War, 1919–1939*, Oxford 1993

Branson, N., *Poplarism, 1919–1925: George Lansbury and the councillors' revolt*, London 1979

Buitenhuis, P., *The Great War of words: literature as propaganda, 1914–1918 and after*, London 1989 edn

Bush, J., 'East London Jews and the First World War', *London Journal*, no. 2 (Winter 1980), 147–61

———— *Behind the lines: East London labour, 1914–1919*, London 1984

Bushaway, B., 'Name upon name: the Great War and remembrance', in R. Porter (ed.), *Myths of the English*, Cambridge 1992, 136–67

Butcher, R. W., 'A regiment at war', *Stand To! Journal of the Western Front Association* xxi/1 (Spring 1989), 21–4

Calder, A., *The people's war: Britain, 1939–1945*, London 1992 edn

Cannadine, D., 'War and death, grief and mourning in modern Britain', in J. Whaley (ed.), *Mirrors of mortality: studies in the social history of death*, London 1981, 187–252

———— 'The context, performance and meaning of ritual: the British monarchy and the "invention of tradition", *c.* 1820–1977', in Hobsbawm and Ranger, *The invention of tradition*, 101–65

Ceadel, M., 'Interpreting East Fulham', in J. Ramsden and C. Cook (eds), *By-elections in British politics*, London 1973, 118–40

———— *Pacifism in Britain, 1914–1945: the defining of a faith*, Oxford 1980

Clark, A., *The donkeys*, London 1961

Clarke, I. F., *Voices prophesying war: future wars, 1763–3749*, Oxford 1992

Compton, Ann (ed.), *Charles Sargeant Jagger: war and peace sculpture*, London 1986

Crouch, M. and B. Huppauf (eds), *Essays on mortality*, NSW 1985

Curl, J. A., *A celebration of death: an introduction to some of the buildings, monuments, and settings of funerary architecture in the western European tradition*, London 1980

Danchev, A., 'Bunking and debunking: the controversies of the 1960s', in B. Bond (ed.), *The First World War and British military history*, Oxford 1991, 263–80

Darracott, J. and B. Loftus, *First World War in posters*, London 1981 edn

Douglas-Smith, A. E., *City of London School*, Oxford 1965

Dutton, P., ' "The dead man's penny": a history of the next of kin memorial plaque', *Imperial War Museum Review* iii (1988), 60–8

Dyer, G., *The missing of the Somme*, London 1994

Eksteins, M., *Rites of spring: the Great War and the birth of the modern age*, London 1989

Encyclopedia of sea warfare, London 1975

Everrard, S., *The history of the Gas Light and Coke Company, 1812–1949*, London 1949

Fishman, W. J., *East End Jewish radicals, 1875–1914*, London 1975

———— *East End, 1888*, London 1988

Furneaux, R., *The first war correspondent: William Howard Russell of* The Times, London 1944

Fussell, P., *The Great War and modern memory*, Oxford 1975

Garrett, R., *The final betrayal: the Armistice, 1918 . . . and afterwards*, Southampton 1989

Green, O., *Underground art*, London 1990

Gregory, A., *The silence of memory: Armistice Day, 1919–1946*, Oxford 1994

Hartley, L. P., *The go-between*, London 1953

Hennessy, P., *Never again: Britain, 1945–1951*, London 1992

Hobsbawm, E. and T. Ranger (eds), *The invention of tradition*, Cambridge 1983

Hughes, C., 'The new armies', in Beckett and Simpson, *Nation in arms*, 99–127

Hynes, S., *A war imagined: the First World War and English culture*, London 1990

Jackson, A. A., *London's termini*, London 1985

Jeffrey, K., 'The post-war army', in Beckett and Simpson, *Nation in arms*, 99–127

Jewish year book [1996], London 1996

Jones, K., *Conan-Doyle and the spirits: the spiritualist career of Sir Arthur Conan-Doyle*, Northampton 1989

Kadish, S., *Bolsheviks and British Jews: the Anglo-Jewish community, Britain and the Russian revolution*, London 1992

———— 'A good Jew and a good Englishman': the Jewish Lads' and Girls' Brigade, 1895–1995*, London 1995

Karol, E. and F. Allibone, *Charles Holden: architect, 1875–1960*, London 1988

King, A., *Memorials of the Great War in Britain: the symbolism and politics of remembrance*, Oxford 1998

Kitchen, M., *Europe between the wars: a political history*, Harlow 1988

Korr, C., *West Ham United*, London 1986

Kushner, T., 'Jew and non-Jew in the East End of London: towards an anthropology of everyday relations', in G. Alderman and C. Holmes, *Outsiders and outcasts: essays in honour of William J. Fishman*, London 1993, 12–32

Larkin, P., *The Whitsun weddings*, London 1964

Leed, E. J., *No man's land: combat and identity in World War One*, Cambridge 1979

Lloyd, D. W., *Battlefield Tourism*, Oxford 1998

Longworth. P., *The unending vigil: a history of the Commonwealth War Graves Commission, 1917–1984*, London 1985

McIntyre, C., *Monuments of war: how to read a war memorial*, London 1990

McKee, A., *Vimy Ridge*, Toronto 1966

Mackenzie, J. M., 'In touch with the infinite: the BBC and the empire, 1923–53', in Mackenzie, *Imperialism and popular culture*, 165–92

———— (ed.), *Imperialism and popular culture*, Manchester 1986

Maclean, C. and J. Phillips, *The sorrow and the pride*, Wellington 1990

Marriott, J., *The culture of labourism: the East End between the wars*, Edinburgh 1991

Marwick, A., *The deluge: British society and the Great War*, London 1965

Mayo, J. M., *War memorials as political landscape*, New York 1988

Messenger, C., *Terriers in the trenches: the history of the Post Office Rifles*, Chippenham 1981

——— *History of the British army*, London 1986

Middlebrook, M., *The first day on the Somme*, London 1971

Moorhouse, G., *Hell's foundations: a town, its myths and Gallipoli*, London 1992

Moriarty, C., 'Christian iconography and First World War memorials', *Imperial War Museum Review* vi (1991), 63–76

——— 'The absent dead and figurative First World War memorials', *Transactions of the Ancient Monuments Society* i (1995), 3–39

Morley, S., *A talent to amuse: a biography of Noel Coward*, London 1985 edn

Mosse, G. L., *Fallen soldiers: reshaping the memory of the world wars*, Oxford 1990

Nicholson, G. W. L., *We will remember: overseas memorials to Canada's war dead*, Ottowa 1973

Oxford dictionary of quotations, London 1982 edn

Palmer, A., *The East End: four centuries of London life*, London 1989

Panichas, G., *Promise of greatness: fiftieth anniversary of the Armistice*, London 1968

Parker, P., *The old lie: the Great War and the public school ethos*, London 1987

Parsons, J., *A short history of Queen Mary's Hospital for the East End*, London 1962

Pedersen, P. A., *Monash as military commander*, Melbourne 1985

Prior, R. and T. Wilson, 'Paul Fussell at war', *War in History* 1 (1994), 63–80

Prost, A., *In the wake of war: les anciens combattants and French society, 1914–1939*, English edn, Oxford 1992

Read, B. and P. Skipworth, *Sculpture in Britain between the wars*, London 1986

Rickards, M., *Posters of the First World War*, London 1968

Rough guide to Venice, London 1989

Shiman, L. L., *The crusade against drink in Victorian England*, London 1988

Shipley, R., *To mark our place in history: a history of Canadian war memorials*, Toronto 1987

Short, M., *Gustav Holst: the man and his music*, Oxford 1990

Sillars, S., *Art and survival in First World War Britain*, London 1987

Simpson, K., *The Old Contemptibles: a photographic history of the British Expeditionary Force, August–December 1914*, London 1981

Springhall, J., *Youth, society and empire: British youth movements, 1883–1940*, London 1977

Stallworthy, J. (ed.), *The Oxford book of war poetry*, Oxford 1984

——— (ed.), *The poems of Wilfred Owen*, London 1985

Stamp, G., *Silent cities*, London 1977

Talbot, G., *The Country Life book of the royal family*, London 1980

Terraine, J., *Douglas Haig: the educated soldier*, London 1963, rev. edn 1990

Theatre Workshop and Charles Chilton, *Oh! What a lovely war*, London 1984 edn

Thompson, P., *Socialists, Liberals and Labour: the struggle for London, 1885–1914*, London 1967

Thomson, A., *ANZAC memories: living with the legend*, Oxford 1994

Thomson, J. A. F., *The transformation of medieval England, 1370–1529*, Harlow 1989 edn

Timms, D. W. G., *The urban mosaic: towards a theory of residential differentiation*, Cambridge 1971

Turner, E. S., *Dear old blighty*, London 1980

VCH, *Essex*, v, vi, vii, Oxford 1966, 1973, 1978

Ward, S. R., *The war generation: the veterans of the Great War*, New York 1975

Warner, P., *Kitchener: the man behind the legend*, London 1985

Watrin, J., *British military cemeteries in the region of Boulogne-sur-Mer*, London 1987

Weinreb, B. and C. Hibbert (eds), *The London encyclopaedia*, London 1992 edn

Weintraub, S., *A stillness heard round the world: the end of the Great War: November 1918*, London 1986

Westlake, R., *The Territorial battalions: a pictorial history, 1859–1985*, London 1986

Wilkinson, A., *The Church of England and the First World War*, London 1978

Williams, G. and J. Ramsden, *Ruling Britannia: a political history of Britain, 1688–1988*, Harlow 1990

Winter, J. M., *The Great War and the British people*, London 1985

————— *Sites of memory, sites of mourning*, Cambridge 1995

Wootton, G., *The official history of the British Legion*, London 1956

————— *The politics of influence, British ex-servicemen, cabinet decisions and cultural change (1917–1957)*, Cambridge, Mass. 1963

Wright, F., 'The Ingles of Limehouse', *East London Record* xi (1992), 15–18

Young, M. and P. Willmott, *Family and kinship in East London*, London 1957, 1972

— *The symmetrical family: a study of work and leisure in the London region*, London 1973

Zhabotinsky, V., *The story of the Jewish Legion*, New York 1945

Unpublished material

Bond, B., 'The anti-war writers and their critics', unpubl. paper given at a conference on '1914–1918: the war experienced', Leeds 1994

Guy, S., 'Back to business: British cinema and society, 1946–1951', PhD diss. London (in progress)

Moriarty, C., 'Narrative and the absent body: mechanisms of meaning in First World War memorials', PhD diss. Sussex 1995

Rose, G. C., 'Locality, politics and culture: Poplar in the 1920s', PhD diss. London 1989

Index

Index of War Memorials

In places of work, schools, colleges and clubs

Civic memorials